TREASURE HUNTER

Diving for Gold on North America's Death Coast

Robert MacKinnon

with Dallas Murphy

THE BERKLEY PUBLISHING GROUP
Published by the Penguin Group
Penguin Group (USA) Inc.
375 Hudson Street, New York, New York 10014, USA
Penguin Group (Canada), 90 Eglinton Avenue East, Suite 700, Toronto, Ontario M4P 2Y3, Canada (a division of Pearson Penguin Canada Inc.) • Penguin Books Ltd., 80 Strand, London WC2R 0RL, England • Penguin Group Ireland, 25 St. Stephen's Green, Dublin 2, Ireland (a division of Penguin Books Ltd.) • Penguin Group (Australia), 250 Camberwell Road, Camberwell, Victoria 3124, Australia (a division of Pearson Australia Group Pty. Ltd.) • Penguin Books India Pvt. Ltd., 11 Community Centre, Panchsheel Park, New Delhi—110 017, India • Penguin Group (NZ), 67 Apollo Drive, Rosedale, Auckland 0632, New Zealand (a division of Pearson New Zealand Ltd.) • Penguin Books (South Africa) (Pty.) Ltd., 24 Sturdee Avenue, Rosebank, Johannesburg 2196, South Africa

Penguin Books Ltd., Registered Offices: 80 Strand, London WC2R 0RL, England

This is an original publication of The Berkley Publishing Group.

Interior maps courtesy of Vibe Creative Group.
Text design by Tiffany Estreicher.

First edition: June 2012

Library of Congress Cataloging-in-Publication Data

MacKinnon, Robert, 1950–
Treasure hunter : diving for gold on North America's death coast /
Robert MacKinnon with Dallas Murphy. — 1st ed.
p. cm.
Includes bibliographical references.
ISBN 978-0-425-24738-9 (alk. paper)
1. Treasure troves. 2. Deep diving. 3. Shipwrecks. I. Title.
G525.M2216 2012
622'.190916344—dc23
2012000974

PRINTED IN THE UNITED STATES OF AMERICA

10 9 8 7 6 5 4 3 2 1

TREASURE HUNTER

BERKLEY BOOKS
NEW YORK

This book is dedicated to the thousands of sailors,
men, women, and children who lost their lives in shipwrecks
along the shores of Nova Scotia; at Sable Island, Scatarie Island,
and St. Paul Island; and in the territorial sea of Nova Scotia.

CONTENTS

INTRODUCTION

It had been an excruciating crossing. Almost from the moment the ship *Astraea* cleared the outer harbor reaches of Limerick, Ireland, heading for Quebec, she had battled strong headwinds and an unrelenting string of slashing North Atlantic gales. She carried 251 Irish refugees from oppression and famine, people who had packed their meager possessions on their backs, bid good-bye to friends and relatives whom they knew they would never see again, then walked from all over Ireland to Limerick, where they boarded the ship *Astraea*, bound for a better life in North America. Most were packed for the duration into the hold (steerage), where circumstances even on easy crossings were atrocious; on this long, foul crossing they must have resembled gulag conditions.

When the end of their voyage was near, the Cape Breton coast would have been in sight, except for the fog, the rain, and the dark. The captain set up his approach through Cabot Strait between Cape Breton and Newfoundland, the only viable entrance into the Gulf of St. Lawrence.

The Cabot Strait is 90 miles across at its narrowest point. That sounds like a lot of sea room, and it's plenty under decent conditions. But after a rough month without a recent position fix, in fog and rain, it's like threading the eye of a needle with ship killers on either hand.

Around midnight on May 7, 1834, the *Astraea* struck Little Lorraine Head just five miles north of Louisbourg Harbor and quickly sank. Out of the 251 immigrants and about 20 crewmen, 3 people survived. Residents of the nearby village of Little Lorraine gathered bodies from the beach and in the surf for two days and gave them a decent burial. It was all the passengers would ever get from their new life in North America, burial in a rocky patch of ground near the wreck site.

The *Astraea* is only one of thousands of shipwrecks that line the Atlantic coast of Cape Breton Island, Nova Scotia, where in some places wrecks are piled three deep. If the sheer number of wrecks is the defining criterion, then this is the deadliest coast in the Western Hemisphere. I know that from the historical record, but far more vividly from firsthand underwater exposure.

I am a treasure hunter. For over 40 years, I have been diving along the Cape Breton coast in search of treasure in the form of gold and silver coins, and bullion, and in the form of everyday cultural artifacts, the lost book and record of our past. I've never wanted to be anything but a treasure hunter since before the age of literacy. And the process of discovery and recovery is as exciting to me now as when I was seventeen.

However, at this writing, as the onshore winds of winter give way to spring and the summer dive season to follow, I am converting my 42-foot workboat from a diving platform to a lobster boat. I like the lobsterman's life, but I'd much prefer to be preparing to excavate the HMS *Leonidas*, *Le Chameau*, the HMS *Feversham*, and especially the HMS *Fantome* fleet. But I'm not allowed. By order of the Nova Scotia government, *no one* is allowed to recover treasure from these waters. Instead, the treasures, some of which I discovered and those from hundreds of yet-unknown wrecks, are to be left on the sea bottom, where they will inevitably be dispersed, destroyed, or simply swept away by the currents and the ice. Government officials, some of whom are competent marine archaeologists and surely know better, call this *in-situ preservation.* These people have used this obvious contradiction in terms to drive commercial treasure hunters from the water, despite the resulting loss to their own cultural history.

How this came to pass is the subject of this book. But because it is also about treasure hunting itself, we'll begin at the beginning, in the pioneering days when nothing much was known about treasure diving, and everything had to be learned from firsthand experience in cold, rough water. So in that sense it's mostly the story of my career in the water, where I always wanted to be, and in the political landscape, where I never wanted to be. Therefore, this story must include a particular place—the coast of Cape Breton Island—because its characteristics, as if consciously designed by sailors' mortal enemy, conspired to kill so many ships carrying tons of treasure.

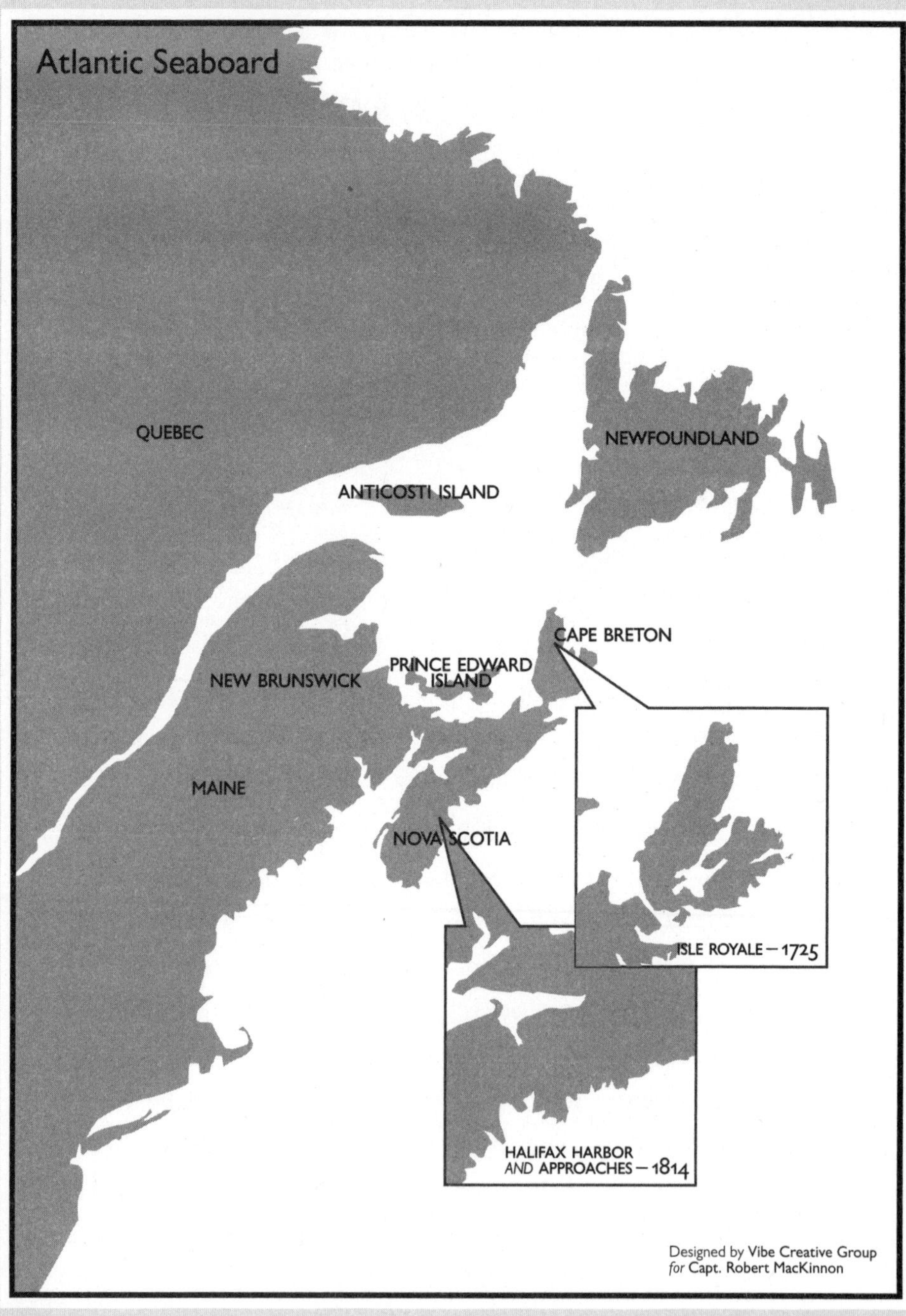

Atlantic Seaboard
QUEBEC
NEWFOUNDLAND
ANTICOSTI ISLAND
CAPE BRETON
PRINCE EDWARD
ISLAND
NEW BRUNSWICK
MAINE
NOVA SCOTIA
ISLE ROYALE – 1725
HALIFAX HARBOR
AND APPROACHES – 1814
Designed by Vibe Creative Group
for Capt. Robert MacKinnon

FOREWORD

R. K. MacKinnon's critics defame his motives as reward driven, particularly that of financial reward. They apply the term *plunderer* to the man who built Nova Scotia's first private maritime conservation laboratory, hired the first archaeologist to ensure professional integrity, respected the permitting and licensing processes in place and those that are painfully evolving. They accuse him of "pillaging" despite sound and costly methodology. But they have not bothered or taken the time to know the man. They see only his perceived seeking of monetary reward and in that tunnel no credence is given to the pure reward R. K. MacKinnon actually seeks and receives from his discoveries and in the sharing of that with the people of Nova Scotia and the world. In the ubiquitous North American culture, a modicum of romance remains. He is not a pirate to be admonished but a patriot to be celebrated. His true success is felt in the legacy he has given us, in royalty payment, in kind, and the artifacts he has harvested from the floors of our ocean and delivered to our museums. This book describes some of that legacy.

Rick Ratcliffe
Former Registrar of Treasure Trove Licenses and Titles
Nova Scotia Department of Natural Resources

TREASURE HUNTER

CHAPTER ONE

HMS *Fantome*

Those ships carried treasure," said the fishing-boat captain as we cleared the harbor mouth at Prospect, Nova Scotia, on a late-fall morning in 1975. "I've heard it all my life," he continued, a man in his 70s who'd worked these hard waters since childhood. He pointed at a line of rock reefs running parallel to the shore about a quarter mile off. Even in this light wind, swells from the open Atlantic exploded in white water when one by one they encountered those ship killers. "We call them the Dollar Shoals, because many, many years ago people found coins on the beach right opposite this place here," he said as he stopped his boat and, moving deftly like a young man, went forward to set the anchor.

"It's a funny thing," the captain said when he returned to the wheelhouse. "Anytime fishing gear is destroyed in heavy weather around here, it always seems to wash up on the beach, right there behind Dollar Shoals." Local knowledge is invaluable; people shaped by the sea in these coastal communities don't forget shipwrecks, even those that happened generations before they were born. I had heard only recently about the "*Fantome* treasure fleet" from two friends who are respected treasure divers, but apparently it was and had long been well known locally. Sport divers from Halifax had been on the wreck in the 1960s, and according to my friends, they had found two 1804 silver dollars, believed to be the most valuable silver coins in the world. But the find couldn't be verified, which is why I was there.

As I rechecked my dive gear and struggled into my wet suit, I felt that familiar flush of excitement. We professional treasure hunters tell ourselves with each dive that we're on the brink of great finds. Sometimes we are. I admit that I was and remain addicted to the excitement of potential discovery.

I sat on the transom, took a couple of deep breaths to regain professional objectivity, and rolled into the cold ocean. I was diving alone. I liked it that way in those days. I had by then complete confidence in my equipment and my ability. The sense of underwater independence pleased me, but of course I knew the practice was inherently unsafe—things can always go wrong down there no matter how skilled you are. And, I should add, there is another reason for diving alone, especially during the initial discovery phase—call it *security*. I needed to keep my finds to myself until I'd registered them with the provincial authorities and received a treasure trove permit. But I'm getting way ahead of the story.

The visibility wasn't great. These northern waters, rich in plankton, tend to be turbid most of the time. That's why they appear green, while clear water as in the Gulf Stream, thanks to a trick of light, appears blue. But since most shipwrecks occur for obvious reasons in shallow water, I didn't need to go much deeper than twenty-five feet. That's well within the range of sunlight—but also within the range of wave action. Shallow-water diving can be violent and frustrating as you're jerked back and forth with each ebb and flow. Anyway, it wasn't too bad that morning.

I had breathed through half a tank without finding any evidence of shipwreck. But then I came upon a cannon, light caliber, like an eight-pounder, in good condition. I felt a renewed flush of excitement as I scrubbed at the marine growth to expose the trunnions trying to find an identifying mark. There should have been an initial stamped on each trunnion, but the marine growth was exceptionally heavy. I kept scraping, but found no marks at all on the cannon. Air was running short; it never lasts long enough, even for experienced divers, in this cold water.

I kicked for the surface and searched the shoreline for *ranges*—that is, two objects (the church steeple, say, and the big boulder) that line up. If you can find two or more ranges at once, then you can visually extend their lines seaward to the point where they cross. Put that together with known water depth and you have a pretty good fix. This eastern stretch of the Nova Scotia coast is low-lying and not generous with features that conveniently align. But I got close enough to return to this spot on the next dive.

Swimming back to the boat along the bottom, I found a large pile of cast-iron ballast bars. These loaf-shaped chunks of cast iron, each weighing about 250 pounds, were placed deep in the ship along the keel to supply stability against the press of wind in the sails. Some bars were broken in half, a sign of the terrible force of the sea on this coast. I searched several bars for an identifying mark. What I really wanted to see was the broad arrow that the Royal Navy used to stamp on everything from the largest cannon to the simplest nail. I didn't, but that didn't matter. All that mattered to me at that moment, while I still had a couple of hundred pounds of air, was: *I was on the wreck*. I had had that feeling before, that intense, sharp-edged clarity to all I saw, and I'll never get enough. Shoreside reality vanishes. At such times, nothing exists except the water, the rocks, the leathery brown kelp lashing back and forth in the wave action, the veins of white sand and shells running between the black rocks—anywhere treasure might hide. Just over there in the field of wreckage, just beyond my range of sight, there was the treasure—I *knew* it was there. But now breathing from my double-hose regulator was becoming laborious, a sure signal that I needed to go on reserve—only 500 pounds of air remaining. I needed to get topside.

I clambered onto the boat, stayed aboard just long enough to transfer my regulator to a fresh tank. The southwest wind was getting up, as the captain was unnecessarily pointing out. I knew I'd need to hurry, even as I reminded myself that divers in a rush often get into trouble. I quickly relocated the ballast bars, and swam seaward following the trail of man-made things barely distinguishable amid the rocks and kelp, to a depth of about 35 feet, where the wreckage faded out.

When I was a young boy reading about pirates, shipwrecks, and treasure, I imagined sunken ships sitting upright and largely intact on the bottom. From the still-standing masts and yardarms hung tatters of sails and seaweed, a shark circling the crow's nest on the mainmast, you know, Davy Jones's locker. In fact, there are intact shipwrecks from the age of sail in the deep, oxygen-less depths of Lake Superior, for instance. But of inshore wrecks on the violent east coast of Nova Scotia—almost nothing remains. The wooden hulls and masts are long gone, almost immediately battered to kindling in the wave action. One good nor'easter blowing hurricane force for days will eradicate all traces of a ship except the heaviest chunks of metal. Unless there are cannon strewn about, it takes a practiced eye to recognize where a ship has died.

I turned back toward shore and the ballast bars by a different route and came across a concretion-filled gorge between two ridges of rock.

It's in these concretions of rocks, sand, and shells that one often finds coins and other small metal artifacts. When I surfaced to take a set of bearings so I could return to this likely looking spot, I saw the captain waving at me. I knew what he wanted. The wind had gotten up considerably since I'd entered the water, and the captain wanted to go. I thought to pretend I hadn't seen him, but when he started waving both arms overhead, I swam reluctantly back to his boat. He was right; the weather now verged on rotten, and it was deteriorating. The deck was pitching too steeply to stand up without holding on. Everyone around here—especially grizzled old captains—know how quickly heavy weather blows in along this coast and how, when it does, conditions turn downright deadly.

The captain didn't want me to go back. I knew I shouldn't go back, but I also knew I *was* going back. I knew, too, that if the captain started his engine and hauled his anchor, there was no way I could stop him. I had to talk fast. I blathered about my vast experience diving in weather worse than this, my safety precautions, and anything else I could think of to keep him on-site for *one more dive*. I was practically beseeching him when he said, "All right, go. But be back here in one half hour."

I changed out my second tank for the third before he could change his mind. As I rolled over the side, I heard him shout, "Half an hour!" He was probably thinking about what he'd tell the police when, just before mounting a search for the damn fool's body, they asked, "Why'd you let him dive alone in *this*?" Pulling myself down the surging anchor line, I searched for my bearings among the bottom features. Visibility had diminished in the surge. Long kelp strings whipped back and forth, and so did I. The surge was impeding my progress to the treasure, and I hated it for that. As I swam into shallower water toward the concretions I'd seen in the gorge, the wave force increased. I was losing my bearings, contemplating turning back to find them, when I saw the concretions. I wanted to examine them for metal objects that sometimes protrude, but I couldn't get there. Each time I reached for the nearest one, my hand inches from it, I got swept backward. Objectively, I could see that I probably looked comical, but I didn't find it funny. The thought of leaving, before I knew what if anything was there—well, I just couldn't let that happen. But my allotted half hour was already up.

Breathing way harder than normal, I picked up two heavy metal pins lying loose near the concretions, for the extra weight, wedged myself into the little gorge, and pulled myself now closer to the first concretion. . . . I felt like shouting for joy into my mouthpiece. Maybe I did. For there before me, within reach and plain sight, was treasure, real treasure. Coins everywhere. And metal household artifacts. Some of the nearby concretions consisted almost entirely of coins. I stopped noticing the cold—about 38°F—I forgot about the weather, about the anxious captain, and about all aspects of my shoreside life, even my present safety. I was *here*, exactly where I'd known since childhood I belonged. Gold fever was running rampant. But I had to calm down, act professionally. Try to identify things in an objective manner.

Without touching them, I saw that many of the coins were silver Spanish reales of all denominations, but mostly there were eight-reale coins, the legendary pieces of eight. Other coins were lying loose on the sandy seafloor. I gently waved away the sand and saw that these were American and British coins, gold, silver, and copper. On some I could see the dates from 1795 to 1800. A little farther along the gorge in a shoreward direction, I made a discovery more thrilling than the coins. Silverware protruded from the matrix of sand, gravel, and shell hash. Straining to stay in place in the building surge, I saw that several utensils were stuck in the concretion with their handles visible. Some were embossed. Several were engraved with the crest of a large bird standing on a mound, holding something I could not make out in its beak, maybe arrows.

Did that mean, as my friends suspected, as I *wanted* to believe, that this was the wreck of the British warship *Fantome* or one of the plunder ships she escorted? In August 1814, British troops embarked from warships and marched inland from Chesapeake Bay, in the face of scant resistance, and invaded Washington. British troops sat down at Dolley Madison's table—set for a banquet before she fled town with only a few precious objects, including the Stuart portrait of George Washington—had a fine dinner, and toasted His Majesty with the president's wine. They loaded the squadron of nine armed vessels with the spoils of war and sent them north, first for Castine, Maine, thence to the British stronghold at Halifax. En route they picked up an armed escort—HMS *Fantome*. She escorted the fleet *almost* to Halifax before she and the other ships ran up on the Dollar Shoals barely 15 miles from the harbor mouth. Because the night was calm, the ships went down without loss of life.

Cold, exhausted, and quietly euphoric, I had in fact listened respectfully to the captain's salty reprimand; he was, after all, absolutely right. In his view, I had risked his vessel's safety and his reputation by risking my life. I felt a little guilty about the fact that I didn't care. I had found the *Fantome* fleet treasure, at least a major part of it. I couldn't of course prove it without a proper investigation that followed sound scientific procedures, but I *knew* I was on the *Fantome* and the small fleet she escorted to its doom.

On that third dive, running dangerously low on air, I had pushed the limits of safety and the captain's patience, making one more pass over the treasure-filled gorges. I caught sight of an ornate handle sticking out of the shell hash and gravel. I gently removed it from its historic resting place. It was a beautiful silver or pewter tankard complete with a flip top, fully crested and embossed with what looked like a stag and a lion. On the bottom of the tankard, after clearing off the black tarnish, I made out the winged griffon indicating that it was of British origin.

Removing the tankard exposed the edge of what looked like a dinner plate. I carefully hand fanned the debris from the rim and saw that it was a silver plate, the topmost in a stack of plates. I carefully extracted the stack from the bottom debris. Without removing the matrix of mud, sand, and shell hash, I could still see the same eagle-like bird holding arrows embossed on the silverware. I was beginning to shake with excitement. I could feel the tank running dry, and pulled the reserve rod, but I just had to stay a few moments longer.

Near the silver plates, I noticed something large, round, and flat sticking out from under several small boulders. It was a large silver serving tray[1] with a fine beaded edge. Inside the bowl of the tray lay countless forks and spoons held in place by years of solidified sediment. I again picked up a couple of iron bars for their weight, since the nearly empty aluminum tank was quickly becoming buoyant, while the underwater conditions were growing steadily more and more hostile.

During the very few minutes of air I had left, I slowed my breathing and my motions, trying to take all of it in. I calmed down, feeling a strong but peaceful connection to the sea and to the past, to events that happened here almost two centuries ago. This was where I belonged, touching the past in this way, and I felt a nostalgic sense of loss that soon, very soon, I would have to leave it. During the last few pounds of air, I reburied or replaced all the artifacts I had disturbed, more a gesture than anything else because the ocean was constantly, violently moving such objects with every spring tide and northeast storm. I surfaced, sad for the end of the experience and for the continuing degradation by the sea of the precious objects on what might be the richest shipwreck ever lost in Nova Scotia waters. A fresh flood of excitement washed over me as the captain bluntly reprimanded me.

As we steamed back to Prospect, I sat alone on the transom. I didn't dare join the captain in his wheelhouse. But about halfway there, he turned his boat over to his deckhand. Then, instead of reprimanding me he embraced me as if I were a trusted mate. "Son," he said with a big smile, "I have seen some crazy buggers in my day, but you take the cake. This place is a pure hellhole in even the best of weather conditions, but you pulled off three dives." He sat down on a fish box and gestured for me to sit on the adjacent box. "Yes, you surely did." He nodded approvingly, and went on to say that during storms from the southeast and east, the waves reach a height of over 60 feet and wash up way past the head of the beach. "That's why there are no trees near the shore." Then, pointing to a strip of relatively flat water off to the north between Betty Island and the mainland, he said, "That's Privateer Passage. The old privateers used it as a secret passage leading to Halifax and to evade enemy ships that may be chasing them. I reckon this was what the captain of your wreck had in mind, a shortcut and a secure route for his treasure fleet. Don't get me wrong, it's a damn dangerous place even with local knowledge, but the Brits would have had that. It's just that your guy hauled up to the north too soon. That's why the wreck's so close to the beach."

Nova Scotia is a fine place to be a treasure hunter. From Black Point near my home on northern Cape Breton, around the corner past Scatarie Island where the coast trends southwestward, past Halifax, Canso, and Lunenburg to Yarmouth on the south coast, and onward into the Bay of Fundy—the 7,597-kilometer-long Nova Scotia coast is strewn with shipwrecks. There are literally thousands of them. I'll bet that for every two known wreck sites, there is at least one yet undiscovered site. I have often seen wrecks layered one atop the other. And the vast majority of the ships in unknown or even known wreck sites will go unidentified forever. There are two reasons why Nova Scotia has claimed so many victims, or, to say it differently, why Nova Scotia is a nautical death threat. One is its geographical position. The other lies in the exquisitely vicious nature of the coast itself.

Nova Scotia sits athwart nearly every shipping lane between Europe and North America. In the age of sail—which is to say most of the entire history of shipping—there were two routes across the Atlantic, both dictated by permanent wind belts. By the southern route, ships typically called at or passed close to Bermuda, the Azores, then on to ports in western Europe, or vice versa for westbound ships. Ships following the northern or great circle route sailed a shorter distance, but they encountered far colder, foggier, and stormier conditions. Because it's the shortest and most direct passage, commercial jets bound, say, from New York to London still use this great circle route. However, the arc of the circle brought ships close to the lurking obstructions along the Nova Scotia coast and its treacherous offshore islands, Scatarie, St. Paul, and especially Sable Island, which has gained the appellation "Graveyard of the Atlantic."

Consider also the nautical jeopardy facing ships bound to or from the Gulf of St. Lawrence. The island of Newfoundland sits like a gigantic stopper at the mouth of the gulf. You can leave (or enter) the Gulf of St. Lawrence via the Strait of Belle Isle over the top of the big island. But the course around the south coast of Newfoundland was far more practical. That, however, required ships to thread the needle through the Cabot Strait between Newfoundland and Nova Scotia's Cape Breton

Island. The Cabot Strait, which has been called the "Home of Fog," lies directly under the west-to-east storm track.

In addition to about 300 years of ships passing close aboard Nova Scotia, almost as many stopped here. Back in the days when it could take two months to cross the Atlantic, Nova Scotia, with its many deep harbors, was a convenient place to water and provision before stepping off into open ocean. Because of its position on the sea-lanes as well as its profuse natural harbors (Sydney in the north, Halifax on the central coast, and Yarmouth in the south being the busiest), Nova Scotia was used as a fleet-assembling area first by the Spanish in the 16th century and afterward by the British. During the colonial period, Halifax Harbor played a vital role in settling what would become the United States, and during the War of 1812, the Americans intended (unrealistically) to capture Halifax because it was so useful to the British. And that of course was the *Fantome* fleet's destination on that fateful November night in 1814.

But far and away the greatest number of ships sailed from and to this coast for fish. When John Cabot sailed into the supposedly unexplored waters of the Canadian Maritimes, he found fleets of Basque fishermen. Arguably, they were in the Western Hemisphere before 1492 (the Vikings certainly were), but in any case, codfish from the Grand Banks fed Europe for centuries. Coastal towns were founded and settled by fishermen to be closer to the fish. Fish fed the people and powered economies in Europe as well as in Canada and New England. One historian called cod "the fish that saved America." Sadly, the cod are gone now, fished out, but during the long heyday of the Grand Banks fishery, millions of ships were built, and the two busiest fishing-ship harbors were not in Newfoundland or New England, but in Halifax and Lunenburg, Nova Scotia.

So Nova Scotia had plenty of ship traffic for a very long time, perhaps the first requirement for multiple shipwrecks. Even so, there are far more wrecks here than on other busy coastlines because this coast gathers the worst nautical conspirators in one place to produce a particularly lethal trap. They are in no particular order: fog, heavy current, and a granite bottom. Fog happens when warm air settles over cold North Atlantic water. In summer, it's not a question of whether there will be fog but of how much fog there will be. Maybe we'll have a luxurious half mile of visibility or maybe none. When seamen say, "It's the black thick o' fog," they mean you can't see the bow of a 40-foot boat from the wheelhouse, and when the old expression "pea soup fog" comes up, they mean you can't see *anything*. Even visitors who've heard stories about Nova Scotia fog before they arrive are astounded when they observe it. Nova Scotia fog made young sailors in engineless, wooden sailing vessels old before their time.

Fog is an obvious nautical danger, but it has a coconspirator—current. Strong tides roar out of the Gulf of St. Lawrence and flow southwest down the coast. Along the way, they encounter head-on other north-setting currents, including an arm of the Gulf Stream. If the currents behaved predictably, it wouldn't be so bad. You'd just get used to it. But the current patterns are chaotic. And they never meet peaceably. They generate rough, confused seas even in the lightest breeze. And when a stiff wind blows against a heavy current, nasty, flat-faced waves get up like rock walls. The wind-aggravated current produces waves that'll loosen your molars, but chances are they won't sink you.

The potentially lethal problem for mariners is that currents can affect a ship's course over the bottom. In other words, currents can take your ship places you don't want it to go. And the insidious part is that from the deck of a ship you can't tell that you're being set one way or the other by currents, unless you have land references in sight. Your bow can be pointing spot on toward your desired compass heading while in fact you're moving sideways. That's not a big problem in the open ocean, but near this shore in dense fog, currents are a very great problem indeed. My heart goes out to these sailors groping blindly by guess and by God as they approached the real monster lurking on the Nova Scotia coast—rocks.

Ice Age glaciers ground Nova Scotia right down to the bedrock. Wherever the advancing ice found a riverbed or a natural fault, it gouged deep trenches in the ancient shoreline. These became fjord-like bays, making excellent harbors, when the ice sheet melted and the sea level rose some 10,000 years ago. The retreating glaciers left behind an unimaginable tonnage of rock, some of which had been carried from central Canada. And much of that rock became, with the floods of melt-water, vicious ledges, reefs, and islands lying sometimes miles from shore. Much later, when ships found this coast, the rocks became nautical nightmares. Worst of all are the sunkers. On fine days, you can see many of the ledges and reefs even at high tide; and if you can't see the rocks themselves, you often see the swells breaking over them. Sunkers, however, lurk just below the surface at low tide. Waiting. You can't see them. They've torn the bottoms out of countless ships for 400 years.

I often think about the people aboard those ships, sometimes when I'm at the wheel of my own boat in a snarling southwest wind blowing dead against a full flood tide with visibility fading fast. I can get a fine fix from my GPS anytime I wish, and my radar will show me where the ledges and reefs lie even in the densest fog. I still need to pay close attention, but I have at hand all the navigation information I need. That electronic stuff has been available for only a blink of the eye in maritime history. It wasn't around when I began my fishing and diving career, so I can relate somewhat to the anxiety and fear aboard a sailing vessel after a rough crossing from Europe, when the captain would have been searching for the safety of Halifax Harbor in heavy weather, big seas, and bad visibility. And I imagine what it was like for a ship in the Gulf of St. Lawrence, outbound for England or the Caribbean, sailing through the Cabot Strait at night, with 30 knots of winter wind on the bow while the sunkers sprawling northward from Cape Breton lay in wait. I understand. I've spent my whole life on these waters, and I've seen the sad remains of many ships that didn't make it. Most left no survivors to tell their tale. Unknown.

It's interesting, however, that the wreck of the *Fantome* and the fleet she escorted was not caused by any of the above conspirators. The night was calm, visibility excellent. The *Fantome* officers were probably doing the navigating, the plunder ships following. I wonder what they saw that they mistook for the entrance to Halifax. I wonder, too, why the captain didn't give the order to stand off until daylight, but it's not fair to judge him from this remove. Those guys were used to traveling this coast at night. What we can only admire as brilliant feats of seamanship were commonplace then. So perhaps the captain took this entry for granted, having made it time and again, and didn't wait to reconcile his position for certain. That still happens a lot. The only reason everyone got ashore alive was that the weather held fair. In a blow, all would have drowned.

I remember now with mixed emotions my pure excitement in 1975 when I found the *Fantome* fleet. Had I known then the effort and trouble, the expense and the unjust criticism I was to incur as a result, my excitement would have been tempered—but only slightly.

NOTES

1. Several years later, in the fall of 1977, while diving on the wreck site of the French pay ship *Le Chameau*, which had been lost just north of Fortress Louisbourg in 1725, I discovered yet another large silver serving tray. I was working with Jim Mullins, engaged in securing the anchor line of our rubber chase boat to some cannon near Chameau Rock. In an attempt to pass the mooring line under the cannon to tie off, I saw the rim of a large silver tray, the rest hidden under two cannon that had, over time, concreted together. I cleared away some of the bottom debris but soon realized that the cannon would have to be removed in order to gain a safe recovery of this culturally significant item from the ship's cargo.

I returned to the surface and explained the find to Jim. We pondered over what to do, not wanting to cause any damage to such a precious artifact. In the end, I decided to call Parks Canada, hoping they would send an archaeologist to help in the recovery. They did, sending Jim Ringer. During several reconnaissance dives, Ringer and I studied the best way to recover the silver serving tray unharmed. We eventually employed hydraulic jacks, lifting the cannon high enough to allow us to remove the silver tray completely unscathed.

Once back on deck, we took a closer look at this unique artifact. It measured approximately 20 inches in diameter, with a very fine beaded edge. The tray was filled to the brim with lead bird shot, which we felt had helped it to keep its perfect shape under the press of the cannon's weight. Turning it over to examine the bottom, we noticed several hallmarks and initials. Here, from the shipwreck, was a rare cultural artifact whose origin and owner should be easy to identify.

Ringer packed the silver serving tray for delivery to Parks Canada headquarters in Ottawa, but not before commenting on the importance of its recovery in an almost-perfect state. Our first request of Parks was that they return it to Fortress Louisbourg for display purposes, in order to represent an actual portion of the *Le Chameau*'s cargo. They agreed. We also asked that we be given all due recognition as the divers who found it. They agreed to that, too.

We made several inquiries, but to the best of our knowledge, the silver serving tray never became part of the Fortress Louisbourg collection. To this day, what actually happened to the silver tray after it arrived in Ottawa still remains a mystery.

CHAPTER TWO

First Shipwreck: SS *Montara*

I was born in Glace Bay, Nova Scotia, in 1950. The French named and settled Glace Bay (*glace*, meaning "glass," referring to ice) about 1720. Like the Basques, Spanish, Portuguese, and English, the French came initially for the fish. And then they discovered the coal, visible seams of it, some 12 feet thick on most every cliff face. When the easy pickings played out, they followed the coal underground, pioneering deep-tunnel mining while inventing the technique called room-and-pillar mining. Later, the steel industry came to Cape Breton Island, and for a century, the mills, located around the nearby city of Sydney, produced more steel than anywhere else in Canada and the northern United States. Fishing, mining, steel—they're all gone now, leaving a hole in the fabric of the economy and society that will never be filled.

My father entered the mine—it was only three miles from our home—when he was 11 years old, and he worked underground for the next 52 years. He and my mother, both of Highland Scot descent, instilled in my brother, sister, and me those traditional values of hard work, honesty, and deep pride in one's ability to support a family that sometimes seem old-fashioned in today's world. Had the industries survived as a context, perhaps those values would still seem in tune with the world. Anyway, I absorbed them and retain them still. Right after high school in Glace Bay, I applied to join the Royal Canadian Mounted Police. As I waited to learn whether I would be accepted, I worked as a lineman's ground hand for the local power company. The RCMP accepted me, and I served five years, stationed in Ontario. The trouble was, there is no ocean in Ontario. The lineman job was a good job, supplied what jobs are supposed to supply, but it was too late for me. The ocean had already reached out and grabbed me.

In a way, it was my parents' fault. In those days on Cape Breton Island a family could own a weekend/summer home on a miner's salary. Ours was in Catalone, overlooking Mira Bay on the ocean. My siblings and I soon became amphibians. We learned to swim right after we mastered walking. My brother, John, and I were hopelessly stricken, practicing for the time when our boyish adventures would become reality. I knew that somehow I would make my living on the water. I had to.

I shouldn't blame it all on my parents. You can't get far from the sea in Nova Scotia, particularly on Cape Breton, where for centuries boys have been imagining an ocean life, where talk of the sea is constantly in the air. Some can ignore the natural ocean attraction and get on in another walk of life. But many of us can't; I couldn't. And it wasn't only the sea stories I heard during my youth. There was also much talk of sunken treasure. Nothing is better than sunken treasure to stir a sea-struck kid's ardor. The media at the time were enthusiastically reporting a treasure-related court case, a squabble over how to divide the treasure between the guys who had found it. The case lingered for almost six years, and from the media coverage, we learned, really for the first time, that our coasts were thick with wrecks from all periods of marine history. Meanwhile, I had a cousin Paddy MacKinnon, who had actually *been* treasure hunting.

It was 1960; I was a mere 10 years old when Paddy showed up in town with scuba gear. Not a lot of divers today remember just how primitive and utterly unregulated diving was back then. No one knew anything. There were no available manuals, let alone schools where people with experience could tell us about, say, embolisms. We never heard of certification. But just look at all that wonderful equipment. I was utterly captivated by Paddy's new gear. *Then* soon after acquiring it, Paddy and another diver found a hoard of coins in a wreck off Louisbourg. Though it took a while to identify the find, the coins turned out to be Latin American silver cobs. The odd-shaped silver coins were inscribed in Latin and Spanish symbols and were mistaken as possibly even Russian in origin. They all had partial dates that made them even more of a mystery for Paddy and others at the time. The only thing the divers were sure of was that the coins were made of silver.

That did it. No sooner did Paddy take up diving than he found a hoard of treasure! Who knew whether it was actually worth anything? The point was that meant there must be a lot more treasure down there, waiting for *me* to discover it. It stood to reason, didn't it, seeing as there were so many wrecks along our coast and many within a short swim off the shore? There could be no question about it. A guy I met working as a lineman some years later—Ace Lynk was his name—was also convinced. We talked of little else at work. Ace and I had gold fever before we ever went diving. Even my father got into the spirit of the thing after Paddy discovered those coins. There was nothing to do but acquire diving gear (*scuba* as a word had yet to be coined). That was an exciting day.

There was no such thing as a dive shop anywhere near Glace Bay, but a sporting goods store had ordered the basics after the discovery of treasure on the wreck site of the pay ship *Le Chameau*. For $110, I bought one 72-cubic-inch tank painted bright orange that turned out to be a fire extinguisher cylinder.

I bought a White Stag single-hose regulator, a quarter-inch wet suit top, fins, a knife, and a U.S. Divers' Pinocchio mask, the same mask I would use for the next 30 years. I went straight from the store to the water. I could breathe and I could get to the bottom. What else did I need to know? Then it was time to collect Ace, who had followed me into the store, and do a proper open-water dive.

It was mid-December, and the air temperature was 30°F, the water temperature, 34°F. I had only half a wet suit, but I didn't care; I was diving. In about 40 feet of water, we poked around on the bottom searching for anything, everything. In those days, tanks came with a reserve valve, because there were no proper pressure gauges. So what you did was breathe until breathing became hard, then you activated the reserve. You had about 500 pounds of air remaining. We used it to swim back to shore, where we sat for a while on the rocks savoring the experience, never mind winter. Never mind either that Ace had not cleared his ears properly and so filled part of his mask with blood or that I had a savage earache that lasted for days. Apparently we still had a few things to learn about this diving business. Like, for instance, the effects of water pressure on the human ear canals. Shortly after that, the ice came in. It took nothing less than that to end our dive season, after only one dive.

The owner of the local sports shop, who appreciated, maybe even respected, my avid interest, ordered me a proper wet suit, though he knew I couldn't afford it. In a way, that act of friendship settled it. When the suit arrived—a beautiful Parkway complete with full farmer John pants, boots, jacket, hood, and a pair of three-fingered gloves—I knew my future—at 17. The rest of that school year seemed to take a decade, during which we talked about nothing but diving, shipwrecks, and treasure. When the ice went out in May, I made the second dive of my life. It turned out to be a valuable lesson in retrospect, but it was scary in the event.

These two local salvage divers of Ace's acquaintance and their boat captain meant to excavate for valuable scrap metals on the wreck of SS *Montara*, a steel ship that had run up on the rocks off Gooseberry Cove in 1920. They invited Ace and me along for the weekend. Our *second* dive. We were bursting with anticipation—this was the big time—as we steamed out of Little Lorraine harbor, not far from the wreck site. A stiff southwest wind and a hard chop were running directly from where we wanted to go. The boat pitched and rolled to windward for what seemed an eternity at four or five knots, but finally we arrived at Gooseberry Cove. The guys had previously fixed a mooring over the wreck, and we tied onto it.

As we suited up, they explained that the water here was 60 feet deep—Ace and I pretended that we were old salts at 60 feet—and they were looking for anything made of copper, brass, or lead. These metals they could readily sell. I didn't exactly grasp how we'd get those heavy items back aboard; in fact I didn't even think to consider the question. I just wanted to get in the water, and I was nervous that they'd call it off for the weather, which was deteriorating. They didn't mention it. I followed one salvage diver to the bottom, and Ace went with the other, quickly disappearing in the murk.

I was amazed at the first sight of the wreck. It was a shambles of steel plates twisted and broken as if the *Montara* had exploded, not wrecked on the rocks. I hadn't expected an intact ship sitting on the bottom, like a model ship in an aquarium, but I did expect it to still resemble a ship.

The stern section lay upside down, and I could see the enormous propeller pointing at the surface. That was the only indication that this was once a ship. Almost none of this damage had happened when she struck the bottom. The ocean had obliterated this ship *after* she sank. The violence stunned me as I swam over it. But there was work to do, as the other diver indicated, pointing toward several red-brass valves, which I understood he wanted me to clear from the surrounding wreckage. He swam away while I worked, then returned with the end of a steel cable and showed me how to "shackle up" the valves. He gave a tug on the wire, and the captain, who had remained topside, winched them up. Okay, that was easy. There was plenty more salvage strewn around; we'd get it on the next dive.

The weather had indeed deteriorated, and we had a strenuous time of it climbing back aboard on the ladder (called a swindle tree, for some reason I never learned) hung over the side. Ace and his partner were already aboard. Ace had had some trouble with his regulator, and they both had gotten cold. Now they were drinking rum to warm up and discussing the weather; soon they'd be talking about leaving.

"Look, let me make one more dive," I blurted before that. I appealed to their profit motive, told them I was feeling fit and was toasty in my new wet suit, why not make some money? I made two more dives, as it turned out, shackling up all the scrap I could get to, tugging the wire, watching it climb away. This was very satisfying. I was getting cold during the third dive of the day, thinking about packing it in, when I spotted a huge bronze valve. I wanted it. I attached it to the wire, gave the "up" signal, and made for the surface.

It was blowing hard by then, swells running eight feet and higher, visibility near nil. Suddenly I felt very alone out there. I wanted to be aboard. But the boat was bucking viciously, and the stern section was slamming down in the troughs with deadly force. I timed the pitch to get a foot and handhold on the swindle tree, and the upswing just about hurled me over the rail. It was hard to stand up on the deck. Guys were crawling around trying to secure loose gear, while the captain and one of the salvers worked at the winch. Something was wrong—the winch could not lift the treasure I'd shackled it to.

Meanwhile, the wind had backed to the south as it had freshened, and the waves started coming, with unlimited fetch, from the open Atlantic, while one of the ugliest reefs I've ever seen lay about 100 feet to leeward. And now the strain on the winch was pulling the boat around beam-on to the waves. Green water poured over the side. We were in trouble. That cable had to be cut, even though it meant losing a lot of expensive iron wire. But no one could find the bolt cutters. It's a nautical truism that it's usually not a single mishap but a series of them that combine to sink you. Maybe that's what happened aboard the ship I had tethered us to, which was now threatening to drag us under. The captain came out of the wheelhouse with a fire axe and began to chop at the cable. When he got tired, one of the other divers took over. They barely scratched the cable.

"Do you have a cold chisel aboard?" Ace shouted in the captain's ear.

Yes, he did. He retrieved it from the wheelhouse, Ace set up a steel backing plate, and with a few deft whacks with the heavy hammer, the cable parted and zinged overboard. Maybe things were starting to go right. Free now, the boat fell away to the wind, and the bow met the waves. She was still bucking fiercely against the mooring line, but that was far better than presenting her side to the waves. We could then cut the mooring line and get out of there—after the captain started the engine. All that was left was to hope it had the power to drive us out of there against the elements.

It started to rain, and with the rain came an avalanche of pea-soup fog.

But the engine wouldn't start, and—for the first time—I was

frightened at sea. I glanced at Ace. He was frightened. If the mooring line parted or if the pitching tore out the deck cleat, then, engineless, this boat would crash in minutes on the same rocks that claimed the *Montara*. The four of us were still in our wet suits and could probably swim ashore, assuming we weren't injured in the crash. But what about the captain? He had no wet suit; we'd have to escort him ashore. Hopeless sounds came topside from the engine. Maybe it would be better to abandon ship before she struck. . . . Even as I tried to devise something like a plan, I knew the chance that any of us would make it ashore in one piece was about nil.

The captain emerged from the wheelhouse. "I've got to go down into the engine room and change the battery banks."

"How long will it take?" someone shouted.

"Longer than we've got," said the captain. His best anchor, he said, was right there under the stern rail. "Make it ready, lay out the anchor road and lash it to the stern tie-up irons." Then he disappeared into the engine room. Night was coming on. All the elements were conspiring against us. The motion down there in the engine room must have been brutal. We counted the minutes while we sweated to prepare the last-ditch anchor.

Days seemed to go by before the captain emerged to announce that he'd changed batteries and that he needed someone to turn the ignition while he sprayed starter fluid into the engine intakes. He was down below again, shouting, "Now, turn it on!"

The engine turned over, but it did not start.

"Okay, try it now!"

The engine started—what a sweet sound—with a big puff of black smoke. But then we heard a shout of alarm from the engine room. What now? "Shut her down! Shut her down!" he bellowed. During one of the savage pitches, the captain had fallen against the engine and got his jacket sleeve caught in a fan belt. He gave a mighty, final jerk to free himself and possibly to save his arm. He was free. "Let her run, don't shut down!" He climbed out of the engine room, his jacket in tatters, and took his place at the wheel. He ordered one of the divers to take the fire axe forward and cut the mooring line; the other passed a life jacket to the captain. "This old girl can make only four or five knots in the best conditions," the captain announced. "We may not have the power to drive out of here against this gale."

Then what? Ace and I glanced shoreward at the waves exploding on the line of reefs. No, we wouldn't have a prayer in that water. So all we could do was wait to see what the old girl could do against 35 knots with higher gusts and 15-foot seas. . . . She tried hard, but, no, she lacked the power to gain sea room. The captain gave up and let the boat fall off to leeward. Then our only chance was to steer inshore of the sunkers in the narrow channel between the reefs and the mainland rocks—in a gale of wind in fog at night—with no navigation equipment except a box compass, no radar, not even a marine radio. At least the seas were slightly flatter in the channel as the waves expended some of their power on the reefs. No one spoke as the captain, outwardly calm, picked his way back toward Little Lorraine harbor. He was making an excellent job of it, and our hopes for survival rose as we neared Little Lorraine. Then hopes plunged when we got a look at the harbor entrance.

It was a scene of terrible chaos, waves and white water exploding over the off-lying obstructions, sending chills through the lot of us. To attempt an entry here would be an act of suicide. The captain turned her away, again trying to gain some sea room to weather. We appeared to make no progress. The boat was rising capably to the waves, but still we were getting nowhere. We had gathered in the shelter of the wheelhouse, and the captain said, "Well, boys, we've got problems now. We can't beat out of here. We're going to have to run with it, and hope we can make

Main-a-Dieu Harbor about seven miles northwest o' here." Then he added words that sounded a lot like a death sentence. "I don't know Main-a-Dieu. Any of you boys know it?" No one spoke.

This was the worst possible nautical predicament short of outright sinking. Since it was impossible to power against the gale, we were putting our stern quarter to it and running with the wind—straight for the land, the dreaded lee shore. Lee shores have killed many times more ships than storms at sea. We'd made a lot of mistakes so far both as divers and seamen, but there was still hope. However, we had to nail the harbor (that no one was familiar with) on the most treacherous coast Nova Scotia has to offer, and once we committed ourselves, there would be no turning back. If we missed it—well, I tried not to dwell on that in detail. And still the weather worsened. How was that possible? We made no better than three knots, the speed of an easy jog, for about two hours while we listened to the engine and to the bilge pump straining to discharge the water coming aboard almost constantly. If either packed it in—no, that, too, was best not considered too closely.

"Look!" said three of us at once. Clear sky, patches of it, anyway, stars. We could *see* the shoreline! We could *see* the harbor lights—we could actually *see* the blinking red light that marked the starboard side of the fairway. The whole episode had been a humbling rebuke to our carelessness, but it finally looked like we wouldn't be paying for the lesson with our lives.

It must be hard for landsmen to credit the relief a seaman in jeopardy feels when he turns behind a lee after a beating at sea. The malicious winds die; the seas flatten. Maybe it's like that point when a bad toothache goes away. We were utterly exhausted by the motion and the tension, not to mention the diving, but we felt giddy. And very alive. When the feeling passed after we'd docked in complete shelter and safety, I began to think of my future in practical terms.

I meant to learn more of diving. I'd loved the time on the wreck. And though scared by the experience afterward, I was not scared off. That was clear. But I would have to do it differently. Yes, I needed a lot more experience, but in the future I couldn't just jump on any boat that turned up. In my headlong enthusiasm to dive, I'd done things without thinking. I'd made a serious mistake down there, shackling onto something that couldn't be lifted. That had set in motion a series of mistakes that might well have killed us had we been a little less lucky. Okay, that was that.

And then there was the weather and also there was the Cape Breton coast. I'd spent my entire 17 years on that coast. I knew how treacherous it was. And I knew how quickly the weather could change for the very worst. But I'd just hopped aboard without even thinking about weather. I would need to demonstrate a lot more respect for those waters and the weather if I wanted a career of any length. And I'd need to take responsibility. I would need to become a captain myself. I wasn't ready yet. I had other immediate plans, but after that, the future was clear. I belonged out there.

I learned one other thing during those three dives. The ship was made of steel when it sunk in 1920, yet the sea had battered it to unidentifiable wreckage. What would the sea do to a wooden ship sunk in shallow water two or three centuries ago? Those were the ships that interested me. Clearly, I would need to adjust my expectations about what I'd see if I found one. Would I even recognize it as a shipwreck?

CHAPTER THREE

The Treasure of Ragged Rock Cove

I was in the water most every day the summer I first went diving. Ace was with me much of the time, and when he wasn't, I dove alone. Though my excitement had not waned an iota after the near-death experience, I took a more professional, studious approach to diving, partly in the interest of survival. (There are bold divers and there are old divers, but there are no old bold divers.) But also I wanted to be a *professional.* More specifically, I wanted to be a treasure salver. That meant I'd be doing most of my diving in shallow water, because that's where most ships wrecked. I honed my techniques in breaking surf and rushing tides in close proximity to reefs and jagged sunkers, absorbing a series of beatings as dues to the learning process.

I was invited to dive on several early-20th-century iron shipwrecks of vessels that had gone down after tearing holes in their bottoms on the reefs and ledges. I spent a lot of time that summer swimming over twisted iron plates, the ruined remnants of undelivered cargo, and a slew of unidentifiable metal objects, reminders of the terrible violence inflicted on these sad ships after they had sunk or run high and dry on the rocks. For those who have not seen them with their own eyes, it's hard to imagine the savage power of the nor'easters, many at hurricane velocity, that slam into this coast every winter. It's harder still to imagine conditions aboard one of those ships when, in the dead of night with a 60-knot blizzard blowing across her deck, she struck the rocks—the terrible noise and the fear. No, these were not the kinds of wrecks I longed to discover. I wanted old wrecks from days before ships were made of metal and powered by engines. I wanted treasure but also history. The iron wrecks were merely modern tragedies. But on one occasion the two intersected, or almost.

Ace phoned to ask if I'd join him and two other guys (whom I didn't know) to dive on a French steam trawler recently wrecked at Kelpy Cove, not far from Main-a-Dieu. The other two divers had already chartered a captained boat. This was beginning to sound familiar, but I said yes. On July 1, 1968, a Canadian holiday, we gathered on the fish buyer's wharf at Main-a-Dieu to meet the others and the captain. The idea was to salvage the bronze propeller, and we'd share any profits equally. That sounded good in my cash-starved state; I liked the other guys, the boat, and the captain, a lobsterman who had plenty of local knowledge. He warned us about the nasty reefs and heavy tidal currents in the dive area, but I was getting used to that by then. Actually, I'd never dove in any other conditions.

As we steamed toward the dive site on a swelteringly hot day, I felt that now-familiar excitement and expectation. Who knew, the dive might be interesting as well as lucrative. But en route it became clear that there was a lot we didn't know. We didn't know whether the ship was clear for salvage or whether the propeller was still on the wreck. And even if it was there, we had no idea how we'd remove it from its shafting or bring it aboard if we somehow managed to free it. On the plus side, the ship had wrecked only a few days earlier, so it was probably still reasonably intact.

It was indeed. We fell silent at the sight: a 100-foot wood-and-steel ship lying on her starboard side a good 20 feet above the high-water mark as if it were a toy left by a child bored with his ship. She sat on the rocks at a bow-up, stern-down angle, and the propeller we'd come for glinted in the unseasonably hot sun. So the plan was to anchor as close as possible to the wreck, about 500 feet away, and swim to it with masks, snorkels, and fins. I was paired with Ace. For safety's sake, the other two divers would swim to the rocks first. Ace and I would stay aboard and stand ready to help the captain get the anchor if they got into trouble, and while we waited we discussed recovery protocol with the captain. We needed cutting gear to remove the propeller, a way to float it off the beach, and then a means to tow it back to the harbor. When we saw the others safely standing on the reefs near shore, Ace and I made the long swim to shore, but by a slightly different route.

Halfway there, the bottom shoaled to about 15 feet, a bedrock shelf hove into view. Suddenly I saw forks and spoons, literally hundreds of them strewn over the ledge as far as I could see in every direction. I motioned for Ace. Where did all this flatware come from? The ship had wrecked only several days before, yet the stuff seemed to have been in the water longer. Could these forks and spoons have spilled from another wreck? Ace and I treaded water to confer. We shouted and waved at the guys on the rocks, but the pounding surf muffled our voices. The divers waved at us in return, telling us to join them. Before doing so, I took a quick set of eyeball bearings to fix the position.

Once ashore, we told them excitedly about our find. They weren't interested. "Who cares? Who wants some old forks and spoons?"

There weren't just "some," I explained, there were hundreds, but that didn't matter to the divers, already frustrated that they had found nothing of value. They insisted that our find was valueless, and we supposed they were right.

"What about the propeller?"

"It's made of steel, not bronze. It's worthless! Like your forks and spoons." They waded in and began the empty-handed swim back to the boat.

Ace and I repeated our incoming route to have another look at the spoons. There were more than we had seen earlier. Our rule even then was to disturb nothing of potential historical value, but I suggested picking up two to show the others back on the boat. But Ace thought we should consult with them first. I came aboard talking about another swim over the stuff; I thought it would be an easy sell. But, no, they had already decided to leave.

The captain pointed out that the tide had turned, the wind had shifted, and now his stern hung within a boat's length of a toothy reef. He wanted to up anchor and get out of here while the getting was good. How could I argue with that? But as we steamed away toward Mira Bay, about 15 miles north, to salvage scrap from a World War II–era plane crash, I had a feeling we were making a serious error, and I didn't want to drop it. I asked the captain where he thought all those forks and spoons came from.

He had no idea, he said, then suddenly: "Wait a minute, boys. You know, it's around here somewhere they found that treasure."

Treasure? "What treasure?"

"You know, the one they fought over for so long in court."

I was momentarily speechless in a flood tide of excitement. Did he mean the treasure case I'd listened to on the radio in high school? "Ah, Captain, do you mean the *Le Chameau* treasure?"

"Yeah, that's the one, *Le Chameau*. There, see the surf breaking over that sunker?" He slowed and pointed away to port. "That's what they call Chameau Rock. I think that's where they found the treasure."

Why didn't he say so before! I begged them to reconsider. That flatware and who knows what else could easily have been washed toward shore by storms away from Chameau Rock. Anyone who knew these waters could see that. But the captain wanted out of there, admittedly a nasty place, and the other two divers didn't see the point—"So what? Some spoons aren't treasure." Even Ace was skeptical. So we left. We left a fortune in treasure, I would later learn, to salvage an airplane that turned out to be useless.

That was the second time I learned the same lesson. I needed a boat of my own. I needed to make my own decisions about where to go and when to leave, but I just didn't have the money. Also, according to my newly signed contract with the RCMP, my fledgling career as a treasure diver would come to at least a temporary end that August when I was to report for training at Regina, Saskatchewan. That summer, however, I took a substantive step in my diving career that made leaving the ocean harder still. I found my first coin.

Having heard about an unnamed wreck near a place fittingly named Ragged Rocks, on the south shore of Scatarie Island, I asked a friend and boat owner to take me there. If the long coast of Nova Scotia presents the worst nautical conditions—low-lying land, fog, fast currents, treacherous offshore ledges, reefs, and sunkers—they all appear in combined and exaggerated form around the 25-mile-long shoreline of Scatarie Island. Protruding from the northeast corner of Cape Breton Island, Scatarie looks treacherous even on the map. In fact, the eastern shore is shaped like the maw of some menacing animal, a snapping turtle perhaps, waiting to clamp those jaws on an unfortunate vessel.

And then there's Scatarie Passage between the island and the Cape Breton mainland, where the tidal current, when squeezed into this mile-wide bottleneck, accelerates to the velocity of a mountain river. When the wind blows against that current, Scatarie Passage, crawling with sunkers, becomes, in neutral nautical language, untenable.

The passage was behaving itself when my friend and I crossed and approached Ragged Rocks in light air and bright sun. We anchored between the rocks and the mouth of Flukes Head Cove, and that offered some shelter from the crashing surf on the rocks. It's a remarkable thing about this coast that even in fine weather swells explode on the off-lying obstructions. This is a good thing for mariners because the surf points out the obvious dangers—at least those that poke their head out of water. But it wasn't much of a shelter as residual seas drove into the cove. The boat bounced to its anchor, and we studied in a kind of reverent silence the exquisite death trap that was Ragged Rocks.

I rolled over the side into about 30 feet of water. The visibility ranged 100 feet. That's Florida and Caribbean visibility, exceedingly rare—and stunningly beautiful—in these plankton-rich waters. The kelp, the rocks and the animals clinging to them seemed to dance and sparkle. Shafts of colored light, as from a stained-glass window, shimmered through the water column, an uncommon phenomenon we call *sun fire*.

In this near-transparent water, the massive black anchor, a design from a time gone by, soon hove into sight. There was no other evidence of a shipwreck; anchors and cannon are among the only things the ocean cannot easily obliterate. I visually aligned the anchor flukes, and using them as a range to begin a search pattern, I swam away until the anchor blurred. Then I swam back in a zigzag pattern, telling myself to remain calm to preserve air and to stick to the organized pattern. Nothing. I swam out the opposite direction about the same distance and zigzagged back. Still nothing. The visibility was so good I decided to swim away from the anchor in a random direction.

I soon came across several cannonballs and some flattened pieces of lead, then a piece of lead about one quarter inch thick in a perfect square, about four feet on a side. Whatever it was, it was wreckage. And there were more cannonballs. Was I on the wreck? Following the debris trail up onto a submarine hillock, I saw it in a shallow crevice—my first shipwreck coin. I pulled myself close to it, consciously stifling the urge to pick it up. I was breathing way too hard. Look around, I told myself. Why was the coin here, not somewhere else? Then I saw two more coins, smaller than the first. Then I ran out of air. I knew it would happen. I flipped the reserve valve. What if I couldn't find this spot again? After trying to memorize the bottom, I placed my dive knife on the rock as a marker; in this visibility, the blade would flash. I hoped. Then with the utmost reluctance, I returned to the boat.

The captain was almost as excited as I was when I told him what I'd found. He hopped to, helping me change out the dry tank for a fresh tank. I was back in the water before I'd stopped dripping. It was easy to find my dive knife on the short hill. And for an instant, I feared that the coins were gone, that they were some trick of gold fever—you want treasure, there it is . . . only it isn't. But this was no fever dream. It was there. I picked it up, stared at it in the palm of my glove. It was a silver dollar–size coin with cut edges, in pretty good condition. I could make out part of a date, "96." I slid it into my glove and looked for more. The very first rock I turned over revealed two more coins. I spent the rest of that tank flipping rocks and revealing coins. I found 18 of them before I had to go on reserve and make for the boat.

We spread them out on the engine box. They were all made of silver. Some were the size of American silver dollars, others were foreign with obscure markings and partial dates, and all were in good condition, at least to my eyes. But the fact was, the captain and I had no idea what we were peering at.

"Are you going back?" he asked.

I had one more tank, but it had only a half fill. I never liked that, going in the water short of a full tank.

"Pretty risky, huh?" said the captain. I knew what *he* wanted.

How could I not go back?

I swam straight to the spot, and began turning rocks and fanning away the sand and shell hash. I waited for the visibility to clear, then repeated the process nearby. I turned up about a dozen silver coins in no time. I moved a slab of rock, and before the visibility cleared I saw a glint of yellow that materialized into a large coin, but this one wasn't silver. It was gold. You don't need to be an expert to recognize gold underwater. It is impervious to time and marine erosion. I picked it up. It really was gold. It shone as if with internal light.

CHAPTER FOUR

Dive Scatarie Project

Consulting an expert, I learned that the gold coin was an eight escudo, with the jeweled cross on one side, waves and pillars on the other, dated 1702. The silver coins, also of Latin American origin, were cobs, eights and fours, all dated earlier than 1700. The gold coin proved to have been minted in Mexico. However, the cobs were of a general mix, from Mexico; Bogota, Colombia; and Potosi, Bolivia. Together they were worth about $30,000, but I did not sell them, I declared them. Their sentimental value as my first real treasure outstripped their actual value. I have them still. However, at the time, I recognized that if I meant to devote myself to this career, I would need to educate myself in numismatics. And as I'd already recognized, I'd need my own boat and a captain's license ("ticket"). It was for want of a boat that I could not return to the site before I was to report for duty in the Royal Canadian Mounted Police.

I enjoyed police work, and I liked my colleagues. But during the five-year contract, I longed almost constantly for Nova Scotia waters and the shipwrecks. Though Saskatchewan is about as landlocked as you can get in Canada, Ontario, where I was stationed, offered me the chance to partake in a few wreck dives at Tobermory in Georgian Bay, Lake Huron. But my targets were all well-known wrecks, bereft both of mystery and treasure. It just wasn't the same thing, and, as time passed, I longed to return to Cape Breton. So I did, declining reenlistment offers to immerse myself in cold salt water. In the summer of 1972, I returned home. However, I was a professional treasure hunter in mind only. I needed a job.

Turning points in one's life and work are most clearly noted in retrospect. Yet even at the time, I recognized two fortuitous events as they occurred: I found a job and I met two actual treasure hunters. I worked as the office manager at a marine and industrial park, run by the Cape Breton Development Corporation, in Sydney, the only city on Cape Breton Island. It wasn't treasure hunting, but I was working in a marine environment, and the job involved some commercial diving. Then I met Ronnie Blundon and Robert "Dewar" MacDonald. These guys were the original Cape Breton treasure hunters who discovered the pay ship *Le Chameau* lost near Louisbourg in 1725, and that made them stars by my standards.

Ronnie, Dewar, and I met frequently after the workday at a local pub, talking for hours about their experiences and about treasure hunting generally. I hung on their words as they educated me. They noticed my enthusiasm and commitment to treasure hunting, and they took me in—but only to a point at first. They had been burned in that court case I'd listened to with such attention as a kid. After their discovery of the French treasure ship, Ronnie and Dewar, representing the Orbit Group, brought in Alex Storm as a partner after he claimed he knew where the treasure was. At some point in the partnership, Storm gained exclusive access to the coveted treasure trove permit held by the Orbit Group. This action by Storm required the original partners of the Orbit Group, who actually found and claimed the treasure site under Part X of the Canada Shipping Act, to seek a legal remedy. Storm subsequently located a portion of the *Le Chameau* treasure trove, which then forced the original partners in the Orbit Group to have their case of claim reviewed in the Supreme Court of Canada. The final outcome: They won back a percentage of the recovery as justification of their rights and first salver status.

> *During their search in late spring of 1961, the appellants found an anchor, cannons, cannon balls and shot, all of which they believed to be part of the debris from the wreckage of "Le Chameau". In accordance with the provisions of the* Canada Shipping Act, *the appellants reported their find to the Receiver of Wrecks for that area, who recorded their claim and assured them that their exclusive right to search in that area (around so-called Le Chameau Rock) would be protected.*
>
> —From *Blundon et al. v. Storm*, [1972] S.C.R. 135 at 137-138

Clearly, the scars of that experience had not yet healed when I met them, and they had no intention of repeating the same mistake. I should stress that in those days treasure hunting in Nova Scotia was wide open; we were making it up as we went along. There were no experts, no dedicated equipment (such as side-scan sonar), and no rules or regulations other than to report any finds to the local receiver of wreck. In fact, no one seemed to care about our discoveries. Admittedly, that pioneering aspect was part of the heady excitement, but I didn't understand then how radically things would change.

My second opportunity came when my employer took possession of a fully equipped 45-foot fisheries patrol vessel, the *Prim Light*. This was the very boat I'd needed, and because no one at the industrial park had any experience with the maintenance and operation of small boats, I became the nominal captain. I gained countless hours of experience handling her in close quarters, working around the park's wharves and jetties.

Shipwrecks and Tourism

As part of an effort to compensate for the loss of jobs in mining and fishing, the Cape Breton Development Corporation, a federally sanctioned entity, was founded to develop tourism and bring new industry to the island. Today tourism is a mainstay on Cape Breton, but in those days it was a pioneering endeavor. I had the rather far-fetched idea that a serious survey of shipwrecks around Scatarie Island might have tourism potential, attracting recreational divers, and the artifacts we recovered might be sold to tourists. Without much expectation, I suggested the idea to my boss, Roy Shawcross, a man I viewed as a kind of visionary. He liked the idea and told me to prepare a proposal to present to the tourism board. I slaved over the thing through the fall and winter. It seemed to make economic sense to Roy and me, but we held out scant hope that the authorities would buy into it. Barely a month later, I received an invitation to present the idea to the board in person. I did so, rigid with tension; after an excruciating wait in the hall outside the conference room, the corporation's chairman, Tom Kent, called me back to say that the board had unanimously accepted my proposal. "Go home and develop a project budget," he said, "and don't scrimp—money is not an issue."

I brought Ronnie Blundon into the fledgling project to help work out details. It was clear that we'd need a guide, and Ronnie knew just the guy, a retired lobsterman from Mira Gut, Jack Steele, who was born and raised on Scatarie Island. Still thinking this had to be too good to be true—that someone would surely tell me at any moment the project was dead—I ordered new dive gear and a compressor, and with Jack's expert help, I worked all winter to convert the *Prim Light* into my ideal dive boat. I bought a 22-foot center console Boston Whaler with twin 120-horsepower outboards to serve as our survey and safety boat.

Scatarie Island is a menacing place, a ship killer, and it looks the part on those rare occasions you can see it through the fog. It's only seven miles long and three miles at the widest point, low lying and boggy with gnarled scrub and clumps of skeletal black spruce. It's a hard place, cold, and offers no shelter at all for shipwrecked sailors. It's hard to imagine, but there were two fishing settlements on this island in the 1880s, at Eastern Harbor and Northwest Cove, that hung on somehow until the 1950s. So many ships wrecked here that in 1839, authorities established one of the first lighthouses in Nova Scotia, on the very eastern tip of the island. The beacon saved some, no doubt, but ships continued to run up on the rocks until the advent of modern navigation aids in the late 1960s.

Jack suggested we use Main-a-Dieu Harbor as our base of operations, but he warned that the harbor was not fully protected from heavy weather. Instead of leaving the boat to pound against the dock, we should set her up with a two-point, bow-and-stern mooring system and leave her out in the harbor. As well as a master mariner, Jack was an amateur historian who knew many of the Scatarie Island shipwreck stories that have been passed down from generation to generation. It began to look like we'd be ready to go diving by July 1.

During June, I hired a crew of four professional divers and a deckhand to help Jack. Imagine, we were actually getting paid to hunt for shipwrecks. And I sat for my captain's license. By the end of that month, we gathered at Main-a-Dieu on one of the most exciting days of my career. But I did my utmost to repress outward signs of excitement, trying to sound the coolheaded captain and leader of the project. I laid out plans based on Jack's advice to begin operations among the offshore reefs and ledges in an area he called March's Rocks on the southeast side of Scatarie Island.

But soon after we'd explored the site on the surface, the spate of warm, calm Cape Breton weather showed that it, not me, was in charge. It came on to blow 70 knots from the southeast. Thanks to Jack, *Prim Light* rode easily to her two-point mooring while boats tied to the dock underwent a savage beating, and a few were holed. The storm raged for two days, offering a renewed lesson—when you think you've seen the worst of this coast, you haven't. But this, like all storms, eventually passed seaward, and in a big residual swell we returned to Scatarie, anchoring off the southern point.

I'd planned to split the divers into two teams and rotate them such that one team would be in the water at all times, while the boat would follow, moving to fresh anchorages as the survey progressed. In 30 feet of water, their bottom time would be almost unlimited, and repeat dives would not cause the bends or any other pressure-related dangers. By this means, I had thought to survey the entire island coastline in one summer, a giddy, unrealistic notion that reflected my inexperience and my underestimation of the riches in these waters, despite Jack's stories.

I remained aboard as the first team of divers entered the water. The Dive Scatarie Project was officially under way. The other team splashed in after a reasonable time. But the first team was surfacing well before their air would have run out. What was wrong? I'd been expecting something to go wrong all winter.

"We have a bit of a problem here," said Ronnie as he came aboard, but his tone suggested that it wasn't a bad problem. He was actually smiling. "There's shipwreck material *everywhere*. Steel plates from modern ships, cannon and other wreckage from old ships—it's all mixed together. I swam a big circle without ever losing contact with wreckage. It's amazing, you got to see it. No kidding. Come on."

The second team surfaced. "Wreckage everywhere!" said one.

"Everywhere!" said his partner. "You can't see the bottom for the wreckage!"

By that time, I was halfway into my gear.

The visibility was poor, but before I reached the bottom, all I could see was the twisted wreckage of steel and wooden ships, centuries of ships entangled in a mass grave. After I settled down, I swam a large orbit over the stuff trying to distinguish the old from the new, anchors and cannon, iron and steel. These ships must have died in their turn right on top of the previous. Ronnie was right. It was amazing. It didn't seem real; it couldn't be real, yet there it was. Could there be another place of this size in the world with so many shipwrecks? However would we deal with this? Part of my proposed service was to document with an aim toward identifying local shipwrecks. Then among countless other objects from the ages, I noticed a pair of enormous bronze rudder-and-stern-post fittings, called *pintles* and *gudgeons* in nautical language. The arms of the brass straps that held the wooden rudderstock stretched some 18 feet. I blew through my tank in record time. My head was spinning when I clambered aboard *Prim Light*.

We were all jabbering and gesturing at once, but Jack Steele wasn't surprised. "Almost every year you'd hear about a shipwreck on Scatarie. I saw many with my own eyes."

I described to Jack the rudder gear I'd seen. "Oh, yeah, that sounds like the old 'rule joint' assembly. That's old. It got replaced years ago by what they call the plug-stock rudder assembly."

I never stopped thanking my lucky stars for Jack Steele. Or for the Dive Scatarie Project.

During that wonderful first season, we averaged six dives a day weather permitting; logging over 800 by the time autumn weather closed us down. And Jack was again right. The south shore was strewn with wreckage all braided together. Cannon—there were so many cannon of different types, periods, and caliber we quit counting at 400. In some places they were piled helter-skelter on top of each other. Further complicating our problem, the sea had, through sheer blunt-force trauma, done savage violence to much of the man-made goods. The largest and most recent wreck we were able to identify was the SS *Cape Breton*, lost on that south coast in 1920. It was made of modern steel, yet nothing remained of it but twisted plates, shafting, and a large propeller. It didn't even vaguely look shiplike. What did that say about old ships, 17th- and 18th-century wooden sailing ships? Nothing was stable down there, and it didn't take that summer's 70-knot blow to disturb the bottom and anything resting on it. Almost nothing of the old ships remained, and every passing year there will be less and less, until soon there will be nothing but some stray cannon to mark an unknown ship's grave; in time, even they will disappear. The old wrecks were essentially gone.

I began that summer to think about the wrecks in new, fresh terms. Yes, I was still interested in treasure of the traditional sort, but the remains of the ships were artifacts, palpable pieces of the past, and as such they had value. If they remained on the bottom, they would soon vanish. They should be recovered, stabilized, protected, and displayed.

Without being too romantic about it, I discovered that summer that I wanted to protect them.

But back to the project itself. The sheer volume and density of material was overwhelming. Our logbooks were chock-full of notes and confusing sketches, and we soon realized we'd need another means of identification besides mere underwater investigation. Sure, sometimes we found the ship's name on battered pieces of wreckage and, on rarer occasions, an engraved bell. But visual investigation would reveal little or nothing about old shipwrecks. We were abruptly introduced to another fundamental aspect of the profession—I was now seeing it in those terms—*research.* History had always interested me, particularly maritime history, but I hadn't thought much about formal archival research as an information source, depending instead on local knowledge and collective memory. Local knowledge can direct you to the site, but it can't identify the ship or the material salvaged from it. And it couldn't help us sort through the tangled victims of Scatarie Island.

In this respect, too, our incredible first-season luck held fast: I met David Dow. His official role was project development officer for the Cape Breton Development Corporation—but his avocation was historical research and analysis; in the Dive Scatarie Project, the two melded seamlessly. Fascinated by the unprecedented number of wrecks in this single area, David accompanied us to the island to see for himself; from then on he was as hooked on discovery as the rest of us. He dove headlong into the research, and soon he was identifying and dating some of the wrecks. Visiting him occasionally in his office, I watched with pleasure and gratitude his mass of research grow. His desk was covered a foot deep with modern and period charts, archival documents, and notebooks. Next visit, the stuff had spilled over the edges of his desk onto the floor. By summer's end, research had reduced his office space to a slim path between high-stacked boxes of documents from door to desk. He had taped to his wall a big-scale chart of Scatarie Island and had marked the wrecks with different colored pins, depending on whether they had been identified. As summer passed, the pins proliferated as wreck sites spread beyond the borders of the chart out onto the wall. His eyes sparkled with excitement when he described how his detective work led to identification.

Meanwhile, the corporation's tourism division was developing a museum at Port Morien, the site of the first coal mine in North America, established by the French in 1672. The director, a retired mine manager, and a project development officer, Don Loney, invited me to Cabot House—a high-rise office building in Sydney, Nova Scotia, that housed the headquarters of the Cape Breton Development Corporation—to ask if we had retrieved any shipwreck artifacts they could display at the museum. Identification, not retrieval, was our purpose, I explained, but we'd be happy to bring them small items from time to time after we had stabilized them. The small display eventually consisted of one 32-pound carronade, silverware, cannonballs, musket balls, shards of ceramics, and small copper alloy artifacts; all items had been restored by the museum staff. The display grew over the summer and attracted happy attention from both tourists and Tourist Board officers. Everyone anywhere near the project was delighted. Public display in a Cape Breton museum: This was precisely what I'd dreamed about doing myself if money were no object. The officials expressed their pleasure by upping my budget for the coming year even before first-year operations were complete.

Just before the close of that first season, mid-November 1974, David Dow made a discovery of his own. When he brought it to me, I could tell before he opened his mouth that here was a man in the clutches of treasure hunting fever. His research had turned up the dates and locations of three British warships—HMS *Feversham* (with three transport ships) lost in 1711; HMS *Leonidas*, in 1832; and HMS *Rover*, in 1798. *Leonidas* had been lost near Hay Island at the east end of Scatarie. "All three carried fortunes in gold, silver, and copper bullion," said David. "And the *Leonidas* carried silverware belonging to several Royal Army regiments stationed in what was then called British North America [Canada after 1867]."

To excavate specific ships was a serious divergence from our original purpose to log as many ships as possible, but David had already submitted a proposal to recover bullion that would then be sold in local tourist shops. It had been enthusiastically accepted. Who can turn down several fortunes in treasure? My crew certainly wouldn't. Our season ended with high expectations for the next.

Historic Context

British North America—Canada—in the early 1830s, suffered a severe shortage of British currency known as *small change*, so much so that the ability to facilitate trade for British subjects living in Canada was seriously affected. Canadians were using hard currency from worldwide sources, but they needed standardized currency to avoid exchange issues. Even officials in Quebec experienced problems when trying to remunerate the British garrison stationed there. Eventually, General Roth, who was in charge of the military at Quebec, spoke to his British superiors, demanding the situation be rectified. As it happened, Roth's requests came at a time when the monarchy itself was in a period of transition. William IV came to the throne after the death of his brother George IV in 1830. As a result, the Royal Mint was very busy changing dies, as the law dictated, so the image of the new king would appear on all British coinage.

Roth's requests from Quebec were set aside until July 1831, when mint officials began to consider the currency needs of North America, according to a document titled "Proposed Copper Coinage for Canada." Tenders were called and copper cake was procured from a Mr. Glascott, who delivered over 30 tons of the material to the Royal Mint. The steam press at the mint began producing coppers of Canada, completing the order of almost 2 million coins in March 1832. The entire minting consisted of pennies, halfpennies, and farthings, all dated 1831. The royal copper bullion destined for Canada was loaded into approximately 350 chests and thus was sent to Canada as a split cargo on two naval transports: HMS *Orestes* and HMS *Leonidas*. The coins assigned to *Orestes* were loaded for transport in April 1832; the coins assigned to *Leonidas* were loaded on June 1, 1832. Both ships were ordered to sail to Halifax and report to the port admiral for further delivery instructions. The HMS *Leonidas* left Halifax for Quebec in August. She traveled up the coast of Nova Scotia, but when rounding Cape Breton Island on her way to the Gulf of St. Lawrence, she ran afoul of reefs jutting from the eastern end of Scatarie Island and was wrecked close to Hay Island, on the Hay Island shoals. The complete cargo of copper coins, well over 1.5 million, and the bullion she carried for private interests were lost. The crew and passengers managed to get off the wreck and make it to the island. They eventually found their way to the British garrison at Sydney on Spanish Bay, and no lives were reported as lost.

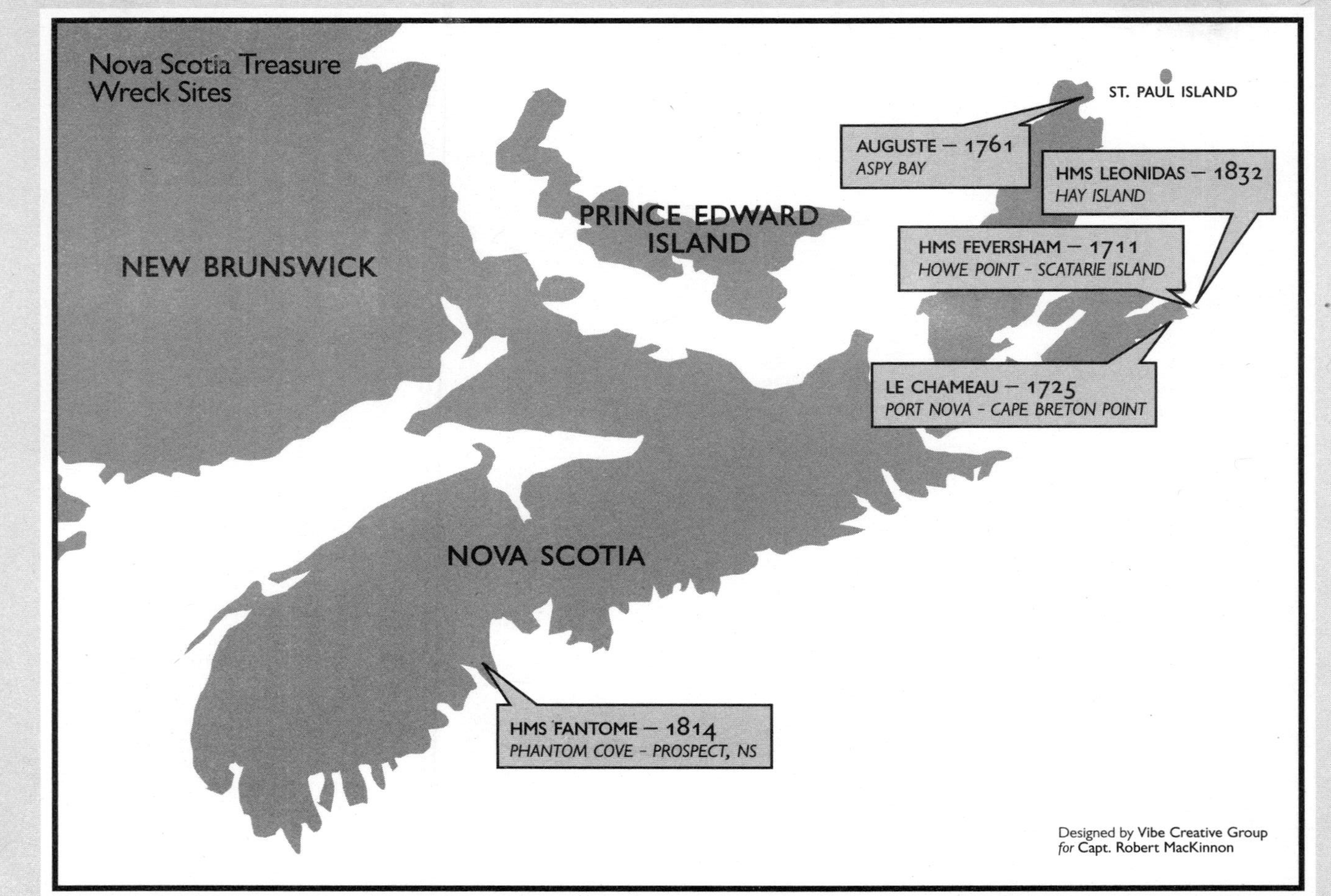

Nova Scotia Treasure
Wreck Sites
NEW BRUNSWICK
PRINCE EDWARD
ISLAND
NOVA SCOTIA
ST. PAUL ISLAND
AUGUSTE — 1761
ASPY BAY
HMS LEONIDAS — 1832
HAY ISLAND
HMS FEVERSHAM — 1711
HOWE POINT - SCATARIE ISLAND
LE CHAMEAU — 1725
PORT NOVA - CAPE BRETON POINT
HMS FANTOME — 1814
PHANTOM COVE - PROSPECT, NS
Designed by Vibe Creative Group
for Capt. Robert MacKinnon

CHAPTER FIVE

Tons of Copper Coins

C*oins! Thousands of them, millions of them, millions and millions!*"

That got our attention.

Four of us, in two teams, were diving on one of David's wrecks. If, as he suspected, this was the *Leonidas*, her manifest could contain over 11 tons of copper coins in chests and several chests of mixed silver and gold coins, mostly Latin American eight reales, eight escudos, and British sovereigns. The silver and gold coins he reported had been consigned for delivery to private interests in Quebec, placed on board at Halifax. The language was still new to me, but the idea was clear—this was a very rich ship and our dreams of discovering treasure were about to come true.

Captain Jack had anchored *Prim Light* in shallow water between the Hay Island shoals and the island itself, but he didn't like it one bit. In fact, he hated it. When Jack warned us about nautical dangers, everyone listened up, and he had been particularly emphatic about Red Rocks and a little passage between the rocks and the island. He pointed to the unbroken wall of white water breaking on kelp-dressed black granite: "That's called Hell's Gates. Boys, I'm telling you now, you get caught underwater in that place, you're on your own—I can't take this boat in there. I about got killed here when I was a kid. No matter what's on the bottom, it's not worth your lives."

"All right," I said before we'd entered the water, "if anyone feels uncomfortable about diving here, he should stay aboard, and nobody will think less of you."

Nobody backed out; I sort of knew nobody would. But what if the trails of debris led us toward Hell's Gates? I supposed we'd follow.

Ronnie Blundon dove first. It was pretty rough that day with heavy surge, the kind that washes you back and forth like a strand of kelp, and the water was barely 20 feet deep over the reefs and sunkers. Ronnie and I separated to the very edge of our visibility and began to search. I immediately saw a short, stubby cannon unlike any I'd ever seen. It was only about 4 feet long, but extremely robust and wide bored. The thing would fire a 30-pound ball. Did *Leonidas* carry such armament? I waved for Ronnie, but at the same time he was waving for me. He insisted, so I swam over to see what he had. Cannon, 10, no, 12 of them, identical to the one I'd found. Wouldn't a ship so armed be positively identifiable? Wouldn't this lot provide more than circumstantial evidence? We surfaced to discuss it. The wind was getting up, and Jack was probably getting anxious. Ronnie and I returned to the boat.

It was then that the member of the second team surfaced shouting, "Coins! Thousands of them, millions and millions!"

Then his partner surfaced nearby. He shouted, "Silverware!" and quickly submerged again.

Ronnie and I hurtled over the side without pausing to put on a fresh tank. We snorkeled over to the diver who'd made the initial find, dove down, and he gestured for us to follow him. He led us about 30 feet away and with a sweeping wave of introduction showed us the stuff of childhood treasure dreams. Mixed with the usual matrix of shell hash, gravel, and small cobble, there were thousands upon thousands of copper coins lying free. Thousands more had concreted into large, individual clumps, virtually covering the bottom as far as we could see in every direction. He stuck his entire arm in a hole at least two feet deep without reaching the bottom of the coin pile. Breath by breath, Ronnie built a pile of coins some three feet tall, and he was still shoveling handfuls of coins onto the stash. I watched in awe. This was so far beyond our experience, if not our dreams, that I had no idea what to do now.

I signaled, with pantomime, for the hole to be refilled and the pile dispersed. Then I pointed emphatically at the surface. Back aboard *Prim Light*, amid excited chatter, handshaking, and backslapping, I called the Coast Guard over the VHF radio to request a landline connection (that's how you did it in those days). I called David at his office. Pretending calm I definitely did not feel, I described our find. He was shocked, silent. What to do? Return to Main-a-Dieu, and he'd meet us there to discuss it. Then his voice shifted to that of a whispering conspirator, telling me not to mark the site with anything that would attract attention from other divers. Other divers? There were no other divers. Never mind, we didn't need to mark the site at all. We knew exactly where it was.

"Do you think it's *Leonidas*?" I asked.

"Yes." Then he hung up.

My colleagues' protests notwithstanding, I asked Jack and his mate to up anchor and head for Main-a-Dieu. At full speed. The divers' excited chatter never died during the 12-mile sprint. About three times, one or another said, "We're going back, right?"

I really didn't know. This find was something extraordinary, maybe spectacular. This wasn't the same as recovering a few artifacts for a museum. This would attract heavy attention with unknown results.

We waited at Main-a-Dieu for three hours before David arrived. "I've been working," he said. "I got official clearance from the local receiver of wreck, Parks Canada, and the corporation to recover a *small* sample for delivery to the park's conservation lab at Louisbourg. They were very specific about that—only a sample for now."

Our team hung together for the rest of the day, too high on discovery to disperse. We refilled tanks for the next day as we discussed how and what we would recover and talked about this vital matter of "stabilizing" objects that have been in salt water for 143 years. Salt water in effect stops time, but if suddenly exposed to the air, metal objects—including coins (except gold)—deteriorate with stunning speed. I had thought vaguely about the accepted science of recovery and preservation, but since things were happening with unprecedented urgency—I had had no time to learn anything about the practical techniques. Parks Canada had provided David with a scanty set of instructions for handling our sample set of coins, not much more than storing them in containers of freshwater. Imagine the magnitude of the job if we were to properly excavate this shipwreck, recovering everything of value and historical interest. I was getting way ahead of myself.

By 7:30 A.M. we were anchored back at Hay Island in clear weather, flat seas: a perfect diving day. I told the divers I wanted to make at least two more sets of reconnaissance dives to learn the extent of the coin piles, marking likely spots with floats from which we'd choose the coins to be recovered. David had stressed that Parks Canada wanted only high-grade samples, which made sense, but how would I recognize high from low grade, or medium, for that matter? I suggested that, given our weather luck, we should expand the search area as far as we felt comfortable. I finished my piece, and then Jack spoke up.

"Boys, I know what happens when you get in the water, you forget about everything else. Well, this time don't forget where you are." He fell silent, stared down at his deck, but he didn't seem to be finished. "This place, Scatarie Island, the rocks and sunkers, it's haunted. I heard the stories all my life. Irish immigrants and fishermen from Newfoundland settled this area, but a lot of them died right here in these waters. Sometimes on days like this when the wind's light from the south, you can hear the dying cries and screams of women, Irish women keening in a sound to tear your guts out. Three hundred Irish women died in a storm not 10 miles from here. I've heard them cry." He paused again, then added, "Don't you boys join them."

We swung tanks over our shoulders, checked our gear one more time, and rolled overboard. Ronnie and I made straight for the silverware. It was everywhere, concreted into clumps with handles and tines, and the bowls of spoons sticking out, thousands of pieces strewn about singly. We saw on the handles of the larger pieces ornate markings and on others the fouled-anchor emblem that is the symbol of the Royal Navy. I remembered the silverware Ace and I swam over years ago, trying to salvage the propeller from that old steam trawler at Kelpy Cove. There was far more silverware on both these wrecks than would be reasonably used in the officers' mess. Were they cargo or currency or what? I would learn a lot more about the meaning of silverware on these wrecks, but for now, David wanted coins, and coins he would get, although I begged him to consider recovering a few samples of the silverware. Just to prove its existence and possible relevance to the wreck. Now we had to decide which coins to recover.

After a quick swim over the mass of coins—without doubting that there were many, many more coins than I saw—I called for a meeting aboard *Prim Light.* To avoid confusion, I wanted Ronnie and me to pick the sample, and I asked the other team to explore inshore as far as they felt comfortable. I asked them not to disturb anything.

We followed the trail of silverware, much larger and longer than I'd ever seen—and the trail led straight for Hell's Gates. We retreated when we felt the tidal current trying to pull us into the passage. Maybe it was Jack's story about the keening Irish women, but searching through the silverware, a new feeling swept over me, far different in kind from the raw excitement at discovery that had first attracted me to the profession. There was treasure here and there was also a palpable history that must be preserved for its own intrinsic value. I was committed to that and happy now to be involved in preservation. But that was not the sort of connection to this wreck I was feeling then. This could have been a grave site. Not all wrecks of the period were fatal—no one died here or when the *Fantome* went on the rocks, but they were rare exceptions. Usually all hands and passengers died when their ship went aground in heavy weather. It was sobering to see—to *feel*—this wreck in the context of human hope and desire, which are always implied by a sea voyage, dashed to a terrible death on Red Rocks. And only sad remnants of lives, their valuable table utensils, marked their tragic end. It changed the way I viewed my work.

I didn't say any of this when I asked the divers not to disturb anything. And of course I saw the contradiction when Ronnie and I swam down to collect a high-grade sample. But, still, this was our first-ever sanctioned recovery of treasure, and I didn't want to lose contact with the day's personal significance. We quickly filled a couple of big baskets with free-lying copper coins in the best condition we could find without digging or disturbing the solid concretions of coins. We hauled them topside where, as per instructions, the crew began counting the coins and one by one placing them in sealable buckets of freshwater.

The team of divers who'd been exploring shoreward came aboard wild-eyed. The leader, Ed Melnick, exclaimed, "We swam as far as we could to a depth of about ten feet before we came on the sunkers—we found coins all the way!" In crevices seaward of the sunkers, he said, sheltered somewhat from wave action, they found huge piles of coins. The piles were two feet high, higher in places.

"Christ," said Jack, dropping a coin in the bucket. "There are something like over eight thousand coins here. I never saw eight thousand coins in my life!"

"You wouldn't believe what's down there, Jack. You just wouldn't believe it."

I phoned David to meet us in Main-a-Dieu. After first inspection, he had his look, dipping out handfuls, studying them. "This is great. . . . Yes, great. These are British pennies, all three types, farthings, half cents, and large cents. Were all the coins copper, no gold or silver?"

"All copper. We also found a huge quantity of silverware," I said, but again he didn't seem so interested in the silverware. We resealed the buckets, loaded them into his car, and he drove them away.

The next day we returned to Scatarie Island to continue our shipwreck survey. We dove every day to the end of that second season. Every day we wondered when we'd see the coins again and when we'd be allowed back on the site. As fall was heading for winter, we retrieved the day moorings we'd laid around the island, returned *Prim Light* to her owners, stored away the diving gear, and I wrote my year-end report, but we heard nothing about coins or the *Leonidas*. I did, however, hear about another ship. She was called *Fantome*.

Dewar MacDonald called to invite me to Halifax to meet the now-famous maritime lawyer Donald Kerr, who had represented Dewar and his Orbit Group during the long, painful *Le Chameau* treasure case. Dewar wondered if I wanted to ride with him to Halifax, where he had some commercial salvage business to conduct (which wouldn't take long), and then have dinner with Donald to talk about treasure hunting. I dropped everything.

The community of treasure divers on Cape Breton was not densely populated, but these guys, Dewar, Kerr, and two or three others, were the pioneers and the most successful members. These were the guys I looked up to and hoped to emulate. That they were inviting me to join them meant they'd noticed and were taking seriously my efforts to do so. I was delighted. And nervous.

I needn't have been. They treated me like an equal, and we talked incessantly through two courses about the business. Then over coffee, Kerr said, "Well, my new friend, have you ever heard of the brig *Fantome* and the plunder fleet?" That was the first time I'd heard the name.

Kerr continued to explain. "We have to go back to 1814," he said. The War of 1812 had been plodding along for two indecisive years. Both sides had been unprepared for war. The Brits were distracted by the naval and continental war against Napoleon, and the Americans, with notable exception, were poorly led and disorganized. But then the Brits, in a combined naval and army operation, invaded the area around Chesapeake Bay and marched inland against little opposition. The Americans figured the force meant to take the port of Baltimore, but, no, they turned left and took Washington. President Madison and his cabinet only barely made it out of town. The Brits plundered the town and set fire to the White House—after sitting down to the dinner Dolley Madison had laid out for 15 guests before she fled from the Red Coats.

Kerr added, "We believe that the plunder from Washington was loaded onto British ships and several American vessels captured at the

Port of Alexandria. They exited the Potomac, and some were sent toward Halifax."

BRITISH NAVAL SHIPS EXITING THE POTOMAC

HMS *Seahorse,* 38-gun frigate	HMS *Fairy,* cruiser
HMS *Euryalus,* 36-gun frigate	HMS *Devastation,* 8-gun bomb vessel
HMS *Aetna,* 8-gun bomb vessel	HMS *Meteor,* 8-gun bomb vessel
HMS *Erebus,* 18-gun rocket vessel	*Anna Maria,* tender
HMS *Manly,* 12-gun brig	

In the Gulf of Maine, the ships sent back to Halifax picked up an armed escort, the brig HMS *Fantome.* A few miles from Halifax, off Prospect, on a clear night, they ran up on the rocks. One plunder ship, HMS *Seahorse,* used as a transport brig, got off the next day, but the others were lost. "The rest of the treasure is still down there. We believe it's the richest of the rich." Kerr spoke in a level, calm voice, but his excitement was apparent. Mine was building.

Donald Kerr went on to explain that since his youth he had heard folktales on this coast about the treasure fleet wrecks. (I had heard none of them because Halifax is 270 miles from my home waters.) Then he said, "In the mid-1960s, local sport divers found one of the treasure fleet wrecks right where the locals said it would be. They came upon gold and silver coins in heavy concretions, which they couldn't break apart. So they resorted to dynamite, recovering less than a thousand loose coins. Frustrated, they left the wreck to the sea."

"Dynamite?"

"Yes," Kerr continued, "can you believe it? Those were the Wild West days. But here's the thing. They found two 1804 silver dollars—the most valuable coins in the world. Does this sound like it's up your alley?"

It did. It did, indeed.

"So if we can arrange for a boat and captain, would you do a reconnaissance dive for us?"

"Yes," I said. "I think I can work that in."

A few days later Dewar called. "Man, we have a chance to get on the *Fantome* site. Donald called me today asking if we were interested. He's found a boat and captain; all he has to do is name the date."

"How about tomorrow?"

Dewer laughed and said, "Tomorrow it is, then."

At the end of October, the day after I returned from that first *Fantome* dive, David called about the coins from *Leonidas*. Would I attend a meeting at Cabot House, the corporation's headquarters?

"What sort of meeting?" I asked.

He was evasive, saying something about delivering my final project report, which I had already delivered. "Look," he said when pressed, "they want to discuss a *top secret* project."

I attended the meeting, along with David and several senior members of the corporation I worked for, which was under contract with the tourism division. David asked me to make myself comfortable, and a senior director of the corporation's tourism development department gave the introductions. "The copper coins we had recovered have been cleaned in the conservation lab at the Parks Canada Fortress Louisbourg facility," said David. "The results were very promising. Most of the coins showed a clear date and most of their original relief. This is far better news than we dared hope."

Then the director who'd made the introductions asked, "How long would it take you to recover a hundred thousand coins?"

"Well," I began, "we could start next July when we'd have—"

"No, no," said the director. "What if you started immediately, how long would it take? Could you do it in ten days?"

"Ten days? It's almost November. Have you noticed the weather? Plus, I have no boat and I have no crew."

"What do you mean you have no crew?" the director snapped. "You had a crew, did you not?"

"That was seasonal work for them. They had to return to their regular jobs."

"All right, say we got you a crew. Could you do it in ten days? I don't exactly see the problem. You collected eight thousand coins in one day. In ten days, you—"

This time I interrupted him. Admittedly, I had a much shorter fuse in those days, but I tried to hide my growing contempt at these landlubbers trying to tell me what I could and couldn't do without bothering to explain their project. With strained patience, I explained that it was an experienced crew that had collected those coins. We had a boat adapted to its purpose. We were diving in late summer in perhaps the most dangerous strip of water in all Nova Scotia. And now it was late fall, the boat had been put away for the winter, and my crew was unavailable. By the end of my speech, I'd almost lost control of my fake patience.

"Look," said David as mediator, "let's clue Bob in on what we hope to achieve." He explained that he'd been investigating the feasibility—cost versus return—of placing single conserved coins in see-through, hard-plastic cases, each containing a brief description of the wreck. These would be sold to tourists from approved shops all over Cape Breton.

"Bob, this is a million-dollar opportunity. Picture the coins you found on sale in the shops. We've cost it out—it can't miss. The profit ratio is five times the cost of conservation and presentation. We need a hundred thousand coins. To begin with."

Okay, then I saw what was going on in that room. These guys had caught a serious case of gold fever without ever getting wet. Also equally clear: They were committed to the idea, and they knew nothing at all about the marine aspects of their million-dollar opportunity. I asked David to speak with me outside the room.

"You of all people should understand that you don't get a competent team going in one week," I said to David after we'd retired to the adjacent boardroom. "And most certainly not in November with no boat, no captain, and no experienced divers—that's impossible."

"I do understand, but look at it this way. The directors are hooked on this idea, and they're going to do it in any case, with you or with someone a lot less capable. Look, money's no object. You can hire any boat and captain you want. Also, we have a diver for you."

"Yeah, who? An *experienced* diver, right?"

"His name's Russell MacDonald. He's a coal miner—"

"A coal miner?"

"But he dives."

"A coal miner who dives? Sounds great." Oh, well, I'd already decided to take on the job. I was a treasure hunter, and retrieval is part of the work. It's just that the lubberly directors had offended my newfound professional pride by telling me what I could do without consulting with me first. "But don't you want to properly excavate the *Leonidas*?"

"Oh, sure, absolutely. We'll excavate her. But with as many coins out there as you say, a hundred thousand is nothing."

"All right, I'll talk to the diver. What'd you say his name was?"

"Russell MacDonald."

Russell had precious little experience, I gleaned immediately, but he was fit and avid, and I liked him. Then I traveled to Main-a-Dieu to meet

Jim Mullins, a prospective captain, and his 38-foot fishing boat. Both these men were to become my valuable partners and friends. Russell and Jim were men of stature who had that quiet strength found in hardworking people tied to the land and sea by the need to survive and the will to bend nature to suit their needs. Between them, they helped me find a couple more divers with reasonable experience.

When I proposed using Main-a-Dieu as our base, Captain Mullins said that would severely limit my time on the site. "The weather's already swung to the north, you probably noticed. First sign it's getting up, we'll have to run for home."

There was a lighthouse near Hay Island at East Point, only minutes from the *Leonidas*. I asked David to inquire of Transport Canada, which administered the lighthouses, if we could use East Point Light as our base of operations. Six people for a week, tops. I hadn't actually come to believe that schedule was possible, but I'd been saying it. Hell, maybe. Stranger things have happened, blah, blah, blah . . .

The lighthouse keeper, Murray Rolfe, and his wife, Eva, welcomed us warmly. We assembled our equipment, built a ramp for the Boston Whaler chase/safety boat, and we found a suitable if not particularly secure mooring site for Jim Mullins's boat, called *Brothers Four*, at Northwest Cove, several miles from the light. That done, we planned to dive the next day. Eva said she'd have breakfast for us at 4:00 A.M. And, man, did she! We awoke on that cold, dark morning to a lavish spread of eggs, bacon, sausages, and more types of bread than I'd ever seen in one place. Throughout our brief, eventful stay, they treated us with utmost kindness. By 7:30, Murray had delivered us and our gear, in a little wagon pulled by his farm tractor, to the *Brothers Four* at Northwest Cove. An hour later, we set the anchor just offshore of Hay Island, back on the *Leonidas* site. I planned to make the first dive alone, a quick survey to select and mark a place to begin recovery. Before I got in the water, Jim

Mullins announced, "I've always wanted to dive. I'm going to become a diver, and you're going to teach me."

It was astonishing. Here we'd anchored about 100 yards from *Prim Light*'s main mooring, but still the coins were thick on the bottom. Just how big *was* this thing? I found several piles of coins lying in the open on a large slab of rock, a good place to start, so I tied off the surface marker float to the remains of a cast-iron gun carriage and returned to the boat. I had devised a simple recovery method and fabricated plastic containers that could be lowered to the bottom and would remain upright after I'd filled them with coins for their return trip to the surface. Russell had some beginner's difficulty with his gear, but he took to it before long, and we collected coins all day. We made three long dives. We filled a lot of containers with coins. This, I thought, may just work out, until Murray met us back at Northwest Cove with some bad news.

"There's a late-season hurricane off the Carolinas heading north, expected to arrive in our area late afternoon tomorrow."

Eva served us another scrumptious dinner that night and breakfast before dawn the next day. We moved with urgency out on the wreck. The wind was light southerly, but the low-cloud sky looked ominous. I'd expected some heavy weather, but not a hurricane. Hand over fist, we piled coins into the buckets, up and down they went, and by the time the wind started getting up in the afternoon, we were well ahead in the recovery. We had 50 three-gallon buckets lashed on deck, each holding, I estimated, 2,000 coins. The wind had a sultry feel about it when it got up around 25 knots. It was time to go.

Again there was Murray waiting at Northwest Cove. He'd been listening to storm reports on his single sideband radio. "They're talking about a cat-two hurricane right now, but it's supposed to intensify and make landfall near Canso tonight. Bob, they're talking about a hundred twenty knots."

"Have you ever seen anything like that out here?"

"Never. No one has."

So we triple lashed *Brothers Four* to her mooring, laid on every piece of anti-chafe gear we could find, ran lines from the stern to a bollard on the little wharf, and retreated to the lighthouse. There was nothing more to do. She'd either make it or she wouldn't. We lashed the Whaler to the ramp with every piece of line we owned.

And the evening marine forecast made it official: The wind would remain east-northeast at 60 to 80 knots that night before shifting to northeast near dawn, with winds sustained for 12 to 18 hours at over 100 knots and then subsiding to 60 to 80 knots the following day.

The forecast couldn't have been worse. And we couldn't have been more exposed perched to a rock island no more than 500 feet wide in any direction hanging out off the northeast coast of Cape Breton in the open Atlantic. The seas would come over East Point—as if it were a sunker.

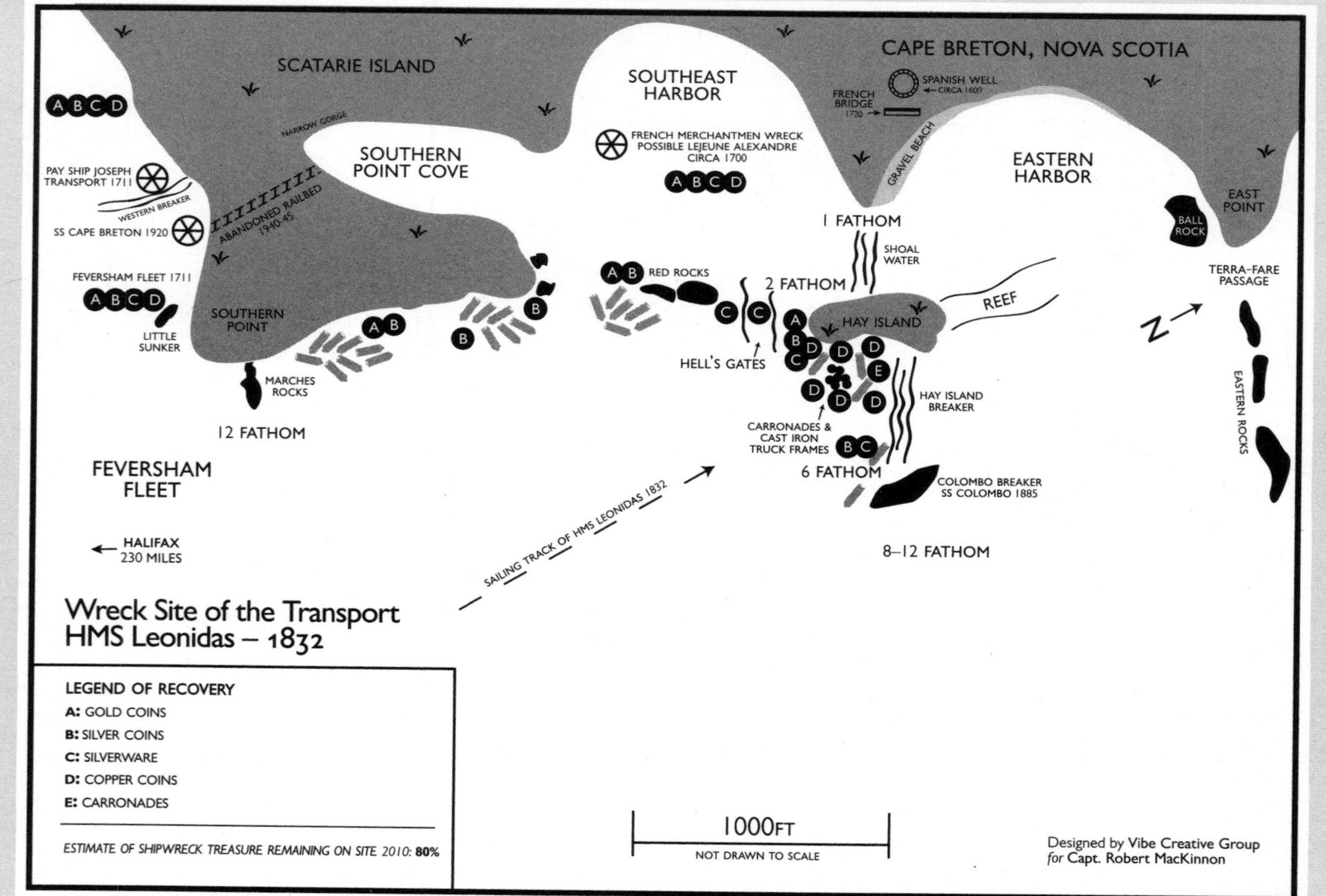

Wreck Site of the Transport HMS Leonidas – 1832

LEGEND OF RECOVERY

A: GOLD COINS
B: SILVER COINS
C: SILVERWARE
D: COPPER COINS
E: CARRONADES

ESTIMATE OF SHIPWRECK TREASURE REMAINING ON SITE 2010: **80%**

CHAPTER SIX

The Hurricane of 1975

I don't think any of us, including Jim Mullins, gave *Brothers Four* a chance in hell if the weather actually came on as predicted, but Jim didn't express his fear and anxiety out loud. Frankly, though no one said it, if this beast shaped up as predicted, then more than the boat would be in danger. We set about securing things in and around the lighthouse, while I tried to imagine what this little island would feel like in 110 knots of wind and 30-foot breakers. Already the wind had taken on that ominous low moan that anyone who's experienced an Atlantic storm knows; it means the beast is close aboard.

Murray rigged a stout lifeline between the lighthouse and the generator shed. "We're on a strict twelve-hour schedule here," he said, shouting, barely audible two feet away. He had two diesel generators; each would run for 12 hours, but after that time, he had to shut one down and manually switch to the other, then refuel the first in order to maintain the light, the fog horn, and the power in the lighthouse. That meant he'd have to venture outside in the middle of the hurricane to make the switch. Tales are told up and down the northeast coast from Newfoundland to New England of the brave lighthouse keeper fighting to maintain the light until that fatal wave swept him away.

We lashed down everything that wasn't part of the island, and then went around adding more lashings. We paid particular attention to the bank of about 30 fuel drums lined up against the generator shed. Eva had already lowered bombproof storm shutters over the windows in the head keeper's home and lower lighthouse. Murray and Russell finished securing the assistant keeper's home and out sheds against the pending onslaught. Now the wind was hard enough to lean against. As I went in for the duration, I glanced up at the tower and the white light blinking as if defiantly. Murray, maybe driven by some personal concern, assured everyone "the buildings of this station, including the lighthouse tower, have taken the best nature can throw at them. Everything here is supported by concrete and steel. The buildings are secured to their foundations by bolts and cable tie downs, we have over five thousand gallons of freshwater stored in the cisterns and plenty of food."

It was a very stout structure. It had stood there since the mid-1800s. If it's your lot to ride out a category-two hurricane on an offshore rock, well, there could be less secure shelters. Murray bolted the doors and ordered no one to go outside during the storm without his permission. It was his ship.

We could barely hear ourselves talk during dinner, so we quit trying and sat listening to the changing pitch of the accelerating wind. Russell went to bed right after dinner, then Eva; David, Jim, Murray, and I hung around in the living room, but I must have dozed. I awoke with a jolt. The building was trembling. Russell was coming down the stairs. He had woken up when his bed started sliding around on the hardwood floor. It was 4:00 A.M., and still the storm had not reached its worst. We sat in our own thoughts trying to ignore the gusts that seemed from inside to bend the tower like a palm tree. Eva made a fresh pot of coffee. She and Murray had tended the light for 15 years, but they'd never seen anything close to this.

At dawn, Murray geared up for the trip to the generator shed. Inside the house, the wind sounded like a freight train that never passed. He didn't want anybody else to go along, but asked for two of us to hold the door against the force of the wind. We were only barely able to do that, and the sound through the open door was terrible beyond description. Was this the worst of it? Murray returned, seawater sluicing off of his foul-weather gear. It took him 15 minutes to un-hunch his shoulders. "No one is to go outside at least until ten this morning when we get the next weather update."

It was dreary. The storm was expected to last all day, wind backing to the north and diminishing somewhat, but gusts were still forecasted to exceed 90 knots. There were local news reports of extensive property damage all along the coast, with boats swept away or driven ashore. One vessel, a long-line fishing boat from the Port of Glace Bay, was reported overdue and missing. (We later heard she was floundering off Scatarie Island, but she managed to survive after pumps were dropped to the crew by air-sea rescue.) Finally, by midafternoon we ventured out to survey the damage to the buildings and boats in 50 knots of wind, a *storm* in technical language, but at least the disturbing roar had moderated, sounding only in the gusts.

The apocalyptic scene brought us up short. The roof had been shorn off the tractor shed, and the 45-gallon fuel drums we'd worked so hard to secure were all but gone. Only 6 remained of 30. We later located a few of the drums scattered over the beach at Eastern Harbor, but they were utterly destroyed, contents lost. The Whaler had been tied down to the last section of the station's slip; it now sat as if suspended in midair, held fast by ropes stressed to their ultimate capacity. The beach gravel that only hours before had lined the shore some 80 feet behind the dive tender, now claimed the area under it and beyond for another 50 feet. The beach had been physically moved inland by the power of the sea; the land that skirted the beach had been stripped bare of topsoil and vegetation. To those not used to witnessing nature's fury up close and personal, the destruction seemed surreal.

Murray drove the tractor out of its ruined shed to take Jim and me to the *Brothers Four.* We carried spare batteries, a gas-powered bilge pump, and the desperate hope we'd have a boat to pump out.

And there she was, in the water and not wrecked on land. We whooped with joy. She was lying very low, with about a foot of freeboard remaining. Her bilges were full, but she was afloat. We were amazed to see that the outer section of the concrete wharf had been flipped on its side and displaced. The shoreline of the cove had been eroded over 100 feet back from its usual location. Giddy with delight, we hauled *Brothers Four* back to what remained of the wharf and got the bilge pump going. When she was dry, we installed fresh batteries, and she started up like a showroom diesel.

My guys were itching to get back home, but the wind held in the 40s all day. Next morning dawned clear and fair with a light breeze from the northwest. It's a strange thing to see the ocean after a storm passes. It's all sweetness and light, behaving itself like a drunk on the day after a violent binge. Actually, it was beautiful, residual swells sparkling in the crisp, clean air. Back at Main-a-Dieu, we loaded the plastic buckets containing about 100,000 coins into a government van that would take them to the conservation lab—at Fortress Louisbourg. We never saw them again.

One day later I got a call from Robert Grenier, the head archaeologist for Parks Canada, who wanted to travel from Ottawa to Cape Breton to dive on the *Leonidas*. The officials were beginning to take notice, and

I thought that would be a good thing. That weekend Grenier and Jim Ringer, another archaeologist, arrived at Main-a-Dieu ready to dive on the wreck site. On a dead-calm day, with the sea flat as a dance floor, Captain Mullins headed the *Brothers Four* to Hay Island. As we talked on the way, I noticed their skeptical attitude. How could there be as many coins as MacKinnon has said? This was going to be fun.

They geared up in their new red dry suits, which looked impossibly cumbersome to me. I was still using a wet suit, and their dry suits didn't make me want to change. Having no idea of their experience, despite their fancy gear, I gave them explicit instructions to stay with me. Fortunately, they proved themselves capable sport divers, and I introduced them to the coins. They examined handfuls here and there, swimming in circles, and I could tell from the steady stream of bubbles from their regulators that those boys were excited. Back on deck, they were nearly speechless.

"You saw only the tiniest fraction of them," I said. I asked if they wanted to see the hoard of silverware we'd found, but, no, they wanted to have a look at the *Le Chameau* we'd been on last season to recover a sample of those coins. It was only an hour's run, so off we went. But I was still mystified why people weren't interested in the silverware.

Grenier asked, "Would you recover as many coins as possible in one dive? I won't make this dive [he was cold], but Ringer here, will go with you."

The water on this site was deeper than usual, about 40 feet, so I stressed to Ringer that he should stay right with me, though in generous conditions like this there shouldn't be any problem; he wouldn't be banged back and forth in the surge. We immediately came upon two cannon and a small anchor lying in the shape of a lopsided cross, a familiar bottom mark for me. At least they hadn't been moved by the hurricane, but the rest of the layout I'd remembered was changed. I led

Ringer to a place where previously I'd found gold and silver coins. I moved some small boulders revealing the usual matrix of sand, gravel, and shell hash. I fanned away the light overburden to reveal round, black, silver dollar–size discs. I recovered about 50 of them in a few minutes while Ringer, the archaeologist—watched. "Was this enough?" I gestured. Ringer wanted more. Before I pulled my reserve rod, I had collected about 150 silver dollar–size coins, called ecus.

Grenier was delighted; you could tell by the way he ran the coins between his fingers, sort of playing with them. I could tell he was seriously impressed, if not momentarily captivated, by the hoard of treasure Ringer and I had just brought to the surface.

"Do you want some more?" I asked, pretending not to notice.

"That's enough for me," said Ringer. "That water's cold."

Back in Main-a-Dieu harbor, I gathered up the coins and stuck them in my pockets before we went for lunch at the nearby coffee shop owned by Jim Mullins's relatives. Before we sat down, Grenier said, "Bob, in my capacity as a representative of the receiver of wreck, I am required to ask you to turn over the coins to me."

We had a local receiver of wreck in Louisbourg. His name was Harvey Lewis. That's who David had been dealing with, but I didn't argue. I emptied my pockets on the table and asked if they'd be returned to me. Robert assured me they would. This was the second lot of coins I witnessed being entrusted to Parks Canada that I never saw again. Some months later when I inquired about them, the director of Parks Canada's Underwater Division informed me that they were believed lost when the conservation lab moved to expanded quarters at Liverpool Court.

By the next season, Jim Mullins, who was turning into a savvy treasure diver, and I dove daily from *Brothers Four* in search of new wrecks while recovering treasure from the older ones—we reported the recoveries of treasure to the district receiver of wreck in Louisbourg. Then in mid-summer we heard that Parks Canada had started a major recovery project at the *Leonidas* site, Hay Island. And the divers, we heard, were being billeted at the assistant lighthouse keeper's residence at East Point for the duration of the project, which was scheduled to last two or three months. When we were in the neighborhood, we decided to pay a visit just to see what they were doing and to say hello. Ronnie Blundon and Dewar MacDonald were aboard with Jim and me.

As we neared the site, with their workboat in view, we saw a Boston Whaler heading for us at speed. One of the junior archaeologists of Parks Canada was driving.

He pulled in abeam of us. Waving a piece of paper at us, he shouted, "This is a government site and no one may come within one mile of operations."

At first I thought he didn't recognize me as the guy who showed them to the site in the first place, so I leaned outboard and identified myself.

"Please leave the area immediately or the Coast Guard will be called." That was his reply.

"What the hell was that about?" we asked each other as we left the area. Some of us said rude things about them, none unwarranted, but I still didn't get it. Why run us off the site like that? It didn't make sense. I soon found out why.

As fall approached, Mullins's family store at Main-a-Dieu took a message from Murray Rolfe out at the lighthouse. The Parks crew had no way to get off the island for the last two weeks to get supplies, it said. Now they were all running out of food, including the lightkeepers, who were digging into their own supplies to help. So of course Jim and I stocked *Brothers Four* full of groceries at the lightkeeper's request and made for East Point.

"I wonder why they couldn't get off the island on their own."

"Their boat must be down."

We unloaded the food, and Murray and Eva invited us in for a quick lunch before we returned to the harbor. Bill Horne, the assistant lightkeeper, joined us. During our conversation over tea and biscuits, I told them how we'd been previously run off the *Leonidas* site over at Hay Island by Parks personnel.

"You want to know why?" said Bill. "It's because they're using explosives on the wreck."

"What!"

"Yeah, they blew it up. Some of the coins from the wreck were blown right up onto the island; God knows what else was destroyed. They've engaged my kids to find them. No kidding."

This could not be true. I felt the crew from Parks may have had a case of gold fever, but not so bad that they would seriously disturb a historic wreck to get at the artifacts. I wanted to speak with someone in charge to get the story firsthand.

"Their boss is gone." Bill Horne continued to report. "They are mighty agitated. He left with the project's Boston Whaler so they have no way off the island until he returns, that was well over two weeks ago. They seem to have abandoned work on the site now most days and remain held up in the other assistant's house across from mine. Murray and I attempt to interact with them, trying to keep their spirits up, but I am sure they would rather be back on the mainland. That's why we almost ran out of food; we needed to share ours with the government crowd."

Jim and I left the island, not knowing what to make of the news passed on by the lightkeepers: the blasting of historic wreck sites and the hiring of children to look for and handle cultural artifacts that may be past the state of fragile after surviving the force of an explosion or a series of explosions. How many precious artifacts were they walking over and destroying in the process? Why weren't professionals called in to save what could be saved of the scores of artifacts most likely thrown up onto Hay Island?

Just as we were struggling with the events at Hay Island, we got a call from the lighthouse. Murray asked if we would return to the island at the end of the week with *Brothers Four* and take what remained of the government crew back to the mainland. He noted feelings within the Parks Canada camp were running high and they wanted off Scatarie Island. After many calls, they had received permission from their head office in Ottawa to return to the mainland by any means available to them. They were dejected both personally and professionally; they had had enough. They just wanted to go home.

In glum silence, we took the dive crew back to Main-a-Dieu.

CHAPTER SEVEN

Discovery of the *Auguste*

We were finding ship's timbers on the wintery, windswept beach at Aspy Bay near the northern point of Cape Breton Island. It was mid-December 1976, and Ronnie had been telling me about a French ship, the *Auguste,* that sank near here in 1761 and the fortune in bullion it was documented to have carried. I had impatiently induced him to drive up here and search for physical evidence of her passing. I hadn't exactly expected to find anything, given time and tide, but there it was. In a brook emptying out of Middle Harbor from a lake behind the sand dunes, we found a large oak timber. Never mind the December cold, I waded in and dragged the timber out onto the beach for a closer look. Bronze pins and large square nails and oak plugs that covered the heads of brass drift pins—definitely from a ship, an old ship. I replaced the timber, and we searched for more in the sand dunes at the top of the beach.

After we'd found huge sections of oak planks and thick frames with bent and broken bronze nails protruding, Ronnie stood up and walked over the dunes back to the high-water line. I followed. Peering seaward for a time, he pointed at an area of shallow water where swells broke over sunkers, and said, "The wreck of the *Auguste* and a king's ransom lies right out there. I'm sure of it."

And so it did.

The life and death of the *Auguste*, unlike most 18th-century shipwrecks, was fully documented by a passenger, St. Luc de La Corne, in a detailed journal that still exists. I spent long days that winter at the Beaton Institute studying the story and the man who wrote it. This was my first in-depth exposure to another aspect of treasure hunting, research. That historical research was integral to the work didn't surprise me. The excitement and pleasure in doing the research did indeed surprise me. The *Auguste* and St. Luc took life in my imagination as I learned their place in the context of events that shaped modern Canada.

St. Luc was born in 1712 into a distinguished military family during the period of French supremacy in Canada, the end of which he was destined to witness firsthand. He fought during the French and Indian War as a militia leader and an organizer of Indian, guerilla-style raiding parties. He was so good at the latter that the British, whom he harried relentlessly and creatively, couldn't help but respect him. He served with General Montcalm at the Battle of Fort William Henry, fought with distinction at the 1758 Battle of Ticonderoga, and in the one that put the end to French domination of Canada, the Battle of the Plains of Abraham.

A keen businessman as well as an avid soldier, he had made a fortune in the fur trade. Under the preliminary terms of the 1763 Treaty of Paris, French loyalists, particularly the aristocracy, could keep their possessions and remain in the previously French-held areas if they'd swear allegiance to the Crown. Or they could return to France—and still keep their possessions. St. Luc, irrevocably French, gathered his valuables in Quebec and waited for a ship to take him home.

The *Auguste de Bordeaux* was a ship, which in the sailing days meant it carried three masts, all rigged with square sails. Ocean-going vessels in those days were much smaller than most people envision from the movies. *Auguste* was only 70 to 80 feet long. An armed merchantman, not a warship per se, she had been captured by the British in 1756, renamed *Augusta*, and then sold as a prize by the Royal Navy. She arrived again as the *Auguste* with cargo for Quebec in July 1761. James Murray, British governor of Quebec and the former New France, commandeered the ship, along with two other smaller ships, the *Molineux* and the *Jane*. A Captain John Knowles took command of the *Auguste*. St. Luc went aboard in Quebec with his two young sons, his brother, and, according to British records, bullion worth several million pounds sterling. The problem was that winter was coming on, a very bad time of year to cross the North Atlantic in those latitudes. They sailed from Quebec on October 15. And, as a kind of foreboding, St. Luc notes in his journal that the *Auguste* was ill-equipped and undermanned.

On November 1, the little fleet of three ships, still in sight of one another, cleared the mouth of the St. Lawrence River and laid a course to exit the Gulf of St. Lawrence between Newfoundland and the north coast of Nova Scotia. On the 4th, while still in the gulf, they were clobbered by a severe northeast storm that blew like hell for three days. When battling the tempest there was no distinction between crew and passengers, and then, after it had blown out, exhausting everyone aboard, the galley caught fire. They managed to douse the fire, but not before it caused severe damage between decks—and ruined their only source of heat and hot food. They hadn't even reached the North Atlantic before the ship was injured and her complement crippled by cold and overwork. St. Luc expresses his concern for his two sons and regret that he'd taken them aboard for this terrible passage.

On the 9th, strong easterlies threatened to set them down on the Magdalen Islands, but working day and night without letup, they clawed their way off the lee shore. The next day, near the south coast of Newfoundland, St. Luc, his brother, and the captain took soundings in 43 fathoms, which by their reckoning put them over Orphan Banks. Maybe things were looking up. They knew where they were, at least generally, the wind had abated, and they caught 200 cod fish. But no, a heavy easterly blew up, setting them back toward the rocks of northern Nova Scotia. Weary and frostbitten, they managed to get an anchor down just in time, and when the wind shifted, they gained some sea room. Hopes were dashed, however, when the heavy east wind returned and blew for two days. Most of the crew had given up and took to their hammocks—and most would die in them.

Fighting for their lives, St. Luc, his brother, and Captain Knowles manned the pumps and tended the sails as best they could, but it was to no avail. Wind and tide blew the ship ever deeper into Aspy Bay. St. Luc wrote:

> *About 11 o'clock we saw a river on the port side about half a cannon shot away. I had just time to acquaint our 5 people when the ship was aground about 40 yards from the shore. [We] tacked about and overturned immediately. [The ship filled with water] so that most of the people were drowned*

before they could get upon deck, and they who did not hold fast when they came there, were soon washed overboard.

But as the ship began to break up, St. Luc saw that the only hope was to try to swim ashore. He clutched his two sons under his arms and jumped into the cold, dreadful sea. No one swims in such waves; one becomes merely an object, like a ship's timber, hurled toward the land. St. Luc dumped ashore largely uninjured, but the seas had wrenched his sons from his grasp, and they were never seen again. St. Luc lay on that rocky beach in despair until dawn, when he knew that if he did not move he would die.

The beach was a macabre scene of death and destruction, strewn with dozens of corpses and wreckage. St. Luc found Captain Knowles, more dead than alive, and five others barely clinging to life. In all, only 7 people survived of the 121 souls aboard the *Auguste.* In addition to soldiers, servants, and common citizens, a cross section of French Canadian nobility died in Aspy Bay that winter night in 1761. St. Luc gathered the little band of survivors and struggled to start a fire, their only hope for continued survival. They couldn't wait on that charnel-house beach, for none would come. They had to find their own way to safety, but where was safety? Cape Breton was still a wilderness. And where were they? North of Fortress Louisbourg, the captain thought. After deciding to head south, St. Luc relates his distress at seeing a few of the survivors collecting useless valuables they found on the beach before beginning their winter march in wet clothes and without food or shelter.

Bedraggled and traumatized, the seven crossed into the woods, slogging through frozen bogs and thick forest and over windswept, naked-rock crags, trying to keep the coastline on their left. After two days of this misery, two of the survivors laden with treasure collapsed in the woods. St. Luc reprimanded and beseeched them to abandon the absurd valuables and get up, but to no avail. St. Luc, the captain, and the others, with no choice but to press on, promised to send help if they found it, and left the two to die of gold fever.

The hardship is barely imaginable today, but they continued moving, starving and in pain, for several more days. About the time St. Luc doubted they could last another day, they came upon a tiny Indian camp at the mouth of a river in St. Ann's Bay. Several Indians emerged from their shelters and stared at the helpless whites. Then someone recognized St. Luc from the war. They welcomed the survivors and shared with them what little food they had (starvation loomed every winter in those days). They were saved, but now what to do? Captain Knowles decided to press on to Fortress Louisbourg, now in British hands, after hearing from the natives that it was only two days away. But St. Luc had other ideas. He meant to walk back to Quebec, 1,200 miles away.

He hired the natives to guide him to the Strait of Canso, the thin body of water that separates Cape Breton Island from mainland Nova Scotia. From there he walked, in the dead of winter, bearing his grief for his brother and two young sons, across Nova Scotia and New Brunswick, through utter wilderness, into Quebec in February of 1762, almost a full half year since he'd left on the *Auguste*. I felt, as I read, a deep admiration for this man's physical and emotional courage.

The period of French colonialism in North America had come to an end, but segments of French culture remained in Louisiana, the small islands of Saint-Pierre and Miquelon, and Quebec and Montreal. St. Luc had participated in one of the signal events in North American history; the French and Indian War (the Seven Years' War in Britain) answered the question that had been lingering for over a century: Who would control Canada, the French or the English? Defeated, St. Luc set off to return to his native France but lost to the sea everything and everyone of value in his life. Then he *walked* back to where he'd started, regained his position of leadership in Canadian society, built up another fortune, and became one of the first senators of Canada. St. Luc died in 1784; he was 72. I never forgot this man as I worked on the wreck of the *Auguste*.

The following summer, supported by divers from both groups, I found the wreck of the *Auguste* almost exactly where Ronnie Blundon said it would be. Jim Mullins and I were partnering with Ed Barrington, a professional commercial salver, and his team. They were working a modern wreck near St. Paul Island and invited Jim and me to join them for a weekend of diving aboard their 90-foot ex–buoy tender. We agreed to split anything we found. The first day at St. Paul went like clockwork, with both groups making several dives. Jim and I found an ancient wreck in Trinity Cove and planned to concentrate our efforts there. But those plans were rudely interrupted the next morning by a severe blow from the southeast.

We had to bolt for shelter in Dingwall Harbor, 20 hard miles across an open stretch of the Cabot Strait from St. Paul Island. The old flat-bottom buoy tender rolled rail to rail that night, sometimes sliding sideways down 30-foot waves, while other waves broke at will across her deck. The power of that summer storm was shocking, and it goes far to explain why almost nothing recognizable as being from a ship remains on these wreck sites. But before dawn, to everyone's pleasure, we reached Dingwall Harbor. We drank multiple cups of coffee in the galley that morning while we waited out the storm, talking incessantly about Cape Breton shipwrecks generally and the *Auguste* specifically.

At the first opportunity, before dusk on July 2, 1977, I borrowed one of the rubber boats and, with Ed's partner, Jerry, I made for the shallow water off Middle Harbor. On the very first dive, I found a cannonball.

I delivered it to the crew back aboard the *Offshore Salver*; it got their attention.

"Say, Bob, have you ever heard the real story of the *Auguste*?" Ed asked.

"Yes, actually I have." I told the crew about Ronnie, whom everybody knew, and our walk on the beach and the unmistakable ship's timbers we'd seen. Then, as I told them the story of St. Luc, his journal, and the fortune *documented* to have been aboard the *Auguste*, I could see the early flickers of gold fever in their eyes. The crew, hard men of the sea themselves, asked me to repeat St. Luc's story, and they, too, admired him and felt for his loss. They asked me to repeat how it was I knew that all that bullion was aboard.

"You have to meet my friend Clayton Dixon," Ed advised. "He's a local fisherman. You'll want to hear his story."

Clayton joined us aboard later that evening. He explained that two years before, the government had hired a company to do magnetometer runs looking for a wreck in Aspy Bay. "The only thing they found was an anchor. These archaeologists came to look at the anchor and declared it modern. Now, I didn't see it personally, but from the description I heard from a guy who was there, it didn't sound modern to me," said Clayton. "I heard it was made of wrought iron."

I asked Jim Mullins how long it had been since anchors were made of wrought iron.

"Good two hundred years."

"Could you put us on that anchor, Clayton?"

"Oh, sure."

"Tomorrow?"

"What time?"

We didn't get much sleep that night, mostly due to the anticipation and excitement; such a discovery, once it becomes a reality, in-vibes. We were up and ready to go at 5:30 A.M.

Clayton put us *right on* the anchor. A quick dive verified that it was not a modern anchor, but a very old one, with a wrought-iron chain.

Now down to coolheaded business—suspend the symptoms of gold fever. Jim Mullins and Bob Anthony made the first dive while I followed their bubbles in the rubber boat. The anchor served as a perfect baseline for our typical search pattern. We decided on a compass course, in this case due east. And the divers followed the course while swimming in 50-foot-diameter circles on either side of the line. By this means, the divers examine a broad but controlled swath of the bottom. That implies of course that they know what to look for on the bottom.

They had barely completed two circles away from the anchor heading east when both divers came to the surface waving their arms. They had found cannon. I told them to go back down to the cannon and, without creating a lot of disturbance, do some hand fanning for further evidence. Within only minutes, both divers found French coins, dated 1734 and 1728. Upon their return to the surface, this news developed into a great crescendo of yells and unbridled excitement. We were on the treasure of the *Auguste*.

We made repeated dives that day, and every one turned up more and more coins, as well as silverware and other artifacts. We disturbed nothing; all that material appeared loose and easy to recover with only minor hand fanning. This was the richest site ever discovered in Nova Scotia. We were finding so much treasure that I called a halt. We had to slow down. We had to establish methods and our own protocols. We had to do it right. My first thought was to keep a detailed log of the things we found, and at the close of each day, we'd all sign the log.

That night I lay awake pondering the magnitude of the find, and what we should do next. This was beyond everyone's experience. In order to get some sleep, I decided to wait to see what the morning might bring. If indeed the next day we recovered anywhere near the quantity of today, then I'd stop and make concrete, forward-looking plans.

Well, we did find as much if not more on the second day of diving. I called a meeting on the aft deck to discuss with the delighted divers what we should do next. This was, I recognized, one of those events that require a life choice. I had a real job and a family to support. Obviously, the decision to quit my job and devote myself full-time to treasure was not the most practical or safe choice. Yet my life had turned in that direction even before I owned a tank and regulator. Now with real opportunity in the work I loved, 20 feet below the deck, should I turn away? Could I? In a word, no. And it turned out I wasn't alone in that. Jim Mullins quit his job as well. So did most of the crew. We agreed we'd use the *Offshore Salver* as a base of operations from Dingwall Harbor, and when Ed had to use her for other work, we'd work around him. We still had the *Brothers Four* on-site. That was an unforgettable day for us—and it proved to be a sharper turning point than any of us imagined.

But there were still shoreside formalities to attend to. Ed and I, as leaders of the respective teams, drove to Sydney the next day to properly claim the wreck. That turned out to be easy. The receiver of wreck, a kindly gentleman, was in his office. He officially recorded our find and our intent to make a claim, which he told us would be forwarded to Transport Canada. Ed and I sailed out of there shaking each other's hand.

"I've been concerned about one thing," I said on the way back to Dingwall. Ed and I both understood the historical significance of the *Auguste* site. "I think we need to bring in an archaeologist who knows how to properly excavate a historic wreck site. I think it's not only in the best interest of the wreck—but in our interests as well. We want to do everything right. And we want to be seen doing it right."

Ed didn't disagree, but he asked the next question, "Where are we going to find an archaeologist who knows what he's doing?"

Today underwater archaeology has taken its place as a serious specialization of the field. In 1977, the science was just getting under way. Some remarkable work was being done at the time by pioneers like George Bass in Turkey, but you couldn't phone up the archaeology department at a major North American university, ask for the underwater specialist, and expect to find one.

"Well, there's Robert Grenier, I worked with him before without any issue. At the very least, Parks Canada might send him down to validate our claim."

"Wasn't it our Parks Canada that blew up the Hay Island wreck last season? You want them to come in?"

"No, I want to see us maintain control over the site; if we are forced to involve Parks—and at some point we will be—it must be on our terms," I said. "That's why we need to do everything right."

"Let me get this straight." Ed took his eyes off the road. "You want to stop all recovery until we see if a marine scientist can be had. You might encounter some, uh, opposition to stopping recovery." He was understating; he knew he was understating. I confronted a potential mutiny back aboard the *Offshore Salver.*

They were working-class guys, like me. I understood how they felt about sitting around waiting for a lubberly scientist while the riches remained untouched, but I tried to suggest the longer view. I tried to explain the historical importance of this site. Hadn't they been moved by St. Luc's story? Didn't they see that the *Auguste* originated from a crucial turning point in Canadian history? Not everyone found that argument persuasive. So I pointed out the other reason for doing it my way. We were a private commercial enterprise planning to excavate a ship that had historical importance to the public. People would be watching to see that we cared about preservation. They had a right to expect that we did. And we did. But not everyone found that compelling, either.

"Look," said a young guy on Ed's crew, "you're not my boss. I can do what I want with the treasure." Or something like that.

"Son, you will have to come through me to do that," I said, bellicosely, I admit. But I was done explaining. We were going to do it my way, and the man didn't challenge me further. The discussion turned more rational, and we talked at length over the scientist question. Should I contact Robert Grenier, head of the Parks Canada underwater team, or try to find another scientist? No one had any idea where to look, and no one wanted the delay required to search. So I phoned Grenier to inform him of our find.

I had formed a partnership with Jim Mullins and local businessman Joe Starr. I had been keeping Joe up-to-date with our recovery and the legal steps we were taking. From the first mention of the *Auguste*, he'd had a singular piece of advice: Be careful, get a lawyer who knows maritime law, and get everything in writing. He'd stressed *in writing*. Lawyers for Ed's company and my lawyer drew up an agreement forming a new partnership and stipulating how the returns from the wreck would be distributed. Neither of our lawyers was a maritime law specialist, however; and Ed agreed that we needed one. He suggested none other than Donald Kerr, who had told me about the *Fantome*. Perfect. Things were working out right, we thought.

Robert Grenier was excited to hear about the *Auguste*. Could he come to Dingwall, look at our recovered artifacts, and dive on the site? If it really was the *Auguste*, he said, then we've found the most important wreck in Nova Scotia waters. Did I know that the ship carried the fortune of St. Luc de La Corne?

"I had heard that," I said.

Grenier showed up two days later. He made several assessment dives with us and pored through the artifacts. There was no doubt about it, he declared, we had found the wreck of the *Auguste.* He immediately phoned his superiors at Parks Canada back in Ottawa. Ed and I were invited to catch a flight to Ottawa the next day to meet the department heads to discuss Parks Canada's possible participation in the excavation. Ed and I were very proud, flying to Ottawa to meet the big shots, but Joe's words—*be careful*—were ringing in my ears as we landed.

We had a pleasant meeting with Dianne Hearst, the director of Parks Canada's Underwater Division; Robert Grenier; and other division representatives. They all agreed unconditionally to recognize our group as the legal owners of the site and everything it contained—this as per admiralty law stating that a wreck left in the water by the owner for over 100 years with no attempt at salvage was deemed to be abandoned and, therefore, the property of those who find it.

Absolutely, stated Hearst and the Parks Canada people, no question about that. Parks Canada then offered to provide scientific and technical assistance in the form of a field conservation lab, including experienced staff and an underwater archaeologist to oversee the excavation. The only stipulation, also per admiralty law, was that we would deliver the recovered artifacts to the receiver of wreck, who would keep them for the mandated one year and a day, an opportunity for the true owner to come forward and make a claim. In that case, we would receive a healthy salvage fee, but of course there were no owners of this 200-year-old wreck, so we didn't worry about it. Also, Parks Canada agreed that day that they would not interfere with any reasonable requests we might make in promoting the recovery to raise money to help support ongoing operations.

Everyone shook hands. They offered us their hearty congratulations on our historic find. Grenier said, "We commend you for putting history ahead of profit. I'm sure you will be rewarded, and your selflessness will have a positive impact on other salvers in the international community."

Ed and I were walking on air as we left that office. How could it have been better? But I was still hearing Joe's words. Get it in *writing*. We hadn't gotten it in writing. Should we go back? But there was no question about the terms. We owned the wreck and its contents. Everyone said so. We had a verbal agreement, didn't we?

Well, of course my partner Joe Starr was right, and I was so very wrong. But we forgot about that because everything was going so well, a dream come true, really.

CHAPTER EIGHT

Enter Parks Canada

A few days after our Ottawa meeting, the first members of the Parks staff and the chief archaeologist, Jim Ringer, arrived in Dingwall. We had a projectwide meeting that evening, salvers and Parks people getting to know each other. Ringer talked about his plans and his methodology. He began his speech this way: "Parks is involved in this project to help promote science, and that is all. We were advised in Ottawa that you, the salvers who found the wreck, own it and everything recovered from it." After that, we all became fast friends.

Parks would eventually set up their mobile conservation trailer at our base of operations, the MacDonald Motel in Cape North. They also set up a field lab on board the *Offshore Salver* and immediately began preserving and cataloging the artifacts we'd already recovered. Everyone was happy; we were comrades engaged in something important. I, for one, was as excited as a kid. But with Ed's support as an equal partner, I was basically in charge of the recovery, and it soon became clear, as the team swelled to close to 20, that I'd have to contend with aspects of the profession I had never considered. Most of the team from away was going to spend the season at MacDonald Motel. This required logistical decisions. How would we eat, for instance? Dingwall was not a major metropolis with a choice of restaurants spanning international cuisine. I took the question up with Ed, who had some experience running crews. He suggested we all eat together in the *Offshore Salver*'s mess room. But who was going to cook?

I went looking for a cook willing to work in a tiny galley aboard an ex–buoy tender feeding three squares a day to almost 20 people with lumberjack appetites. They aren't thick on the ground. As it happened Robert Grenier knew just such a person who had worked in restoration at Fortress Louisbourg and had just been laid off. Her name was Jocelyn Marchand, and because we needed a cook immediately, we hired her sight unseen.

"Are you kidding!" she exclaimed upon first laying eyes on her galley. "You guys *eat* in here? I can't work in this dump. Get someone down here now to clean this up—to my satisfaction."

There's an old nautical saying that the captain is not the most important man on the ship—the cook is. I went back to the motel to collect a gang of volunteers to clean it up to her standards. By the end of the day, the place was spotless. You could have performed an appendectomy in that galley without fear of secondary infection. Meanwhile, I went food shopping. *Everything* was working out.

The next morning Jocelyn was hard at work in her galley at 6:00 A.M. when my crew and I (Parks staff were eating at a local restaurant) arrived for a hearty workingman's breakfast of eggs, potatoes, flapjacks, and lots of meat. The table was set like a fine restaurant, flowers in the middle, places all labeled with names on the chairs. We took our places, and the cook dished us up with—

"What is that?" I asked.

"That's muesli."

"No, I don't think you understand. We don't eat—what did you call it, 'muesli'?—we don't need grain and nuts. We need meat. We're going to spend five or six hours in cold water doing real labor. We need—"

"This is my kitchen, and I set the menu. If anyone doesn't like it, he can go eat at the restaurant."

I started to tell her, look, you work for me, so I have a say, but I stopped when she turned on me with a heavy muesli-stirring spoon.

"Either I'm the cook or I'm not. If you want something special, say so. If not, eat what I put in front of you. Of course, you can try to find another cook. I'm sure there's dozens would like to work in this closet of a galley."

Ed was kicking me under the table. "Bob, don't piss off the cook," he said as we headed toward the restaurant for some bacon and eggs. "Who else is there? Besides, I paid a month's rent on her cottage in advance." What's a captain to do? "Let's talk nice to her. She'll come around."

She did, too. She worked all summer in that closet galley. She even cooked some meat. And a few of us came to like muesli.

Meanwhile, the diving was like a gold-fever fantasy. Silver coins in near-mint condition and some gold ones flowed aboard by the thousands, seemingly with no end in sight. We were advancing meticulously through the area where we'd made our initial discovery, on the reasoning that because we owned the site and time was on our side, a complete recovery mattered more than a speedy one. Plus, we were enjoying every minute.

According to Jim Ringer's plan, we laid in a permanent baseline running from the shore past where we felt the debris field ended. In our opinion it led straight to the spot where the *Auguste* struck, as a complete ship. The stern section, main hull, and bow section were still intact. We had learned on other wrecks we'd worked that debris moved shoreward, not seaward. This made sense because the wave action capable of disturbing debris also moved shoreward. My brother, John, a qualified surveyor, established two cairns in a range on shore that led to the baseline, so we could find the line if we were blown off the site and all floating markers were lost. John also surveyed and marked a line running perpendicular to the initial line for triangulation purposes. This, remember, was before the days of GPS.

We delivered the coins from the bottom directly to the *Offshore Salver*, where Parks Canada people performed initial cleaning and stabilization in a makeshift lab set up in the cargo hold, a room about 40 feet by 15 feet, with tables, bins, desalinization tanks, and storage boxes. That summer was hotter than normal, which the divers appreciated, but not the conservation people working below deck in an airless room thick with the usual shipboard smells, plus the stink of rusting steel plates and things Ed had salvaged from some long-forgotten shipwreck that defied all efforts to clean out. We respected them for their unwavering work in truly rotten conditions.

After we laid in the offset lines, we built a mobile control grid made of steel rebar held together with clamps to form three squares three meters on a side. This gridding technique, common also in land archaeology, precisely locates the artifacts before recovery. With one grid section completely excavated, the control device can be moved to an adjacent section, and the process repeated. We used smaller grid squares to maintain optimum control over a particularly rich area. And when recovery required excavating deep into the subbottom, we used single squares for the same reason. The work went on square by square every day, weather permitting, with the divers making five or more dives a day. Since the water was not deeper than 20 feet, bottom time was unlimited, without risk of the bends or any other pressure-related sickness. We never turned off the weather radio. If the forecast for the next day was threatening, we dove until dark and sometimes beyond using lights, but they didn't work very well because they couldn't penetrate the cloud of sediment our work always kicked up.

Early on in the excavation, we encountered a deep sand cover and struggled to clear it away while fighting the constant swell action that reburied our grid squares. This problem needed to be addressed immediately. We designed air lifts, giant vacuum cleaners, driven by powerful 300-cubic-feet-per-minute (cfm) diesel compressors that, after some experimentation, proved invaluable. We were then able to clear the sand out of the grid areas within minutes. The pace of the excavations increased considerably, allowing each diver to easily hand fan through the subbottom.

Clearing this sandy overburden led to another fascinating discovery. There were freshwater springs filtering up through the ocean floor. This fortunate phenomenon explained the almost mint condition of the artifacts. They were surviving in a freshwater bath, under the cover of a saline sea.

The divers and scientists alike were puzzled at first by the freshwater found so far from shore, but not old salt Clayton Dixon: "Boys, I thought you were book learned. Look behind the beach—there's a lake of freshwater forcing its way under that narrow strip of shore, and then coming up through the sand that covers the site. Everyone knows that."

At that moment, one of the divers broke the surface and yelled, "I found a bell here, the biggest I've ever seen," and quickly resubmerged. His air lift was still spouting sand and water in a plume that rose some

30 feet in the air. We could see he was increasing the air flow; he must be excavating something buried very deep.

Before the end of day, all six recovered pieces, those of a large German silver bell, were assembled on deck to represent a complete and rare artifact, a large gray bell dated 1749. The bell was embossed with a raised Christ on the Crucifix set under a Latin inscription *Sit Nomen Domini Benedictum* (Blessed be the name of the Lord). It stood over three feet high with a circumference at the base of over 30 inches; no one on board had ever seen such a thing. Before the week would pass, two more bells of lesser size but just as impressive made their long-awaited return to the surface.

After some preliminary research on the part of the site archaeologist, it was confirmed that these were indeed church bells. The set of three were called chimes. They were cast in France for the Catholic Church at Trois-Rivières (Three Rivers), Quebec, and placed on board the *Auguste* by the La Corne family. They were the original benefactors who commissioned their casting and supplied them to the church. Ringer went on to explain that such items were more valuable than gold to the passengers of the ill-fated *Auguste*: "They were an integral part of their religious heritage, representing, in sound, their struggles in a new land." At that moment, thanks to the rare glimpse into the minds of long-dead men and women provided by the significance of the bells, we privately mourned the passengers of the *Auguste*.

During a weather day, Ed asked me to chat with him in the wheelhouse about money. We were funding the recovery work with our own money and money Joe Starr had raised from private small investors. Excavation was costing us about $3,500 a day all told. Ed wanted to raise some money on the material already found, and he had an idea.

We had found two spoon molds in excellent condition. Ed suggested we contract a prominent Canadian silverware manufacturer, say Rogers Brothers, to press spoons using a reproduction of one of the 200-year-old molds. We were sure we could sell them in Canada to help defray costs. What a great idea, I thought. We took it to Ringer, who saw no problem, but he wanted to run it by his superiors in Ottawa.

Ottawa said no, he reported. *No? What do you mean no?* Ringer rattled off a litany of reasons why that would be bad for the project, the whole public-private partnership would be suspect if such replications of artifacts were sold, even if the money would be going right back into the excavation. This was not Ringer's doing; he was only repeating Parks Canada's position.

Wait a minute. Did they use the word *partnership*? As in public-private *partnership*? This was no partnership, and they knew it. Technically, we didn't need to ask permission from Parks Canada. We had only informed them out of courtesy.

Joe Starr was still more skeptical. "Maybe you can trust Jim Ringer and the people working the site," he said, "but be very wary of authority in Ottawa."

This was a sour note in what thus far had been a nearly ideal project. It irked us all. I began to worry about money and about overlapping authority. The province of Nova Scotia seemed strangely absent in this so far. The *Auguste* wreck site lay several hundred yards off the coast of Cape Breton, which is part of the province of Nova Scotia. Did Nova Scotia have any jurisdiction? Didn't I file the claim with the receiver of wreck in Sydney, Nova Scotia? I brought up the question more than once with Ed and our lawyers. We put the question directly to Ottawa, who told us equally directly and without question that they, federal not provincial authority, had jurisdiction. But what of the fact that I'd registered the claim in Nova Scotia?

Oh, that was no problem; Parks Canada said via Jim Ringer that they had gotten a "dispensation" from the head receiver of wreck in Ottawa. It was all worked out. This, we later learned, was an oversimplification of the facts. Nova Scotia had standing. I recall these events with a mixture of anger and embarrassment, tempered by passing time, yes, but still present. I was naïve, still clinging to the notion that this was the government of my country talking. These people weren't going to misrepresent or mislead me. Plus we had a very clear agreement, and all any of us wanted to do was dive and recover treasure.

One memorable day during the latter part of the season, Jim Mullins found a cache of silverware mixed with large gold coins. As he excavated within his grid, he discovered signet seals used on personal communications to stamp the sender's name in sealing wax. By matching that name to the still-extant passenger list, we could prove categorically we were on the *Auguste*. But the seals also added a personal quality to the recovery, enhancing its historic value. As our work continued, we found more than 20 silver seals, and we were thus able to identify almost one third of the passengers who left Quebec on their last voyage in 1761. Further, we were able to identify the owners of individual artifacts, particularly the vast quantities of silverware being recovered. The wreck seemed to come alive, and our respect for the people who died here grew almost daily.

Near the close of the 1977 season, Parks invited Ed and me to a meeting. Because so much treasure was coming ashore, overwhelming our mobile ship's lab, this was causing some security anxiety. Parks asked if we would be amenable to allowing the artifacts to be transported by Brink's truck to Ottawa for further conservation and safe storage? They would sign an official receipt. We could retake possession with a few days' notice anytime we wished. We, too, had been concerned about security, since our work was attracting a lot of attention from the public and the media.

We called a meeting and took a vote. It sounded like a good idea to most everyone except Joe Starr, who said, "If we lose control over the recovery, we will never see it again." We just didn't believe that, and besides, the quantity of treasure was in fact overwhelming our facilities. We shipped thousands of precious and nonprecious artifacts to Ottawa in 1977.

That winter a representative from *National Geographic* magazine called me to ask if they could send an expert to assess the recovery. We met at the Parks facilities in Ottawa. When we arrived, conservators had already laid out a large sample of the artifacts for his inspection. A highly knowledgeable guy who had covered most of the treasure-recovery stories for the magazine, he spent most of the day examining our find. When finished, he said, "Robert, you have a great wreck here. This material is as fine as any I've seen all over the world in twenty years. Congratulations."

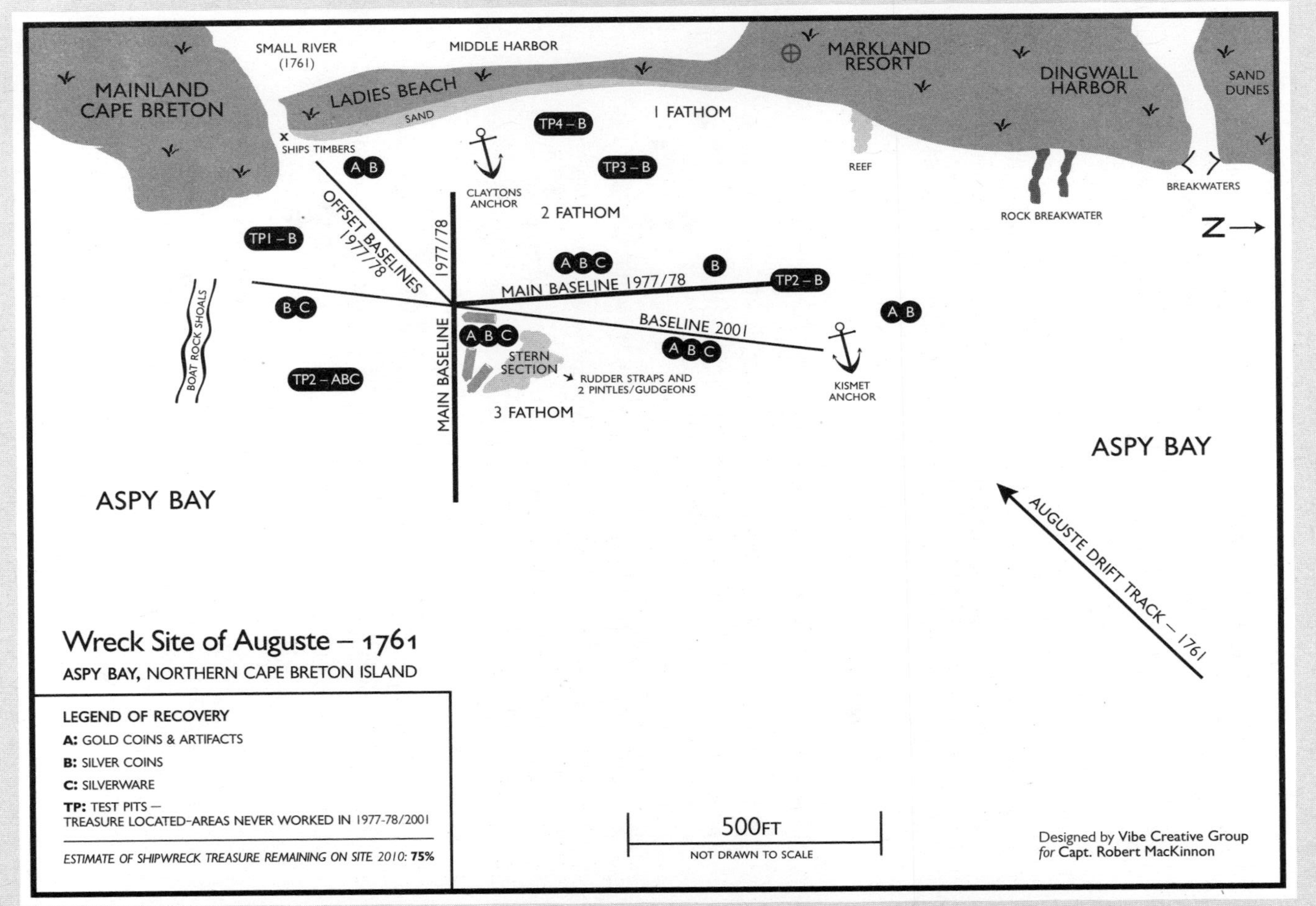
MAINLAND CAPE BRETON
SMALL RIVER (1761)
MIDDLE HARBOR
LADIES BEACH
SAND
SHIPS TIMBERS
MARKLAND RESORT
DINGWALL HARBOR
SAND DUNES
1 FATHOM
2 FATHOM
3 FATHOM
TP4 – B
TP3 – B
TP1 – B
TP2 – B
TP2 – ABC
CLAYTONS ANCHOR
REEF
ROCK BREAKWATER
BREAKWATERS
Z →
OFFSET BASELINES 1977/78
1977/78
MAIN BASELINE 1977/78
BASELINE 2001
MAIN BASELINE
BOAT ROCK SHOALS
STERN SECTION
RUDDER STRAPS AND 2 PINTLES/GUDGEONS
KISMET ANCHOR
ASPY BAY
ASPY BAY
AUGUSTE DRIFT TRACK – 1761
Wreck Site of Auguste – 1761
ASPY BAY, NORTHERN CAPE BRETON ISLAND
LEGEND OF RECOVERY
A: GOLD COINS & ARTIFACTS
B: SILVER COINS
C: SILVERWARE
TP: TEST PITS – TREASURE LOCATED-AREAS NEVER WORKED IN 1977-78/2001
ESTIMATE OF SHIPWRECK TREASURE REMAINING ON SITE 2010: 75%
500FT
NOT DRAWN TO SCALE
Designed by Vibe Creative Group for Capt. Robert MacKinnon

CHAPTER NINE

Betrayal

Like excited kids off to summer camp, we assembled our equipment and our dive vessels in Dingwall Harbor to open the 1978 season. The Parks Canada crew arrived in July and set up their new mobile conservation lab, in a secluded spot behind the MacDonald Motel. We had a happy reunion that night, and the next day we were back in the water to relocate the site and reestablish the original baselines. The following day Jim Mullins found a cache of gold coins, and that—with treasure pouring in after every dive—set the tone for the season. Only foul weather kept us off the wreck.

As the recovery increased, the divers, even the cook, began to take an interest in the artifacts' fate and conservation. What happened to them after they left the water? What was the process site conservators referred to as *final stabilization*? The strangeness both groups—private and public alike—felt toward one another during the first season took time to dissipate. Early on in the first summer, we were nothing more than two groups of professionals, struggling to work together for the common good of the enterprise. Fortunately, that strangeness quickly melted away early in the second season, molding the interests of private and public sectors into one cohesive working unit of specialists.

The less-than-ideal conservation facilities of year one, in the hull of the *Offshore Salver*, were moved to the new mobile lab set up at the MacDonald Motel. As a result and by mutual agreement, the whole crew had access to the conservation work being carried out there. Everyone wanted to help, to be involved in more than just recovery. The crew wanted to be part of it all, and I agreed they could be. The bond between the government team and the salvers reached such a level that they began to discuss future projects they could work on together.

There was even an apparition of developing a special heritage team of maritime experts from this group. The private sector would lead the discovery and recovery aspect, and Parks would supervise all science, including interpretation, research, and final conservation. The crews took it so far as to come up with a unique but fair way to compensate the private and public sector from these future recoveries. I had no choice but to admire their zeal and dedication. Both teams complemented each other on and off the site. The salvers were learning the scientific way to properly set up, recover, and conserve cultural material from a maritime heritage site. The Parks team had a firsthand opportunity to witness and learn the ways of private salvers, how they searched for and recognized such shipwrecks. Throughout, Jim Ringer was a knowledgeable if not always patient influence.

I could see that getting close to each other in such a way was having a positive effect on morale and, even more important, on the everyday atmosphere on the job. The spoon mold issue slipped into the abyss. We were becoming a family, not in the genealogical sense of the word but through a love of what we did, respective of ancient shipwrecks. We were laying the foundation for a strong and viable research community. A band of brothers molded in the fires of desire and tenacity, one that Canadian shipwrecks, their stories, and humankind in general would most surely benefit from.

As time passed that year, all doors were thrown open. Any lingering sense of suspicion long abandoned, we were one on the job, for the job, and for each other. The *Auguste* recovery project took on an innate pride of its own. We were aware of it and enamored by it. The site began to take life and we talked of it as a living entity. A divine spirit of maritime history that revealed its glory with each artifact that broke the surface was finally, after centuries, entered into the knowledge of modern man.

During a weather day, while Jim Mullins and I were having a tot of rum in my cabin, a strange site appeared in the motel parking lot. There before us was a tricked-out, fully customized three-quarter-ton, yellow-and-brown Dodge van. It was fitted with smoked-glass windows down both sides and a special airbrushed paint job; oversize chrome wheels gave off a continuous illustrious glare in the noonday sun. We had never seen anything like it before. Was it a mirage; was it a trick of the rum? It sat motionless for a while, then a beautiful young woman stepped out from behind the wheel, looked in through the open door, and asked for Robert MacKinnon.

"That's me. Who are you?"

Wordlessly, she turned on her heel, returned to the van, and opened the door for a distinguished, nattily dressed man who walked to the still-open cabin door and introduced himself as Gilbert Grosvenor. He asked if we were the men in charge of the *Auguste* operation. In a jovial mood, Jim and I offered him a drink and a seat. He had a genial way about him, so we were soon chatting about the ship, the wreck, and something of our findings. But he seemed to know a lot about what we were doing. He was way too well informed for a tourist or idle visitor. How come he knew so much?

"You don't know who I am, do you?"

"Gilbert Grosvenor, right?"

"Don't you gentlemen have a funding agreement with *National Geographic*?" he said with a smile.

Oh my God, *the* Gilbert Grosvenor, the very face of *National Geographic*! Jim and I began to babble apologies in unison, but he said none was necessary. He said he'd enjoyed the drink and the chat and was familiar with Cape Breton hospitality, having spent many a summer at the family property in Baddeck. Everyone in Nova Scotia knows about that place, called Beinn Bhreagh, perched like a small castle on a mountainside overlooking the Bras d'or Lakes. It was originally the home of Grosvenor's relative Alexander Graham Bell.

"Mr. Grosvenor, the crew would love to meet you. May I bring them around?"

He'd be pleased to meet them, he said.

I asked Jim Mullins to round up our people, and I found the Parks crew at the restaurant mid-meal. They dropped everything to meet our famous visitor. Grosvenor spent the rest of the day with us, touring the site from the beach and carefully examining the artifacts and chatting with the conservators. He was impressed and glad to be playing a small funding role in the recovery and preservation. Our cooperation with Parks Canada also impressed him as a prototype for the future. Then he invited the entire operations team to dinner at the world-renowned Keltic Lodge—a famous government resort in nearby Ingonish. Morale the next day was as high as I'd seen since the initial discovery.

However, the weather didn't cooperate that summer. We were blown out more days than anyone wanted to count, and people were showing signs of impatience as we fell behind. But behind what? we asked ourselves. This was our wreck; we had all the time we wanted. Having worked in the area of the original find, we still didn't know the extent of the wreck. To find it, Jim Mullins suggested that we do some *test pitting* as a way to search for the site's extent. Basically, you dig some holes along a fixed baseline and search in them for evidence of wreckage, especially treasure. If you find it, you keep working outward from a fixed point until you don't. Ed and I liked the idea, and the timing was right as late summer came on, so we informed Ringer of our plan.

He didn't like it. He gave us a litany of unconvincing scientific reasons why we should continue working in the original area. Though he knew it full well, I explained that it was always useful to know the extent of the wreck site. He carried on objecting until I said something to the effect that it would also be good for us—who were paying for all this recovery—if we had some idea just what we had in order to raise the money to continue. Unless, I added sarcastically, Parks wanted to kick in some cash. Anyway, we thought this odd behavior coming from Ringer. There was no good reason not to test pit.

"I'll run it by Ottawa," he said to close the unsatisfying exchange.

We were getting tired by that time of hearing about "running things by Ottawa." It had been happening too much that season, and it was beginning to chafe, again renewing our almost-forgotten aggravation about how they killed the spoon mold idea. We loved working with Ringer and the Parks people here on the site—we were a team—but Ringer seemed edgy of late. If he was getting pressure from Dianne Hearst or her people, we wished he'd tell us about it.

But then, next morning, before we boarded the *Offshore Salver*, he came around to apologize for his mood the day before. "I have no problem with test pitting. Parks doesn't need to be consulted."

Well, okay. We got right to it. We ran an offset baseline parallel to the shore for about 300 feet and began pitting every 25 feet, along both sides of the line. It took all morning to set the baselines, anchors, and floats marking the assigned test-pit locations. Jim Mullins turned up 200 mixed silver coins by lunchtime. Unfortunately, I was doing our banking and buying supplies in Ingonish and missed his afternoon discoveries.

You could tell something had happened. Our little community was abuzz. I hurried down to the dock as the *Offshore Salver*'s lines were coming ashore. Everybody was smiling. *"What!"* I almost shouted.

"I found a few coins in each of the test pits," said Mullins. "And I was near the end of the line when I saw a likely looking rock outcrop." (Artifacts often gather around the base of prominent rocks.) "I moved the rocks and there they were—" He removed the lid from a large bucket nearly overflowing with silver coins. It was a spectacular moment that I'll never forget.

As we later learned, he had collected a total of about 800 Spanish milled dollars in mint condition, each worth at least $250. So one diver in one afternoon, in about an hour and a half, recovered $200,000's worth of treasure. "The thing is," said Mullins, "there's thousands more. The rest of the treasure is right there!"

But Ringer was adamant that, nonetheless, we should stick to the original area, that there was still much to be recovered, and that all our good science would be compromised if we were to shift the excavation.

And then on the other side, there was Ed and the crew. Mullins stated their position clearly: "What the hell gives, Bob? There's a fortune in those test pits. The first three I dug were *full of coins*! Don't let them do this to us. We've done everything they wanted for two years. We're an easy fifty percent behind in recovery because of the weather, and you know it."

I did know it. The trouble was I agreed with Ringer. I wanted us to proceed in a meticulous manner. We were recovering fine historical artifacts as well as the coins. I wanted *all* artifacts cataloged and preserved, instead of letting the divers pluck out the ones that looked the most valuable, *high grading*, as we called it. But, of course, the crew was right. This slowed recovery by about 50 percent, just as Mullins estimated. The issue was becoming a rub between Ed and me. I knew someday we'd have to settle it between us, but not right then. "Look," I said, "the season's almost over. Let's stick to what we're doing. We could start first thing next season on the test-pit area."

We'd had a fantastically successful second season. But people were getting tired. We were working hard in cold water every day, the first-stage conservators were still working in the only slightly improved cargo hold, the others were doing the same back in the mobile lab. People were getting homesick living in a motel full-time. Besides, the weather had been punk. Maybe it was time to pack it up for the season and be back here first thing in the spring. We took a vote, and it was so agreed.

Jim Ringer had scheduled two armored cars—we needed both—to arrive in a couple of days. Meanwhile, we collected our surface buoys and moorings, while the Parks crew tended to the artifacts, readying them for their ride to Ottawa. The armored trucks arrived in the morning, and it took us nearly all day to pack everything in. Ed and I signed the receipts and invited the drivers to dinner, after which they were off.

I was ready to go home as well, but I felt a twinge of nostalgia watching people pack their gear. I loved this work, and I'd have been happy to do it forever.

Just a half day before we were bound to disperse for the winter, Ringer stopped by my room to tell me that Hearst (from Parks) and several other officials would be in Dingwall the following day to meet with the whole team, divers and Parks staff alike. Would I ask everyone to stay on long enough to meet her?

"What's this about, Jim?"

"I don't know. She just asked me to request the meeting."

I went to talk with Ed after Ringer left. "What's this about?"

"I don't know. Jim didn't know. Maybe they just want to discuss the plans for next year."

So we assembled at three o'clock the next afternoon, laughing and joking together, in the largest motel room. The treasure was rich, morale was high. But the mood in the room was not lighthearted. Hearst stood behind a table flanked by members of her staff and two security officers. We looked at each other around the room. Security? You don't bring security when you come to tell us what a bang-up job we're doing.

Hearst thanked us all for our cooperation. Then with barely a pause, she said, "Our department lawyers have studied our arrangement and the laws pertaining to such shipwrecks. Parks feels within its rights to notify the salvers that they have no standing or rights to the wreck or its artifacts."

Silence. We stared at her. She couldn't have said what we'd just heard.

"If you have any issue with the department's position, then you should avail yourself of the opportunity to talk with your lawyers. You have the right to challenge the department's position in court."

They'd let us excavate the site while they lawyered up, all without our knowledge or notice. As a private-sector group, working with Parks on-site every day, we'd been lulled into a false sense of well-being. Good idea to bring security. Our Parks people sat in stunned silence, but the divers rose at once and seemed to advance on Hearst and her lackeys. The security pair went rigid, well-founded fear in their eyes. There was violence in the air. Ed and I glanced at each other—we had to break this up before our guys set upon the Ottawa types, not that Ed and I wouldn't have been happy to participate. Ed and I started talking at once, both to the effect that we should get the hell out of that room before violence erupted. We walked out as a group, but we were seething.

I went looking for our so-called friend Jim Ringer, who'd been helping them set us up. I didn't exactly mean to assault him, but if he gave me any lip that could change. I found him on a nearby porch with most of the Parks crew, and I could plainly see at first glance, by his dejected look and slumped shoulders, that neither he nor any of the Parks people knew in advance about this underhanded move. That at least was good news. Meanwhile, our guys were walking around in circles trying to shed some of their anger. Then as a group they decided they needed to get themselves away from the motel grounds. I went along, feeling thoroughly embarrassed as well as irate at the heavy-handed betrayal (the term *robbery* was kicking around). It had been beyond my ken that my own government would do this to us. In that, I felt unjustly compromised. Obviously. But I wasn't alone in that. Ottawa had annoyed us at times without provocation and beyond reason. No one suspected they'd act in such a manner, taking property that by their own words and verbal admission, on day one in Ottawa, was not theirs to take—no one except Joe Starr.

We stayed on for a few days trying to figure out what to do next but finally left, totally demoralized and without any sense of direction for the future. We now became, together with men and women through the ages, one more tragic sea story.

Alone, alone, all, all alone,
Alone on a wide wide sea!

—Samuel Taylor Coleridge, "The Rime of the Ancient Mariner"

We were shipwrecks of another kind, wrecked on the reefs and sunkers of indifference, suffering a misplaced faith in fair play and human nature.

Years would pass before the divers who found the *Auguste* site, legally claimed and declared theirs with all it contained, saw some form of resolution at the hands of the federal government of Canada. A split of the recovery was finally proposed by Parks Canada. They did so reluctantly but not before having all of the specie, literally thousands of coins recovered from the site in 1977–1978, high-graded out for the best specimens. Parks proposed to take the rarest, most valuable coins and return the rest to the salvers. Parks further proposed they would take all the precious artifacts that made up the bulk of both the recovery and value. They did. That alone represented over 75 percent of the fiscal benefit from the overall recovery.

The salvers knew it was just another raw deal meted out by an authority that proved totally hostile to public-private partnerships. I was the only one who wanted to reject it flat out. I begged the partners to go to court and seek justice. We needed justice. The other salvers were beat down to such a point; they just wanted it over with.

Totally demoralized and degraded, lashed into submission by the bureaucratic whip of an entire country, the remaining partners, although very reluctantly, accepted the offer from Parks Canada.

It would be several years before I discovered another major treasure ship. That time, with the Parks Canada affair still fresh in my mind, I took a totally different approach to the recovery of shipwreck treasure. I would never again step outside the authority of the receiver of wreck, and as it finally turned out, Natural Resources, the jurisdictional authority of the province of Nova Scotia.

With ownership now an unresolved question as far as the *Auguste* shipwreck was concerned, we had no choice but to quit the site until some form of resolution was achieved. I worried over the fact that the site was now left unprotected from unscrupulous divers scavenging it with no care for culture or scientific protocol. The same issue that kept us off-site and unable to raise operational capital to secure our find, protect our rights, and continue recovery left the site open to the very rape we had hoped to see avoided by involving Parks Canada in the first place.

During the period from 1978 until the final division of artifacts was forced on us and eventually accepted by the majority, Ed and I received reports of ongoing and unauthorized recoveries from the wreck site. The untenable actions of Parks Canada against the original salvers in this case set in motion a sequence of events that in years to follow destroyed the archaeological and historic integrity of the *Auguste* site.

Another tragic result with long-term consequences and of no less importance was Parks Canada's failure to keep the unique working partnership developed on the wreck site alive and improved. The archaeologist in charge—Jim Ringer—introduced the idea at an Ottawa meeting I attended, stating, "So much more could be accomplished if Parks were to work out a formula to hire the *Auguste* team under Bob MacKinnon's direction searching for and cataloging wooden shipwrecks. It would be a win-win for everyone, with the private sector doing the actual recovery in the field and leaving Parks to deal with the science protocols."

Parks felt there may be a conflict of interest so nothing came of what in fact was already in place on the *Auguste* site, a proven strategy to study and recover maritime artifacts scientifically by a combined team of professionals. Ringer realized that each group had certain areas of expertise that, when combined, better served to protect our maritime shipwreck heritage. He realized that the costs related to searching for a shipwreck versus recovery and conservation could be prohibitive. He also felt such activities should be left to proven industry professionals, not government archaeologists.

Personally, I never forgave the government of Canada for what they did to the innocent; I'm sure I am not alone. In this case, Parks failed to respect the rights of modern men.

CHAPTER TEN

Finding HMS *Feversham*

We stayed on for a few days consoling each other. I was touched at how hard our Parks science team took the betrayal and how sorry they were for us. (At least one would reenter my professional life after quitting Parks Canada totally disheartened.) But after that it was time to go our separate ways.

Ed and I had spent a lot of money on the recovery, not to mention legal fees, and it would be years before we saw any return.

Finally, the federal government of Canada offered what seemed to us no more than an underhanded deal after they had high-graded out the most valuable coins. Parks further proposed, besides a selection of the best coins, they would keep all the precious artifacts. This alone decreased the total value of what was recovered by 75 percent. Take it or take us to court was their attitude. I was itching to do just that, to tell a judge the facts and see how they sounded out loud. But the partners, who just wanted the whole distasteful episode closed, voted me down.

I saw their point, and a court fight would be expensive, but I didn't share their opinion then and still don't.

Here's the other galling thing: After 1978, in the best interest of historical preservation, nothing of any consequence from a government perspective was ever implemented to protect the integrity of the site. They just left it abandoned to the mercy of the sea, which everyone knows has none. No doubt this was for budgetary reasons, but doesn't that say something about the value of commercial salvers' involvement? (They had no compunction about letting us spend our money.) I never had an interest in doing anything but serious, scientific excavations, and they knew it. Never mind. This is the case I should have made in court.

But it was around that time we began hearing the phrase *in-situ preservation* bandied about by Parks Canada and those reflexively prejudiced against commercial treasure hunting. This must be a rationalization, I thought at first; they couldn't take seriously this contradiction in terms. In-situ preservation? In the ocean? That might make sense for an archaeological site in a dry cave, but there is nothing *in situ* in the ocean. This is Cape Breton Island. Were they unaware of the ocean's violent power on this coast? Further, the discovery and excavation of the *Auguste* was big news locally and beyond. Sport divers, who couldn't be expected to resist a treasure wreck, pillaged the site over time—it was in situ just waiting there for them.

It was too depressing to hash and rehash the story and the might-have-beens; we had to leave it behind. I was fortunate to be aided in this by discovering another, still-richer wreck. Well, more precisely, I *re*discovered the HMS *Feversham.*

When Barry Gross, president of a New Jersey dive club, called me for about the 10th time, I realized he wasn't going to take no for an answer.

His club wanted to charter my boat for a weeklong dive tour of Cape Breton Island. They wanted to dive on modern wrecks to retrieve brass portholes. They were serious collectors and sellers of portholes. To each his own, but I wasn't interested in running sport diver charters. I was too set in my diving ways to accommodate any but my own crew. I had long ago learned the necessity of captaincy, and I'd grasped the lesson too long and hard to break it. Besides, I wasn't interested in modern wrecks (or portholes). I'd already explained to Barry that dive chartering just was not my thing, but he kept calling.

For about the fifth time he told me what experienced guys they were. New Jersey wreck divers were a special breed, he assured me, who were used to rigorous conditions. Most New Jersey wrecks lie in open water over 100 feet deep, sometimes 50 miles offshore, in big current and poor visibility. I wouldn't have to babysit his guys and shouldn't worry about that. They had heard about the wreck-rich Cape Breton waters and so the profusion of portholes. They just *had* to dive here.

Okay, the only way to get rid of Barry and the boys was to price myself out of the market. I named an outrageous fee. Barry jumped at it. They arrived at Main-a-Dieu Harbor, with an astounding load of dive gear, in late August 1982. They had gauge panels on a single high-pressure whip. They had an extra second-stage regulator, called an *octopus system*, a new take on buddy breathing. They had stuff I'd never seen before, not to mention amazing camera equipment. After they'd loaded it aboard, I called a meeting to explain my way of doing things on and under the water. Maybe I was a little rigid sounding, but the techniques I'd developed were tried and they were safe. Maybe by insisting that they dive in groups of two to four, adhering strictly to the buddy system, I insulted their experienced-diver egos. But that's how my crews and I always did it, and besides, a lot of guys are expert divers on the dock.

I had developed an extraction system that I also intended to stick with. My mate George Steele (Jack Steele's son) would follow the divers' bubbles from a Zodiac inflatable tender, and when a diver was ready to leave the water, he'd come to the side of the tender, pass all his gear—tanks, weight belts, buoyancy compensators, cameras, everything except fins—to the tender, and only then climb aboard. The thing about diving is that it's so engrossing, so fundamentally liberating, that you take its inherent dangers for granted. (In this, gold fever can be particularly dangerous.) The way to combat that tendency is to adhere rigidly to very concrete procedures. Besides, boarding the tender in full gear is a good way to damage the rubber pontoons and thus lose the chase and safety boat. As I told them the way it would be aboard my boat, I couldn't help but remember the angry captain of the boat from which I first dove to the *Fantome* fleet, when I defied his instructions. They were affronted, I could tell, when I called for a practice dive in the harbor, but nobody squawked. I didn't want to come on like Captain Bligh; nor did I want to come back from our first dive to say, "Yes, we found some very nice portholes; trouble is, we lost two guys somewhere."

Truth to tell, they *were* experienced, capable divers, but I took the time to inform them of the law, noting that all finds had to be declared. We made our first dive on the SS *Cape Breton*, wrecked in 1920 near Southern Point on Scatarie Island. I felt comfortable putting them on the wreck; let them have at the portholes while I looked at another, far-older wreck. It so happened that the SS *Cape Breton* lay within a short swim of the resting place of the Royal Navy frigate HMS *Feversham* and three armed transports that went aground with her late in 1711. I knew this because we had located and logged the *Feversham* site back during the Dive Scatarie Project, but we had not examined her in any detail. Local stories told of treasure aboard, so I thought I'd have a quick look before checking back with my New Jersey charterers. I put my boat's bow into a light southwest wind and eased her back on the anchor line until the stern lay almost directly over the SS *Cape Breton*. Visibility was pretty good; I could almost *see* my guys from one wreck to the other, which shows you the wild extent of wrecks along this coast, one within underwater sight of the next.

I came on a large bed of concreted cannonballs. I had time to do a little hand fanning between them. Coins—small silver coins—lots of them. I picked one up and read the date, 1652, as clear as yesterday's minting. I had been reading enough about numismatics to know that this was a very rare and valuable coin. On the reverse side, there was the distinct image of a pine tree. This made it one of the first coins minted in North America, by John Hull at the Saugus Iron Works outside Boston. I filled my dive glove with as many coins as it could hold and headed back toward my charterers, who were vainly trying to extract a porthole from a broken steel plate that once was the side of the SS *Cape Breton*. We surfaced together, and as we doffed our gear into George's waiting tender, I debated with myself about whether to involve them in my discovery. Truth to tell, I was too excited to keep it to myself.

As they discussed the difficulty of extracting portholes, I nonchalantly removed my glove and dropped it on the engine box with a gentle clatter. Conversation ceased in midsentence.

"What have you got there, Cap?" asked Barry.

"This?" I emptied the glove. "About a hundred thousand dollars' worth of coins. They're called New England coins, minted in 1652."

They were flabbergasted. "In a half hour you recovered a small fortune?"

"Yes, boys. This is Cape Breton Island."

They wanted to buy some; they wanted to get back in the water right then; they wanted to participate in whatever future plans I laid.

"But I thought you were interested in only portholes."

"Portholes? What portholes?"

I promised to show them the site, but not today. I had to deliver the coins to the receiver of wreck in Sydney and stake my claim. I explained the year-and-a-day wait under the rules of maritime law, but once the coins were returned to me, I would share a few with them.

"But surely, Cap, you're going to excavate the wreck. We'd like to participate."

"We can talk about that, but I need time to formulate a reconnaissance plan and find some serious financial backing."

I phoned Barry Strang, head of Transport Canada and senior receiver of wreck for the Sydney region, including Scatarie Island. To my surprise, Barry said, "Bob, keep the coins in your possession—we don't have secure facilities for your find. Keep a catalog, and when your charter's over, I'll officially post your claim."

As promised, we returned to the site the next day, and during a single dive, we recovered another 300 coins to make about 500 total. We found different kinds of coins: Spanish cobs, Dutch lion dollars, and English crowns mixed with New England coins. But instead of the easily recognizable pine tree stamp, there were images of other unidentifiable trees. Clearly, I needed to do some research. The Jersey guys were so impressed, I thought they might be moving en masse to Cape Breton. Maybe not, but they left talking about nothing but their return next season.

The next day I took the coins to Barry's office in Sydney, and he, with a staff member to witness, counted and cataloged them, and then returned them to me. Barry said that he had been in contact with officials in London who stated that "they had no direct interest in the *Feversham* or the recovery. England won't interfere, but they may ask for a site report." This was important because of the so-called sovereign immunity rule, which states that a warship lost in foreign waters remains the property of the nation she originated from. I was off again, getting ready to salvage another treasure, and this time I would take all possible steps to protect myself as well as the wreck site itself. That winter I dove into the research.

The Royal Navy, like others, holds a court-martial when any one of its ships is lost or damaged, to learn exactly what happened and to append blame, if any. And *Feversham* was not just any ship. First, she was a frigate, one of the fast, versatile ships that served the same general duty as modern destroyers, to escort convoys, enforce blockades, and deliver messages. Frigates were highly valuable weapons in the 17th and 18th centuries because of their combination of speed and heavy armaments. And *Feversham* was a special frigate because she carried huge quantities of bullion; in addition, she was escorting the transport ships *Joseph*, *Mary*, and *Neptune*, also loaded with bullion, that went up on the rocks right along with their escort.

HMS *Feversham* was a member of the now largely forgotten Walker Expedition, the largest fleet of warships ever to cross the Atlantic until World War II. Under the command of Admiral Hovenden Walker, the fleet was ordered to sail up the St. Lawrence River, attack Quebec, and once and for all drive the French from North America. The expedition, which had swelled to over 150 ships by the time it assembled in Boston Harbor in June 1711 and headed north, is largely forgotten because it was utterly unsuccessful, defeated not by the French but by the sea. However, the remarkable thing about Walker's fleet, in addition to its size, was its wealth. His ships took prizes en route to New England, and the colonists contributed money to the cause. Victory a foregone conclusion, Walker would need plenty of ready money because he planned to occupy Fortress Quebec over the winter after expelling its occupants. Captain Robert Paston of the frigate *Feversham* was ordered to collect all the supplies and funds he could muster, load them into the three cargo vessels, and escort them to the Cape Breton coast, where he was to stand off and await further orders. The *Joseph*, a fleet pay ship along with the escort frigate, was carrying, according to an article in the *Boston News Letter* and *Boston Dispatch* of November 1711, "five millions in gold."

Late leaving New York, *Feversham* and her charges were ordered to take up station off Cape Breton in early October. Two months earlier, the body of Walker's fleet had entered the St. Lawrence River (then called the Canada River). To imagine that over 100 sailing vessels could con their way up such a poorly charted, ever-narrowing river and then en masse attack a heavily fortified installation was a classic instance of military overreach that always cost seamen their lives. A total of 900 were lost when on the night of August 23 a segment of the fleet went aground at a place called Ile aux Oeufs (Egg Island), miles from Fortress Quebec, essentially ending the expedition before it had fired a shot. After that, Walker decided his operation was compromised so severely that he had no choice but to retreat and make for Spanish Bay (now called Sydney Harbor) to regroup for the passage back to England. Meanwhile, the *Feversham* and the transports were standing into danger.

Most of what we know about the fate of the *Feversham* comes from the court-martial testimony of her gunner John Knox. Knox tells us that the noon sight on October 7 fixed her position at 45 degrees north by 39 degrees west, or about 25 miles off the Cape Breton coast southwest of Scatarie Island. You don't need local knowledge to picture the nautical problem; its recurrence is the reason Cape Breton Island is dotted with disaster. The fleet, positioned line astern, with *Feversham* leading the way, was heading northwest running before a stiff southwest wind probably making about eight knots in gathering darkness. Each ship was following the stern light of the ship ahead. At 7:00 P.M., they sighted Scatarie Island, a dark mass to leeward, and so with that landmark, the sailing master knew exactly where he was. Now all Captain Paston in the lead ship had to do was bend his course to starboard and head north by east to gain sea room.

Because I know those waters well, I could visualize, as I read Gunner Knox's testimony, the sad inevitability in the sequence of events leading to disaster. *Feversham* did in fact turn right, from northwest to north by east, and the transports dutifully followed. But it was too late; the strong winds had veered to the south and strengthened, pushing them ever closer to land. The other member of the nautical conspiracy—tidal current—already had them in its teeth. You see, Captain Paston might have been steering *due* north, maybe even a little east of north, but he wasn't going north over the bottom. I've seen the current around Scatarie run at 5.5 knots at max flood and ebb, and it was setting the fleet northwest, even as their bows pointed north by east.

First *Feversham* crashed on the rocks. Seeing this, the transports tried desperately to claw away from the ledges and sunkers, but one by one, each a little farther west than the last, *Mary*, *Joseph*, and *Neptune* went to their deaths. The *Feversham* was totally wrecked along with one of the transports, and their treasure went to the bottom. The other two ran up on the rocks and were "bilged," as Knox put it, "but standing on their keels." Before long, of course, the waves reduced them to splinters, spewing their treasure over the sea bottom. The story of the 300-year-old accident casts events in human terms, anxiety building to terror, but it also tells the modern treasure hunter where to look. Treasure hunting and history are always inextricably linked.

There is a sidelight to the story that has little to do with the search for treasure but reveals the state of relations between the nations in the fight for control of North America that, among other things, resulted in sunken treasure. Because the weather was moderate when the ships wrecked, the loss of life was also moderate. The survivors of the four crews, however, were stranded ashore—without food or dry clothing, trapped on a truly inhospitable coast. They built and maintained signal fires at both ends of the island; without rescue before the onset of winter, they would be doomed. After many days of pain and privation, salvation in the form of a French fishing brig hove into sight. (A brig, by the way, is a two-masted vessel square rigged on both masts.) The French captain put a boat ashore and learned of the riches that had been aboard the ships. Naturally, he wanted some.

When Captain Mathews of the *Joseph* came forward with several thousand Dutch silver dollars and promised the payment of 2,000 more if the Frenchman would take the survivors to New York, the French captain's humanitarian instincts kicked in. The brig was too small to take everyone, but to make room for the British officers, a few French sailors agreed to wait with the remaining English on Scatarie for a relief ship that would be dispatched from New York. It took the brig a week to reach New York. When it sailed into the harbor under a flag of truce, the Brits promptly seized the ship and threw the captain and his crew into jail. They were later exchanged for British prisoners of war. To one of the officers he had rescued from certain death, the French captain said, "Of this ill treatment all Frenchmen must know and be forever fearful."

Naturally, the British tried to salvage the treasure on Scatarie but it was too late in the season to mount such an expedition. The following year, 1712, Captain Augustine Rouse of the frigate HMS *Sapphire* stationed at Annapolis Royal, Nova Scotia, on the Bay of Fundy, was assigned the job. He dispatched another ship, a salvage brig, to head for Scatarie, and he would follow a day or so later in *Sapphire*.

However, the lead ship was captured, while standing off Scatarie Island, by a French privateer, which seriously delayed the salvage attempt. When Captain Rouse arrived on the scene, the early fall gales had already set in. He mounted a search, but the weather and dangerous shoals that surrounded the wreck site plus the constantly breaking and heaving huge swells against the shore combined to thwart his every effort. In his log, he wrote, “In the name of God and man, I abandoned the wrecks and their respective cargos to the sea”—where, as a treasure hunter, I found them three centuries later.

CHAPTER ELEVEN

New England Silver

But as I had learned on the *Auguste*, finding treasure, the part that had attracted me from childhood, was not enough. There was the bureaucracy and there was the funding, the parts that interested me least. I had duly reported my find to the proper authorities and, in the person of Barry Strang, the receiver of wreck for the Sydney area. Goverment authorities had been cooperative and congratulatory. But I still needed money to begin the mapping and reconnaissance of the site before I could think approach, recovery, and restoration. And then just when I needed one, another of those fortuitous meetings within the small world of the Cape Breton salvage community changed my course.

A French geophysics company and their Canadian partners chartered my workboat, my mate, and me to run a series of seismic studies between St. Paul Island and Scatarie Island. They needed a captain who knew the area and a boat able to tow a 2,500-foot streamer from the dangerous inshore water out to about 60 miles offshore. Among the Canadian technicians hired to coddle the gear, I was surprised to see John Oldham. John was one of the Parks Canada conservators we ferried ashore during that strange time when he and the others were left at the Scatarie Island lighthouse. All of this, after their team used, from our perspective, less-than-scientific recovery methods on the wreck site of the HMS *Leonidas*, leaving nothing in situ. I would like to have heard the whole story, but I didn't want to put John on the spot if, as I assumed, he'd signed a confidentiality agreement. Or even if he hadn't—you could tell he was uncomfortable with the subject.

"That's why I resigned from Parks," he said. "I'd had enough of their imperious attitude even before the *Leonidas* debacle." And naturally he'd heard all about their takeover of the *Auguste* site. "What are you working on now?"

There was no reason not to tell him about the *Feversham*. I had clear title, and besides, I trusted John. His eyes lit up when I described the wreck site—and the coins I'd recovered. Clearly wanting to get back in the water, he asked if he could join us as a diver when and if we began recovery. We exchanged numbers and parted company at the close of the survey project. Several weeks later, he phoned to ask if I would take him and a friend from Vermont, "an experienced and knowledgeable guy who may be able to help with funding," out to the *Feversham* site.

"Sure," I said, "but it better be soon." We both were familiar with the storms of October.

"We could be in Cape Breton day after tomorrow." He showed up at my home two days later, with one Eugene Brunelle, to see the New England coins I'd recovered from the site. Brunelle was indeed a knowledgeable guy. He referred to the coins in slang I'd not heard until then, *Mass silver*, for coins minted in Massachusetts and dated 1652. "Bob," he said, "some of these early Mass silver coins are worth five figures apiece. Tell me, are there more on the site?"

"Many," I said. I took them to the site to demonstrate that fact.

They were trembling with excitement as they came back aboard after the dive. Signs of Mass silver coins were everywhere. When they calmed down enough to speak in complete sentences, Eugene explained that he would be diving with the group that had found the pirate ship *Whydah* in shallow water off Cape Cod. The discovery had been getting a lot of press in those days, and Eugene knew one or two of the backers. "Would you allow me—no strings attached—to represent the *Feversham* discovery to potential investors either on the Cape or, possibly, in New York?"

I agreed. I didn't expect much to come of it, but in that I underestimated his desire to hunt treasure. It reaches out and grabs a certain kind of person and never lets go. I knew John Oldham was of that sort, and so apparently was Eugene Brunelle.

Only a few weeks after that dive, there came a stranger knocking on my door. "Hello, I'm looking for the man who found the *Feversham*."

I took him for a tourist, since he'd come in a large motor home, which he parked in front of my house.

"My name is Michael Emmerman. I've driven up here from New York with my family to meet you and discuss my interest in possibly funding a recovery project."

"Come in. Bring your family."

It took a little while to find chairs for everyone. After introductions, he got right to the point. A friend of his, Judge John Levin, investor in and financial adviser for the *Whydah* group, had met with Eugene Brunelle on the site in Cape Cod. "Judge Levin puts a lot of credence in what Eugene says, and he says that the *Feversham* site could produce some of the rarest coins in North America. Therefore, I'd like to invest in the recovery, and I'm prepared to leave a deposit with you to demonstrate my interest." He slid a checkbook from his jacket pocket.

"Well, Mr. Emmerman, I'm—"

"Call me Mike."

"Well, Mike, we don't need to discuss money right now."

But he was busy writing a check, which he placed on the coffee table near where my wife and I were sitting. Her eyes widened when she had a look at the numbers. She slid it in front of me. There were six numbers on the check. I liked the way this man, Mike, did business. I told him the deposit would not be necessary. I would develop an operations budget and send it to him for his review. That day began a lifelong friendship.

So over the dark and stormy Cape Breton winter, with inevitable cash in hand, I took the first step toward recovery by hiring a dive team. I spoke first to John Oldham and Eugene, both of whom would drop everything to dive. Then I called Barry Gross, the New Jersey diver, who had sworn his interest. He was still keen. He recommended a young diver, Ed Hayes from New Jersey, whom he had trained and who would be available for the entire coming season. Bob Anthony, one of the best divers from the *Auguste* project, also wanted in. I met Judge John Levin in person that winter when he visited Cape Breton to discuss technical details. We spoke the same language; I was pleased to learn we shared that treasure hunting thrill.

Guys like Levin, who could likely find more predictable investment opportunities without leaving Manhattan, invest serious money in sunken treasure for the pleasure of participation, not the capital returns. John recommended the last member of the team, Phil Masters, a Florida diver with some scientific diving experience. When Judge Levin proposed that Masters could serve as liaison between me, Levin, and the other investors, saving me the obligation to write endless reports, I jumped at the offer. This turned out to be the best dive team I'd ever had the pleasure to work with. The *Feversham* Recovery Project was under way. I tried to suppress my excitement and temper expectations given the potentially high disappointment quotient, but I gave up, expectant excitement being one of the basic attractions of this profession.

The weather was exquisite on opening day, August 1, 1985. I took the glimmering sunlight on the flat, inviting water as an omen of hope as we set our first mooring at the southern point of Scatarie Island right beside that bed of cannonballs. (A mooring serves as a single semipermanent anchor instead of deploying the boat's anchor every day. This saves work as well as protects the site from anchor damage.)

The guys had struck up an air of camaraderie even before we got in the water. Phil Masters had gained enough experience to think like a chief archaeologist, already familiar with the techniques I used. Its depressing ending notwithstanding, I had learned a lot during the *Auguste* project about archaeological practices and procedures. Phil nodded avidly as I explained the careful, meticulous process I wanted to exercise on the *Feversham*. All artifacts, not just coins, would be given a precise position on the bottom in relation to a baseline tagged every meter with reference numbers. Nothing would be removed until it had been assigned a location number and distance from the main baseline. Phil was generally familiar with that technique, so I asked him to help me teach the others.

And I had a grunt-work job for Ed Hayes, the youngest and least experienced diver on the team. What I wanted, I explained to him while watching his reaction, was to build a protective wall of small boulders on the seaward side of the excavation. We would be in for some heavy surf action, and this wall might cut some of it down.

"You got it," said Ed. This kid was going to work out fine.

Bob Anthony and I made the first dive, a long, slow, back-and-forth survey of the site looking for prominent features of the wreckage such as a cannon lying at an unusual angle that could be used as a baseline anchor. The bottom, I'd noticed on my few previous dives, was terribly rugged, but it was more so now. Winter storms had rearranged the seabed. Boulders the size of compact cars were strewn across the site, along with what seemed like hundreds of smaller, pumpkin-size rocks. These would have to be removed, a job for great young, You-Got-It Ed, who could use them to build the wall. And then there were rough geologic features that had been there since the last ice age, some rising 10 feet off the bottom, with valleys and box canyons in between. These would need to be worked around. It took most of our air on that initial dive to find a flat patch from which to begin mapping the site.

Even without looking for it, we were seeing treasure. Every crevice we swam over seemed to contain something valuable and interesting: coins, silverware, and other precious artifacts. We exclaimed over them in sign language, but we didn't pause to look closer. Near shore in very shallow water, we found dozens of cannon and cannonballs in a mass, about 25 feet square. The natural tendency of sand, mud, and shell hash combined with electrolysis is to concrete around metal objects, and that term *concrete* is apt. They are hard, solid things. I'd always suspected that their frustration when facing stubborn concretions had induced Parks to resort to less-than-acceptable disturbance methodologies on the *Leonidas* site. This concretion of cannon and shot would be beyond our by-hand capabilities; we'd just have to work around it.

The other issue that brought us down to earth was the bottom topography's nasty effect on the swells. The ocean is never still even when it appears dead flat as it did that day. The smallest swell rolling in from the open ocean rose up into a real wave that broke against the near-vertical 30-foot cliff, which resulted in a savage backwash. This would be tough work and dangerous.

Further, the site was bracketed by two sunkers large enough to have names: Little Sunker and Cape Breton Sunker. As the swells tried to squeeze between them, they compressed, swelled twice their normal size, and accelerated. The water between the sunkers was in constant turmoil. In addition, at our position here on the unprotected southeast point of Scatarie Island, with deep water so near, the tidal current ran at four knots, more when a stiff wind blew behind it. Where to begin amid such violence on such a rumpled site?

I decided to postpone that decision for a couple of days, let everybody get familiar with the site and the dangerous diving conditions, then do some test pitting in two-man teams. But the concretion bed seemed to be in the middle of things. We were turning up silver coins in little digs all around it. I remember kneeling on the bottom and pondering the damn thing. Coins all around, we should find out what lay below it. But how?

Before we were satisfied with the test results, a heavy onshore blow rolled in and rampaged around for two days. Only the guys from away were surprised by its sudden arrival, its intensity, and its duration, but they quickly absorbed the weather lesson. And they learned the attendant message when we returned to the site after the storm and found the bottom altered by wave action. I was familiar with that fact of life on this coast, but I had never seen such a dynamic, unstable, and therefore dangerous stretch of bottom. This would haunt us repeatedly, even after Ed had built a wall seaward of the site about 80 feet long and several feet high, which effort earned him everybody's respect. It wasn't long before I had a firsthand experience of the danger, and the scariest incident of my career to date.

It was on a rough day but only a little rougher than usual, when a boulder that appeared to have been there for a few thousand years toppled over and pinned me hard against the base of the Cape Breton Sunker. I was uninjured, just stuck, and struggles with all my strength seemed hopeless. There was no way I could gain any leverage to move the rock an inch. Fortunately, Bob Anthony was nearby and, not only that, was carrying a long prybar. As he heaved and jerked at the rock, I couldn't help imagining what would have happened if I had been alone—the process of death, my energy spent, watching the ascending bubbles from each exhalation, knowing they were numbered. Then the hard pull on the regulator as my life dwindled down to a few final breaths. Bob managed to move the rock, but not before both of us were thoroughly shaken.

The *Feversham* wreck was unique in my experience, presenting not just one or two of the usual local nautical conspirators, but all of them at once, with jaws wide open. My guys were really tough and avid, thinking nothing of diving in hostile conditions, and that was all the more reason to install stringent safety measures. Treasure is one thing, death quite another.

We would need to remove the larger boulders by some brute-force means, but on this site we could not allow, as we sometimes did on the less dynamic sites, guys to dig deep holes under the rocks. There's a high temptation to do so because coins and other artifacts knocked around by waves tend to collect in the shadow of boulders. Anytime we dug a concavity under anything big, we would shore up the object with rocks or other stout bracing. I preached constant vigilance as the most dependable lifesaver. Don't get carried away by the riches in your hands, but keep focused on your immediate surroundings. My guys all knew to do this, and so did I, but that didn't keep me from ending up under a falling rock because I had ignored the precept in my excitement. Gold fever can kill, especially here on the *Feversham* site.

We also needed practical means to deal with the four-knot tidal currents. On the first day we delivered the divers from my workboat via the inflatable to the site, over they went drifting past the main work area, but never again. They were swept off the site before they could get to the bottom. So we marked sections of the wreck with *down lines* tied off to cannon on the bottom and to a big, bright orange surface float. The inflatable tender would deliver the divers to a specific area and tie off to the down line (using a bicycle tire as a *snotter* to absorb the snap load on the tender). That way the diver could fight off the current by handing his way down the line, and he knew his exact location on the wreck. Should a diver get into trouble, he could make his way up one of the lines and find a reliable source of buoyancy at the surface, should the tender be working elsewhere.

We also rigged underwater travel lines from the down line positions that spiderwebbed over the wreck site, by which divers could pull themselves against the current and which they could hold on to once they got where they were going. Times were rare when we could actually swim over the wreck or remain in one place not tethered while working on it.

While some of the guys were laying down the travel lines, others were test pitting with almost unbelievable results. I kept returning to the cannonball concretion, attracted by all the coins we were finding in close proximity. It was a brute.

I was working with John Oldham cataloging and stabilizing the artifacts in the temporary conservation lab we'd set up in my garage when I got a call from a Rick Ratcliffe, registrar of mineral and petroleum titles at the Nova Scotia Department of Natural Resources, and my heart sank. What now? He understood that I was running recovery operations on a wreck called *Feversham* in Nova Scotia waters. His records showed that I did not have a provincial treasure trove license.

A *provincial* license? "Oh, no," I said, "I recorded the *Feversham* with the federal receiver of wreck. Parks Canada had told me during the *Auguste* recovery that the feds had authority, and that the province had no jurisdiction over—" Then I stopped to listen to myself. *Parks Canada* told me that.

"No", said Ratcliffe, "they're wrong. It would surely be unethical for them to have told you that. Nova Scotia was the jurisdictional authority over shipwrecks lost within a hundred miles of her coast, according to the British North America Act of 1867."

A wave of fear washed over my head, not the same sort of fear as when pinned to the bottom by falling rocks, but not a lot less intense.

"But don't worry," he said. Though it was well within his rights to shut me down, he had no wish to do so. He would prefer to see me in compliance, and if I submitted applications for the proper license, he would expedite them.

"Fine, thank you," I said. "I'll do so immediately, and then that will do it, right?"

"Well, not exactly." There was a new law that was now in effect called the Nova Scotia Special Places Protection Act. It stipulated that in order to excavate a heritage site, people like me needed a special heritage research permit from the Nova Scotia Museum. I would be hearing from Robert Ogilvie, manager of Special Places for the province of Nova Scotia.

No, I didn't want any of that I'll-be-hearing-from-someone trap. If

I had multilayer bureaucracy to climb through, I wanted to get started. "What's his number, this Robert Ogilvie?"

Ogilvie told me that there would be a royalty of 10 percent of any precious artifacts payable to the province under terms of the Treasure Trove Act. Further, I would need to turn over to the province, in a conserved state, all nonprecious artifacts recovered each year. Because I was already working the site, his department would extend to us the same courtesy as Natural Resources and issue the necessary heritage permits immediately upon application. "As long as you're compliant, we have no intention of interfering with your current or future salvage operations."

Whew, that was not nearly as bad as I'd feared. Then why did I still feel so uneasy . . . ?

I called Ratcliffe back. What about previous discoveries? The *Auguste*, for instance. Would the province be inclined to make any claims on them, since I had willingly and honestly reported them to what I was informed, at the time, was the appropriate jurisdictional body?

"No," he said, "now that you know who the appropriate authority is, this department will not be looking at your prior recoveries—as long as all the required permits and licenses going forward are up-to-date." I'll bet I set records for immediate compliance.

The Nova Scotia Museum Group was responsible for the protection and administration of the province's cultural resources under the terms of the Special Places Protection Act. Trouble is, the act was written to apply to terrestrial archaeology. Underwater archaeology essentially didn't exist in Nova Scotia at the time. When I started recovering cultural artifacts, the Special Places manager tried to adapt to the new kind of archaeology, but it was never anything but a square peg in a round hole.

I needed three separate permits after I had established, at my own expense, that the site was archaeologically worthy of the designation *special place*. I then needed the Class A Heritage Research Permit to enter provincially owned land above or below water to carry out nondisturbance reconnaissance surveys. The Class B Heritage Research Permit allowed for the disturbance and recovery of cultural artifacts from either the land or sea. However, no recovery operations could be conducted without scientific supervision. There were all kinds of reports and accounting procedures required under Permit B, but the most expensive stipulation required that I have access to or own a fully functional conservation laboratory, and it had to meet Special Places inspection and approval before a Class B Heritage Research Permit would be issued.

The Class C permit was needed when an archaeological assessment was required. On all shipwreck sites, this was a standard requirement before continuous excavations could proceed. This form of scientific assessment could be carried out only on-site by a provincially approved marine archaeologist. Once the archaeological assessment process was completed, the final reports accepted, and the site declared culturally significant, only then could the archaeologist apply for a Class B permit to begin excavations.

Once a shipwreck site had been assessed by a marine archaeologist, this process did not have to be repeated. However, all other Nova Scotia heritage research permits required yearly renewal, in effect from January 1 to December 31 of any given year.

A Class B permit had its own special regime of compliance requirements before a final site report would be approved. If it was rejected, the archaeologist involved had the opportunity to modify. However, no new Class B Heritage Research Permits would be issued for the following season until all the previous permit-reporting requirements were met and approved to the satisfaction of the Nova Scotia Museum.

Back on the site of the *Feversham*, the hulking mass of concretion was impossible to ignore and very hard to work around. And even before we could seriously try, we'd have to remove two boulders the size of small cars perched atop the concretion. We did some excavating around its edges to see just what we were dealing with. We didn't find a bottom to the damn thing until we scratched down five feet. I was pulling off the last dregs of air on the last dive of the day when, digging, I dislodged a large chunk of the thing. Coins fluttered to the bottom, sliver flashing with each spin. I picked one up.

It was a New England coin of 1652. They were all New England silver coins. We were in about 30 feet of water on a reasonably gentle day. A few of the guys swam around to see what was going on. Did they hear my heart pounding? *Look!* I held them out in both hands. *Look!* That did it, of course; we had to attack the concretion and without damaging whatever artifacts it contained. But how?

"We could call Parks Canada for advice," someone joked as we discussed the problem back aboard my boat.

"First, we have to move those damn boulders, right? We could use come-alongs," said Bob Anthony.

It might just work. Come-alongs, common in mining and other industries where really heavy objects needed to be moved, were readily available. A really serious one could move 50 tons.

Bob, an experienced commercial diver, thought he could rig it underwater easily enough. "We should probably use two at once pulling at angles. Trouble is, what are we going to use as a shore fast underwater?"

A come-along moves heavy things efficiently, as long as it has something to pull against, something heavier than the thing being moved. What?

"How about the Cape Breton Sunker?" I suggested.

They laughed.

"No, no kidding. What if we wrapped cable around the base of the sunker and used it as the shore fast? Cape Breton Sunker's not going anywhere."

"Okay," said Bob, "we'll need about a thousand feet of half-inch soft iron cable and the stoutest come-alongs in Canada."

Before we could put our plan in the water we were blown off the site again. Well, more precisely, we were washed off the site. *Blown off* implies heavy weather. As I mentioned, even when a moderate wind blew southwest, the prevailing direction, it set up huge swells between the sunkers, creating such a backwash that after the water broke against the cliff, diving was out of the question. Sometimes a storm passing way east of Sable Island and the Grand Banks heaved up impossible swells on an otherwise perfectly calm day. Unless we were lucky and an offshore wind calmed them down, the swells would roll in for days after the storm that had caused them had moved east halfway to Europe. And then there was the dungeon fog in which a diver could be swept out of sight by the tide. *Feversham* didn't welcome us aboard.

With Bob Anthony's expert guidance, we wrapped cable around the sunkers, set up two come-alongs on the first rock, and heaved on the ratchet mechanism. God, it was hard work. We sweated in our wet suits, and then when paused in the actual labor, we froze. Finally, after days of drudgery, we managed to winch the boulders off of the concretion. That's when a full-on easterly storm drove us ashore.

While in that familiar state of waiting, I came up with a tactical approach, and Bob with his technical commercial experience thought it just might work. We would use bottle jacks similar to the sort used to jack up cars. We'd dig under the concretion, lay in several small hydraulic jacks, and gently try to wrench the mass from the bottom, ideally in reasonable-size chunks. To make a long, laborious story short, it worked.

We felt this great sense of accomplishment when, as Bob and I cranked the jacks, a crack developed, and a cloud of gas and black sediment belched from the concretion. Then coins trickled out. We repeated the process, and as the close of the season drew near and the weather worsened, we had broken a portion of the thing into smaller chunks, some of which could be lifted off the bottom and aboard the boat. Soon, however, we had more chunks than we were able to deal with by our present reduction methods. We had to devise another way.

Still, during this time, the ongoing test pitting was turning up hoards of coins, much to everyone's pleasure, including of course our investors. However, everyone noticed that we had lost day after day to weather. Since we paid our divers whether they were in the water or waiting onshore, overhead costs were getting out of hand compared to the return, as our investors gently pointed out, even as they assured us that they fully respected the work we were doing when weather permitted. It's just that Mother Nature was very stingy with her permission.

Well, I said, this is Cape Breton Island, after all. There is always another wreck. And in fact I knew of one that lay in deeper water where it was not so vulnerable to inshore surf. And so it would manifest almost 10 years later, during the 1995–1996 season, that I would then be working two sites at once: the HMS *Feversham* and *Le Chameau* claims.

The 1985 and 1986 diving seasons came to a successful conclusion, both in recovery and the development of new and proven recovery methodologies. The investors were totally satisfied, and we agreed should the opportunity arise, the team would be willing to continue excavations on the *Feversham* site. But for the present, it was now time to test the market and present our finds for auction. It took a few years to conclude the bureaucratic process of delivery, royalty selection, and a return to the salver of the remaining 90 percent of the treasure trove. Once this was accomplished, we were required to apply for a Cultural Export Property Permit to allow transport of the treasure out of the country. In February 1989, all of these efforts culminated in New York City with an auction of our 1985–1986 finds from the HMS *Feversham* site.

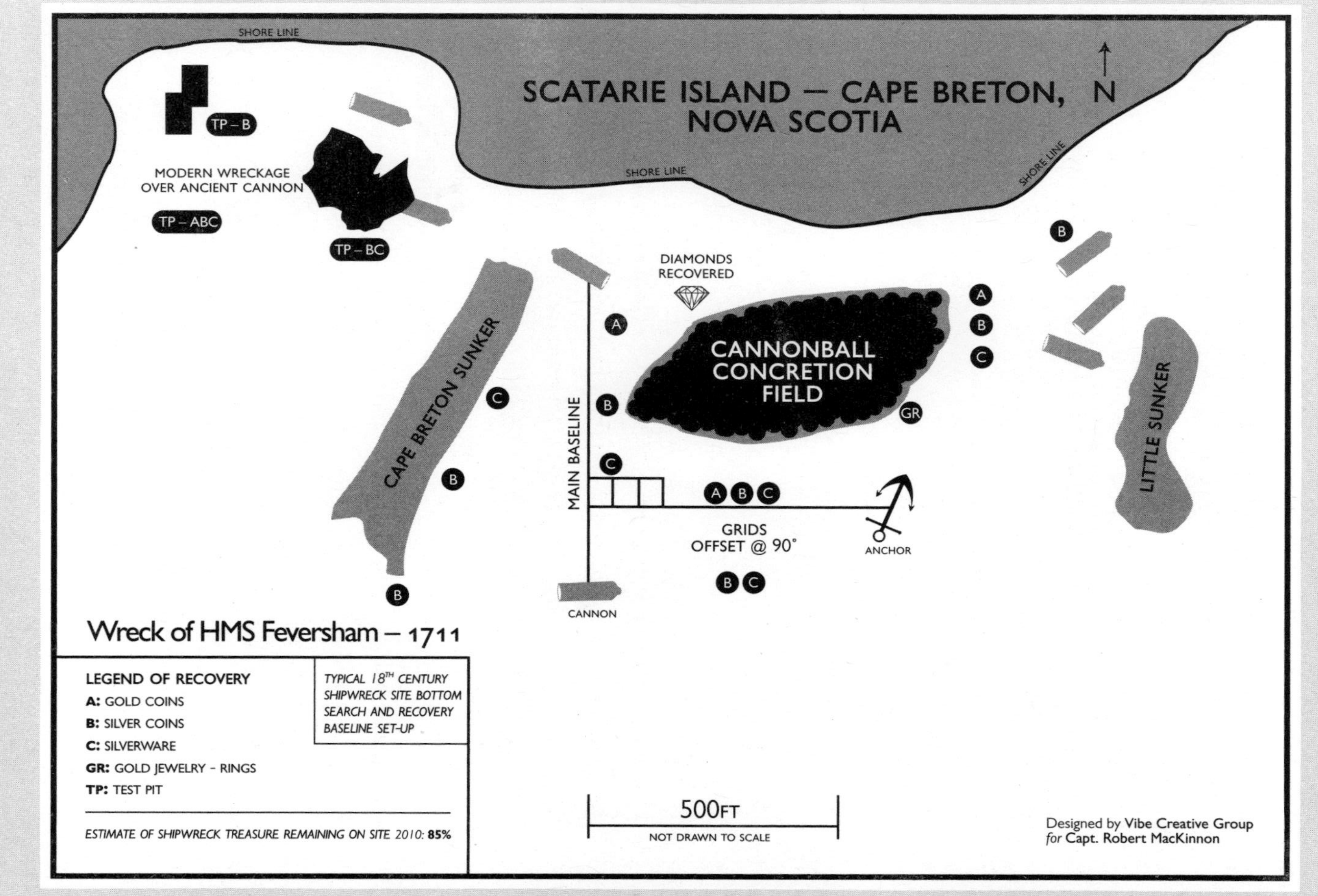
SCATARIE ISLAND – CAPE BRETON, NOVA SCOTIA
N
SHORE LINE
SHORE LINE
SHORE LINE
TP – B
MODERN WRECKAGE OVER ANCIENT CANNON
TP – ABC
TP – BC
CAPE BRETON SUNKER
DIAMONDS RECOVERED
CANNONBALL CONCRETION FIELD
GR
MAIN BASELINE
GRIDS OFFSET @ 90°
ANCHOR
CANNON
LITTLE SUNKER
Wreck of HMS Feversham – 1711
LEGEND OF RECOVERY
A: GOLD COINS
B: SILVER COINS
C: SILVERWARE
GR: GOLD JEWELRY - RINGS
TP: TEST PIT
TYPICAL 18TH CENTURY SHIPWRECK SITE BOTTOM SEARCH AND RECOVERY BASELINE SET-UP
ESTIMATE OF SHIPWRECK TREASURE REMAINING ON SITE 2010: 85%
500FT
NOT DRAWN TO SCALE
Designed by Vibe Creative Group for Capt. Robert MacKinnon

CHAPTER TWELVE

Le Chameau

In the spring of 1725, the armed transport *Le Chameau*, under Captain de St. James, was ordered to sail from La Rochelle, France, to Quebec via Louisbourg. Quebec, then in a state of economic turmoil, badly needed and anxiously awaited *Le Chameau*'s arrival. She carried millions in specie[1] and general cargo to be used in trade, to pay the soldiers, support the Catholic Church in Quebec, and to forestall the illegal trade in bullion with the New England colonies. She also carried over 51 first-class passengers—the crème de la crème of French colonial society: wealthy merchants, senior church officials, scores of Catholic nuns, and second-son aristocrats. The 104 contract soldiers destined for Quebec would also help shore up French influence and authority in North America. Add the crew and officers, and altogether, some 316 people embarked from Brittany. Not a one of them made it ashore alive. *Le Chameau* crashed on sunkers only a few leagues north of Louisbourg

Harbor after a two-month passage. The only reported survivor was a chicken that floated ashore in a wooden crate.

It's hard to remember from this remove in time and nautical technology the extent to which both the French and the English settlements, isolated in Canada, depended on their mother country for economic and political survival. Of course the settlers farmed and fished, and, though life was hard and every winter a tough struggle, it wasn't a matter of physical survival that rendered them so dependent. But any vestiges of the European way of life, things such as money and household items that softened the hard realities of the vast wilderness—all had to come from Europe *by ship*. The fur trade, for instance, was well under way in the 1720s, but a ton of beaver pelts was of no value unless the goods could be shipped back to a market in Europe. Today, when we can cross the Atlantic in just a few hours, it's easy to forget that dependence on ships was one of the facts of life in colonial North America. And shipping was a perilous business in 1725.

The ships of the time were small—*Le Chameau* was only 125 feet long on deck, 29 feet at the beam—and, of course, utterly dependent on wind. Further, it's worth remembering, they lacked all navigation gear except an astrolabe, quadrant, lead line, and compass. This was no problem in the open ocean where it didn't matter if their position fix was several miles off, but it mattered a great deal when the ships approached the terrible shores of Cape Breton as they sought to enter (or exit) the Gulf of St. Lawrence.

Under this light, it's interesting to note the unity among the *Auguste*, the *Feversham*, and *Le Chameau*. The *Auguste* sailed from Quebec with French refugees and their belongings after the French defeat at the Plains of Abraham in 1758. Only 47 years earlier, HMS *Feversham* sailed to Quebec as part of the Walker fleet sent to expel the French. Then 14 years after that, *Le Chameau* tried to deliver specie, bullion, and people to Quebec to bolster France's North American sovereignty. None reached their destinations, all three dying on Cape Breton (then called Isle Royale by the French), one on the same tiny Scatarie Island. And they all died of the same cause: faulty navigation that landed them on some of the most lethal lee shores in the hemisphere.

Around midnight, about nine miles northeast of Louisbourg Harbor, *Le Chameau* tore out her bottom on a line of reefs, now called the Chameau Rocks, rising from deep water less than a half mile from any safety running onshore might have provided. The next morning, locals found the beach and the shallows at Kelpy Cove strewn with corpses and wreckage, including the ship's figurehead—a camel (*Chameau*)—by which they made a positive identification. That afternoon, officials from Louisbourg, who arrived to inspect the sad scene, found the lone survivor, that chicken. Bodies continued to wash ashore for days afterward.

In a sad coda to the story, the French immediately set in place a plan to dispatch another ship to Quebec loaded with coin of the realm to replace what was lost on *Le Chameau*. It was her sister ship, *Le Elephante*. She made it through the choke point that caught *Le Chameau*, only to wreck in the St. Lawrence River in 1729. It's an exaggeration to say that the very expensive loss of these two ships caused the decline and eventual loss of New France, but it's none to say that the losses weakened the French position in Canada.

The major difference between treasure hunting in Nova Scotia and, say, the hunt for Spanish treasure ships in Florida waters is that the actual location of many Nova Scotia wrecks is known and has been known, sometimes for centuries. I didn't need to hunt for most of them. This is

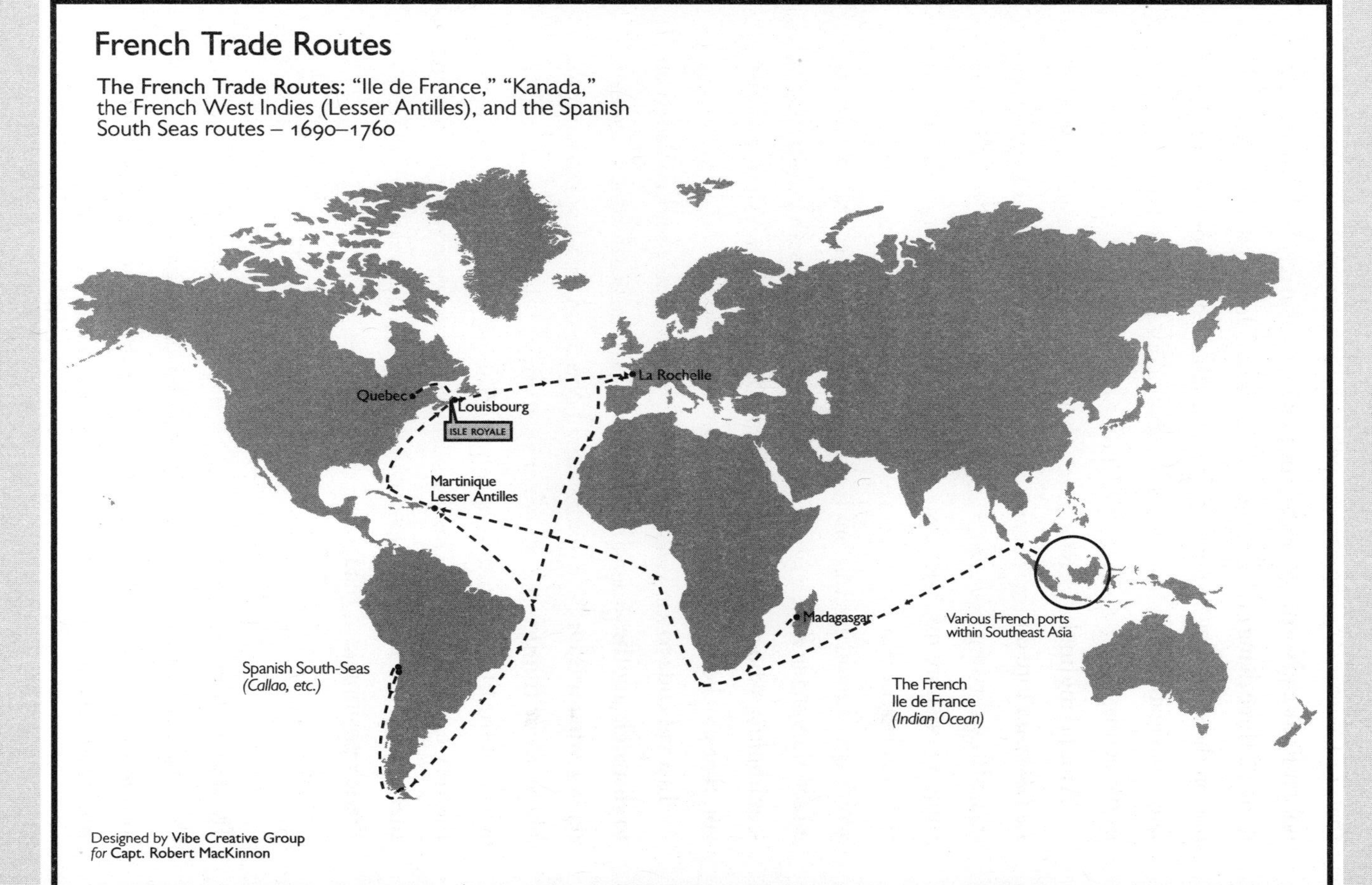
French Trade Routes
The French Trade Routes: "Ile de France," "Kanada," the French West Indies (Lesser Antilles), and the Spanish South Seas routes – 1690–1760
Quebec
Louisbourg
ISLE ROYALE
La Rochelle
Martinique
Lesser Antilles
Madagasgar
Various French ports within Southeast Asia
Spanish South-Seas
(Callao, etc.)
The French
Ile de France
(Indian Ocean)
Designed by Vibe Creative Group
for Capt. Robert MacKinnon

because the ships went aground in shallow water well within sight of land and the awareness of local residents.

By the time we turned to the *Le Chameau* wreck, while working the *Feversham*, I had treasure trove permits for 10 other wrecks. Over the years since that brief dive on her bones back in 1975, I had never forgotten about the *Fantome* fleet. And I'd always suspected that those ships would prove to be the richest of the rich, with one of the most fascinating historical contexts: the sacking of Washington and Alexandria in 1814. After that first dive on the *Fantome* fleet, I applied for a treasure trove permit, but it had already been claimed. However, the claimants had not initiated any known recovery before their permit expired, at which point I successfully applied for my own permit. The trouble was that the *Fantome* wreck site was a good 270 miles south of our base of operations at Main-a-Dieu, whereas the *Le Chameau* site was only 5 miles across an open bay from the *Feversham*.

Recovery operations were growing more complex and considerably more expensive. The Special Places branch of the Nova Scotia Museum was forcing me to jump through their hoops, and they kept moving the hoops. But I didn't want to worry about that; I wanted to concentrate on the exciting changes and developments. I had two rich and important wrecks to work, and I had people with enough faith in my future to put money on it. I was learning a lot of history and numismatics from books, and marine archaeology from hands-on experience. And I admit to a certain pride in the fact that people in Canada, the United States, and Europe were taking notice, including a man who would become my new business partner.

In 1994 Steve Farrell, a local mining engineer well respected in the community, and I invested $50,000 each toward a piece of property in Main-a-Dieu Harbor where we meant to build a real marine archaeology and preservation center, including a wharf, storage and stabilization sheds, and air compressors complete with a high-pressure air-delivery system to the dive boats. It was the sort of facility I'd dreamed about for years. The following year we hired a professional marine archaeologist, Rob Reedy from North Carolina, and additional divers and we acquired new equipment. By August 1, 1995, we were ready to begin dual operations.

We were astonished by the condition of the *Feversham* site. It was chaos. Surf, tides, and ice had done savage damage over time. The area where we'd been working on the concretion was almost entirely covered with huge boulders that nothing short of a tugboat could drag away. But that was out of the question for sure because indiscriminately dragging them off-site would surely damage any artifacts in their path. The cannon and other large cultural features we had charted so meticulously back in the mid-1980s were either buried or knocked way out of position. New cannon had been exposed. Everything had changed. We'd need to start over in a different area with a new set of baselines and test pits. And then, barely starting the new work, we were blown off the site. Again. So we turned as planned to the *Le Chameau*.

That site presented its own technical demands. Since the northern Cape Breton coast was both our home and our workplace, we sometimes lost sight of its unique dangers, but as I try to tell this story, I'm keenly aware that the coast itself is a major character. We oughtn't to call it the villain, because reefs and sunkers and severe tidal current, fog, and sudden heavy weather have no intentionality. They just are. But here, the natural threats, gathered en masse, seem to be the result of a conscious conspiracy to kill ships and sailors.

On a night in August 1725, Captain de St. James of *Le Chameau* knew just where he was. Even on dark, moonless nights at sea, there is always some degree of light in the sky, while land appears dark black. The captain could see the deep, broad cove with low-lying land behind it. And he could see the distinctive island perched in the mouth of the cove. Broad reaching before a southerly wind, all he had to do was keep that island about a ship's length off on his port hand, and he'd safely enter Louisbourg Harbor. Perhaps he breathed a sigh of relief before he ordered the helmsman to stand on. Then only minutes later he ran hard aground on a vicious sunker invisible several feet below the surface. It's now called Chameau Rock.

His navigation would have been spot-on had he actually been entering Louisbourg Harbor, but he wasn't. He was entering Kelpy Cove, about nine miles northeast from Louisbourg, which had the same appearance: a deep, bowl-shaped cove with low-lying land behind and a distinctive roundish island marking the mouth. He in fact was trying to pass between Port Nova Island on his port side and Cape Breton Point to his starboard, and right in the middle of that "channel" lay the then-unnamed Chameau Rock. This configuration of a deep cove with rocks and an island at the mouth is fairly common on our coast, having been subject to Ice Age glacial activity.

French officials who investigated the wreck site from shore the following day surmised that after she struck, the ship broke up in at least three pieces. They also noted the moon was full on the night of the 23rd and that there were strong southerly gales on the night the ship was lost, the 27th. The tides were still in flood.

The stern section, now between wind and water, battered by the huge swells and strongly influenced by the tides, floated off to the north, maybe even a bit east, before it sank. The port and starboard sections forward of the aft deck, which contained most of the deckhouses and the really heavy gear, including cannon, probably drifted away under the influence of the wind. One section broke up and sank in shallow water near the southern arm of Kelpy Cove, which the locals call Woody

Point, and the other went to the bottom near the center of the cove in about 50 feet of water, spewing out wreckage all along the way. Then for the next three centuries, the wind, waves, and ice spread her bones and her treasure over a vast and varied sea bottom.

I've long found it useful to try to visualize a wreck as it happened based on what I know about navigation, sailing-ship handling, and the lay of the bottom. For instance, we found a large pile of cannon and two of her lesser bower anchors piled around the base of Chameau Rock. In other situations this might suggest the presence of the bulk of the wreck, but not here. All the heavy stuff at the point of initial impact suggests that the ship didn't break up immediately. Instead, the violence of the sea took no time unshipping the cannon, their shot, and the anchors; thus each huge swell that broke over the decks lightened the ship, creating *achieved buoyancy*, in nautical parlance.

Knowledge of the ship's rig and structure is also useful in deciding where to look for the bulk of the treasure. The weakest position on a three-masted sailing ship lies at the foot of the mainmast (the middle one). The standing rigging that supports the masts exerts a downward force on the hull, and over time literally bends the keel like a bow. So when a ship goes up on the rocks, it tends to break in half at the weak point, letting the contents of the hull spill out near the point of initial impact.

But it didn't happen that way to *Le Chameau*, because she didn't break up all at once; instead, her dismembered parts drifted off on their own before sinking. And for our purposes, this meant that the contents of the ship were spread over a very wide area of bottom. And it meant that we wouldn't be able to go at the recovery in the old low-tech way. We needed electronic intervention, which, in turn, would require a new step in my career.

We decided to hire a local geophysics company, Canada Seabed Research, to run mowing-the-lawn patterns over Kelpy Cove using my boat to tow a magnetometer and side-scan sonar fish in tandem. The magnetometer is essentially a sophisticated underwater metal detector (though the good Seabed guys might blanch at that oversimplification), and the side-scan sonar is a torpedo-shaped pod of acoustic transmitters that paints a shadow image of the bottom and anything lying on it. The weeklong survey cost us $25,000, and was well worth it, producing hundreds of metal targets and vivid sonar images of the work cut out for us. But we had an interesting little experience, a kind of intersection of past and present, while running the survey with our newly implemented technology.

"Look at these things," said one of the onboard technicians, waving me over to his computer screen, which was receiving real-time images from the magnetometer and sonar. "There are literally thousands of these things all over the place. Look at the sonar image, you can even pick some of them out, the magnetometer is going crazy."

"They look like pipes, don't they?"

"Yeah, they're round and about two to three feet long. At first glance I imagined they were gold or silver ingots. But whatever they are, they're sure messing up the survey. They're overwhelming everything else."

"I'd better go have a look." Then it dawned on me. I had been reading about just such things. I had most recently acquired a translation from the French of *Le Chameau*'s passenger list and her manifest. On it, I remembered, was listed what I took to be a small cargo of cast-iron pigs, but apparently not so small. It was basically scrap iron and would have been used as raw material for foundries in New France. (That the raw materials to forge metal tools, weapons, and implements had to be imported from Europe shows the settlements' degree of isolation from and dependence on the Old World.) Unfortunately, all that valueless stray iron meant that we couldn't depend on the sonar or magnetometer to distinguish between the pigs and the treasure.

"You need to look at each one. There's no way to sort this out from the surface. I can set the baseline for larger targets, like over fifty-two thousand nanoteslas, and ignore the pigs. But there may still be treasure under the pigs that wouldn't show up on the scan. And, well . . ."

"What's on your mind?"

"We'll know more when we assemble the imagery back in the office. But it looks to me like there's more than one shipwreck involved. One of the targets just outside the Chameau Rock to the southeast is so large it must be an iron shipwreck. Then, out in the middle of the cove, closer to Woody Point in about seventy feet of water, there's another target that sure looks like another iron shipwreck. That's really going to confuse the electronics."

Layering, we called it, a case of more wrecks than there is room on the bottom. I felt sometimes in the evening twilight heading back to Main-a-Dieu that the wreck, speaking in low tones from across the centuries, was saying, "It won't be that easy, boy, to learn my secrets."

We would find the same conditions back on the *Feversham* site as we followed the trail of artifacts into a new area through that season and the next. We were recovering almost every day an assortment of shipboard and household artifacts and coins, including large Dutch dollars, Latin American eight-reale cobs, and New England coins (mostly from the pine and oak tree series). We were also finding odd bits of silver that seemed to come from neither a coin nor a broken piece of silver service. They seemed to have been intentionally cut to various sizes. We collected and preserved each one, hoping we might figure out what they were. Then one fine day, a diver found gold coins. Gold always gets attention.

The diver passed them to the tender operator, who delivered them aboard my boat, and we gathered around. They were small cob-shaped Spanish-American coins with strange inscriptions. But there weren't many, and they were in one place. Naturally, we kept looking, finding silver coins but almost no gold ones. That could mean that they were some poor nameless soul's personal property.

I shuttled back and forth between the *Feversham* and *Le Chameau* sites, depending on diving conditions, over the next two seasons. This was a heady time for me, a high point of my career. For the first time, I think, that word seemed to apply. This was a *career.* Though I felt a twinge of regret that, for the same reason, I wasn't doing as much diving as I used to. Sometimes I envied the young divers wide-eyed with the thrill of actually discovering things as I sped off to do this or that on dry land.

And then during the 1996 season, John Burnham, another admired star in our small sky, traveled from New York to observe our site. John was one of the leading colonial-era coin experts on the continent, working then at Stacks Auction House, famous in numismatic circles. On the first morning John was aboard, a diver discovered on the HMS *Feversham* site a very special coin. I followed John into the wheelhouse for a closer look at it in its so-called wet state. I stood silently by as he examined it. Then he turned to me, his face glowing.

"Bob, you have here, I am sure, without the benefit of it being cleaned in your conservation lab ashore, an exquisite willow tree shilling. What a thrill this is to me—here I am holding the rarest of the rare colonial coins directly over the wreck site. You can't beat that for provenance. And we're the first to lay eyes on it since 1711. This is one of the finest moments in my career." And that was only the morning of his first day. Coins came aboard all that day, though none quite as rare and valuable as the willow tree shilling. By the time we dropped the mooring and headed back to Main-a-Dieu, he had identified those odd pieces of silver.

"They were makeshift currency," he said. "Hard currency was very rare in early-eighteenth-century North America, and in its place colonists cut up silver plate and other silver objects to specific weights to use as legal tender. The smaller pieces were used as change."

On *Le Chameau*, we found other strange silver pieces. They were dated and had what looked like a Greek god holding a rock tablet stamped on one side and the bust of Louis XV on the other. Despite the dates, they didn't look like coins. Later we learned from John that they were jetons, used as gambling chips for cards and other games of chance. The king was known to make gifts of gold and large silver jetons to church, civilian, and military officials. They were sort of the Monopoly money of the early 18th century, but in the case of the jeton, it was made from a precious metal and had real value.

Still following the *Le Chameau* trail, the divers found a cultural gold mine: a complete chest of swords and daggers. Though most of the iron blades were gone to the ravages of the sea, the hilts, guards, and pommels, made of silver with gold gilt, remained in decent condition. Nearby, diver Joe Fiorentino found several gold louis d'or coins dated 1725, an extremely rare find.

Back on the *Feversham*, we followed the treasure right up to the edges of the wreck of the iron ship *Cape Breton*, to which I had led the New Jersey divers on the day I rediscovered the *Feversham* back in 1982. There is every reason to believe that some significant portion of her treasure lies layered beneath the *Cape Breton*'s massive, twisted steel plates. If so, I doubt it will ever be recovered.

Near the close of our second season, John Burnham called to tell us that a major auction of the *Feversham* and *Le Chameau* treasure was scheduled for January 12, 1999, at Stack's Auction House in Manhattan. There had been earlier auctions of rare New England shillings and other coins we had recovered from the *Feversham* site at Christie's, among other places, but I had been unable to attend due to work-related commitments. This time, my partner Steve Farrell and I headed south by car, excited and a bit anxious, not so much about the transactions themselves but about going—country Canadians in the big city, a foreign land. Where would we park? Could we even find the hotel where the auction was to be held? We studied city maps en route as if they were wreck-site charts, and as the actual cityscape hove into sight, we joked about our urban anxiety, but that didn't make it any less real.

Well, as a lot of visitors before us have discovered, the city isn't all that hard to navigate. We found the hotel (admittedly with some help from one of my longtime lead divers, Joe Fiorentino), and nobody stole our vehicle.

All dressed up in our auction-going duds, we arrived early at the top-floor auditorium in the Le Parker Meridien Hotel to peruse the catalog. It contained, among others listed for sale, coins from both wreck sites, and Mass Silver, those first-ever coins minted in English North America, were most prominent. We learned that coin collectors were very specialized in their interests, and many of the 200 prospective bidders in the audience (and others making phone bids) were committed collectors and serious students of colonial-period coins. It was clear chatting with a few of them before the action began that they deeply appreciated the unique historical significance of these coins.

It became easier to pretend we belonged in this company when we were ushered to our front-row reserved seats, and still easier when John Burnham stepped to the podium and said, "We also have the very special privilege to have on hand in the audience, the divers who located the colonial shipwreck coins presented here this evening. They are part of a

Canadian team of renowned salvers led by Captain Robert MacKinnon, an internationally renowned treasure hunter and personal friend of Joseph R. Lasser, one of our best-known coin experts and collectors in the New York City area. We are proud to present this group in person, at such a prestigious numismatic event, one of the highlights of the auction season."

The audience actually stood up and applauded us.

Then the bidding began in earnest, as they say in auction circles. It ran far into six figures. A single piece of Mass silver in not-great condition went for near $20,000. In all, we made expenses and a modest gain for the investors. Steve and I, city slickers, headed home buoyed with new confidence and success to undertake the research and recovery of the vessel I'd been dreaming about for years—the *Fantome* and the little fleet she led to their deaths off Halifax Harbor in 1814.

Before this would happen, in 2004, it would be my pleasure to be back working *Le Chameau* with professional and experienced marine archaeologists Dr. Duncan Mathewson III and James Sinclair. Both had worked for Mel Fisher on his famous discovery of the Spanish treasure ship *Atocha* off Key West, Florida. Duncan, Fisher's chief archaeologist, taught us recovery techniques he had essentially pioneered. Jim Sinclair introduced us to several innovative ideas about dealing with concretions as well as recently established scientific excavation procedures. The raw pioneering days of underwater archaeology had passed by with the mid-1990s, but it was by no means complete, and I was pleased to be part of its development on this coast.

That year, 2004, we recovered some of the finest treasure we had taken from the site to date, several mint double louis d'or coins; scores of single louis d'or coins; a 1693 cross of St. Louis[2] in perfect condition; silver plates and other assorted religious utensils, including a hoard of silverware; and lesser copper, silver, and gold coins. With 2005 now looming, I would push hard to place a team on the *Fantome* fleet site. In fact, I would insist on it.

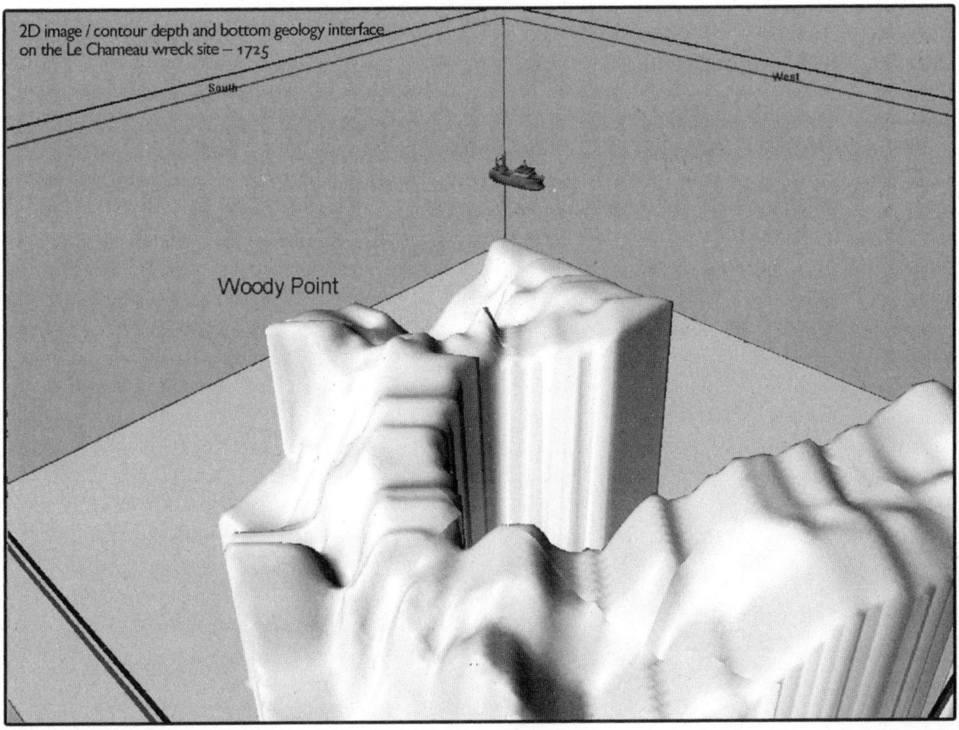

2D image / contour depth and bottom geology interface on the Le Chameau wreck site – 1725

South

West

Woody Point

Redesigned by Vibe Creative Group
for Capt. Robert MacKinnon

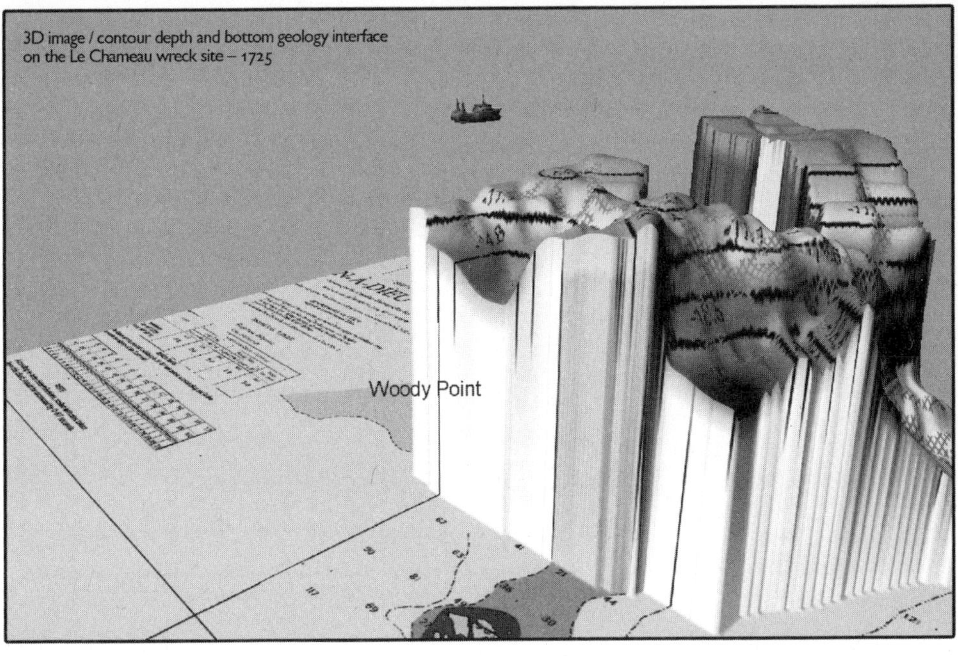

3D image / contour depth and bottom geology interface on the Le Chameau wreck site – 1725

Woody Point

Redesigned by Vibe Creative Group
for Capt. Robert MacKinnon

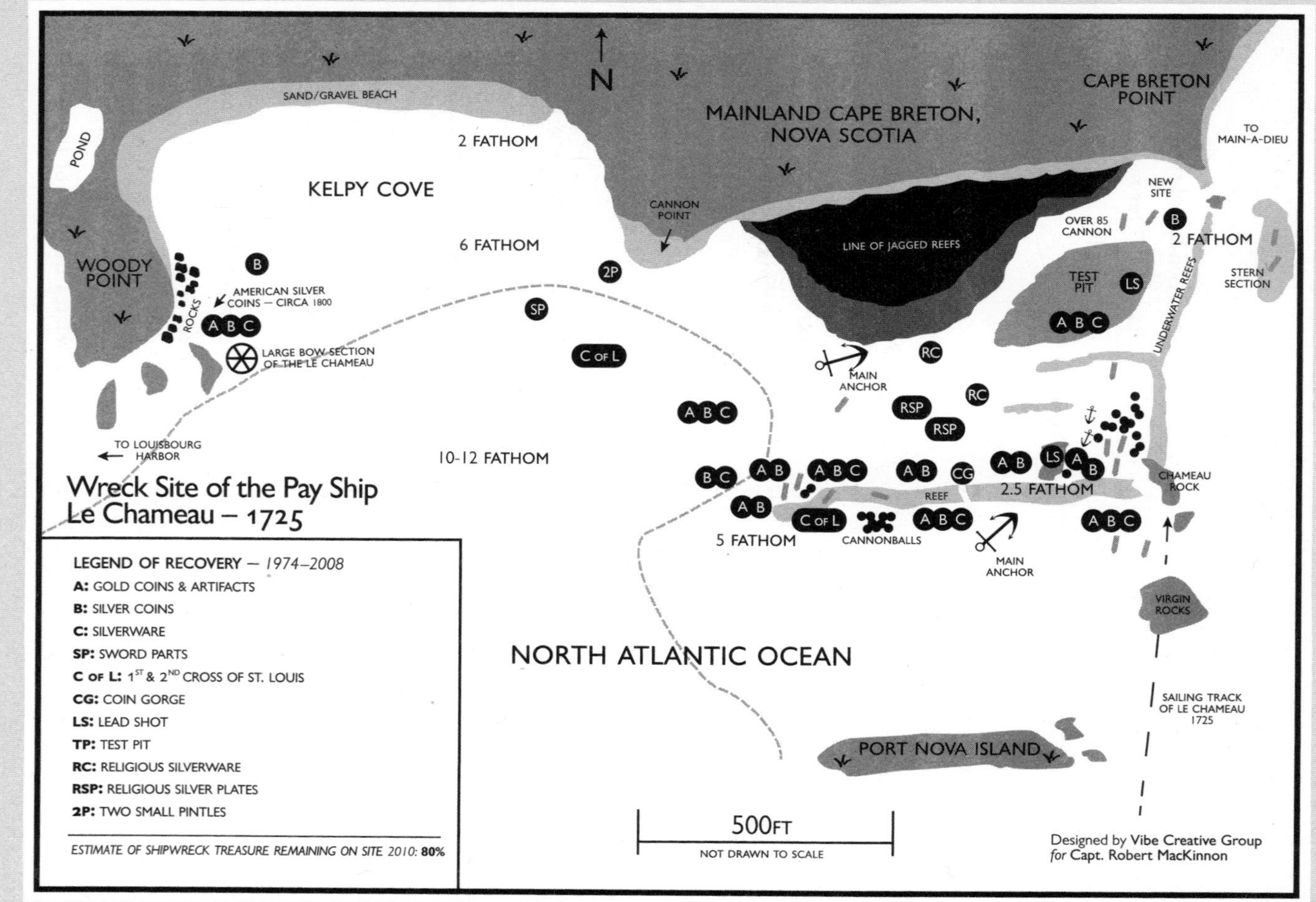
Wreck Site of the Pay Ship
Le Chameau – 1725
MAINLAND CAPE BRETON, NOVA SCOTIA
CAPE BRETON POINT
TO MAIN-A-DIEU
N
SAND/GRAVEL BEACH
POND
KELPY COVE
2 FATHOM
6 FATHOM
10-12 FATHOM
WOODY POINT
ROCKS
AMERICAN SILVER COINS – CIRCA 1800
LARGE BOW SECTION OF THE LE CHAMEAU
TO LOUISBOURG HARBOR
CANNON POINT
LINE OF JAGGED REEFS
NEW SITE
OVER 85 CANNON
2 FATHOM
TEST PIT
UNDERWATER REEFS
STERN SECTION
MAIN ANCHOR
REEF
2.5 FATHOM
5 FATHOM
CANNONBALLS
MAIN ANCHOR
CHAMEAU ROCK
VIRGIN ROCKS
SAILING TRACK OF LE CHAMEAU 1725
NORTH ATLANTIC OCEAN
PORT NOVA ISLAND
500FT
NOT DRAWN TO SCALE
Designed by Vibe Creative Group
for Capt. Robert MacKinnon
LEGEND OF RECOVERY — 1974–2008
A: GOLD COINS & ARTIFACTS
B: SILVER COINS
C: SILVERWARE
SP: SWORD PARTS
C OF L: 1ST & 2ND CROSS OF ST. LOUIS
CG: COIN GORGE
LS: LEAD SHOT
TP: TEST PIT
RC: RELIGIOUS SILVERWARE
RSP: RELIGIOUS SILVER PLATES
2P: TWO SMALL PINTLES
ESTIMATE OF SHIPWRECK TREASURE REMAINING ON SITE 2010: 80%

NOTES

1. Research indicates the cargo of mixed specie carried on board the pay ship *Le Chameau* at time of loss may well exceed 1 million livre. Our research and recoveries also prove the shipment of coins was destined for many different recipients inside New France, as listed below:

Known Specie Shipments on *Le Chameau*

a. Funds for the Academy of Sciences in Montreal: 61,000 livre
b. Funds for the General Hospital at Quebec: 102,000 livre
c. Funds for the General Hospital at Montreal: 200,000 livre
d. Funds for the Seminary at Quebec and Trois-Rivières: 60,000 livre
e. Funds for the Quebec government (loan from the Compagnie des Indes): 547,000 livre
f. Payroll specie for troops at Quebec: 82,010 livre
g. Funds for the fortress at Louisbourg: 50,000 livre
h. Funds for the fortresses at Michigan and Quebec: [?]
i. Funds from Paris pensions for St. Louis cross holders: 48,000 livre
j. Funds for the Quebec government: 289,696 livre

In 1725, one ecu (French dollar) was equivalent to six livre or one Spanish eight-reale dollar.

Broken down into small change—½ and ¼ ecus, sols, billon coinage, copper sous, and deniers—it is very possible the individual number of coins lost on this shipwreck could easily exceed 1 million.

There is another dynamic at play here: How much of the specie shipment was recovered by the original salvers? In specie value at time of loss, I suspect close to 30 percent. In total of all the coins carried on board *Le Chameau*, I suspect no more than 20 percent was recovered in the 1960s. However, there is yet another important factor to consider; it relates to rarity of the coins involved, in a modern auction setting.

Most of the coins carried on board the ill-fated *Le Chameau* were only minted for a short period, the gold coins referred to as *louis d'or mirlitons* for only three years, from 1723 to 1725. The majority of the silver coins lost in the wreck were 8 L ecus minted in 1724 and 1725. This alone, including the fact many of those coins minted were lost in a single maritime event, increases their current numismatic value.

One single louis d'or mirliton may fetch a few thousand dollars, while a double louis d'or mirliton could sell for $10,000 and higher, all depending on rarity and condition. From the modern-day salver's perspective, these facts alone warrant the cost of recovery. The other factor that supports the effort financially lies in the belief additional public funds would be involved for trade and commerce.

2. **Cross of St. Louis—Ordre Royal et Militaire de Saint-Louis.** The order was created in France by Louis XIV in 1693 and dedicated to Saint-Louis. The cross was awarded to French Catholic officers having served at least 10 years in the army. Recipients were not required to be noble. There were three ranks: chevalier, commandeur, and grand-croix. The king was Grand Master; the dauphin or heir presumptive was automatically a member.

The medal was a gold Maltese cross edged in white, with large fleurs-de-lis between the arms. On the obverse was a coin-shaped medallion bearing the effigy of Saint-Louis with the legend "Ludovicus Magnus Instituit 1693." On the reverse was a sword held upright with flaming blade through a laurel wreath, and on a bordure azure was the motto *bellicae virtutis praemium*: "rewarding valor on the field of battle." The cross was worn hanging from a short red ribbon on the breast for knights, from a red neck ribbon for commanders, from a large red sash and accompanied by a metal or embroidered breast-star for grand-cross. (Edict of March 1694.) *Courtesy Trident Research.*

Crosses of St. Louis—Recovered from *Le Chameau*. It is reported that in the recovery of the 1960s, one cross of St. Louis was discovered. I recovered one in the 1970s, and one of our divers, Matt Nigro, recovered a near-perfect specimen in 2004. The cross recovered in 2004 now belongs to the people of Nova Scotia and resides with the Nova Scotia Museum of Natural History, Halifax.

The cross I recovered in the mid-1970s was also a near-perfect specimen. It was later officially offered to Parks Canada for a small recovery fee, one quarter its market value. However, Parks responded that they were not interested as they had purchased a similar cross in France. Their decision still perplexes me considering the provenance.

Some prestigious passengers on board the ill-fated *Le Chameau* were chevaliers who were awarded this distinguished honor by their king:

Chevalier de la Gesse
Chevalier Francois Aubert de la Chesnaye-Bois
Chevalier Charles Potier
Chevalier d'Argenteuil
Chevalier de Louvigny
Chevalier Dubuisson
Chevalier d'Esgly et Saint-Martin
Chevalier M. d'Loges
Chevalier Jacques L'Hermitte

With every award of the cross of St. Louis came the establishment of a pension for the recipient; many were in the range of 2,000 livre a year for life. In 1725, there were many recipients living in New France who depended upon ships like *Le Chameau* to deliver the pension funds related to their position of chevalier. Many were years behind in payments due.

In 1725, there were also many French officers living in New France who were awarded the coveted cross of St. Louis just prior to the loss of *Le Chameau*. Records indicate that *Le Chameau* carried a small box containing these crosses and award documents. Another carried the pension payments for those already inducted into the order and for those newly appointed recipients. The number of crosses involved is not known, with only three recovered from the wreck site to date.

CHAPTER THIRTEEN

Back on HMS *Fantome*

In the spring of 2005, when winter storms still slashed the Cape Breton coast, we held a partners and investors planning meeting in Portland, Maine. The question was whether we would devote full attention to the *Fantome* fleet or work the site along with *Le Chameau*. I understood the investors' reluctance to turn away from a known, producing site to an unknown one, but that's what I would have preferred. Besides, we wouldn't be abandoning *Le Chameau*; we had all kinds of time to return. However, based on their insistence, we were now folding in another important wreck site. The investors were convinced of the unprecedented riches aboard the *Fantome* fleet, supported by extensive research and what I'd seen on three rushed dives 30 years earlier.

So we finally decided at their behest to work both sites, and I was to supervise both operations. This had been pretty demanding when working *Feversham* and *Le Chameau* at the same time, and they lay only 5 miles apart. East Dover near where the *Fantome* fleet grounded was 270 miles from Main-a-Dieu. We would need an entirely new dive crew. And we'd need a full-time archaeologist overseeing recovery, a principle investigator (a PI, in their language).

Jim Sinclair would be perfect for that. He was excellent at his job, everybody liked him, and he had already been approved by the province. He moved up from Florida to take the job, and he brought with him the new dive team. Things had changed considerably in the dive world. Talented amateurs had formed companies and turned professional, going wherever the work called. Deeptrek, based in Houston, Texas, had just finished a job in England. Their superintendent, Jay Usher, was a well-known guy whose reputation had already crossed the Atlantic, since he'd excavated a wreck site on the English coast in conditions (shallow, cold, rough water) not unlike Nova Scotia. He'd also done some notable work on shipwreck sites off the Florida coast. This was a new one for me. Up to that point, our divers were unquestionably of pro quality and had made up for their initial inexperience with ingenuity and avidity. Now we had a team of full-on pros. Still, I admit, I was silently skeptical, with that old feeling that I couldn't be sure about unknown divers until I saw them in the water dealing with the current and waves.

Jim Sinclair, Jay Usher, and I met to hammer out the financial arrangements and discuss the *Fantome* Fleet Project, the areas of responsibility, and my ultimate responsibility.

Our first obligation under the license requirement was to carry out an archaeological assessment of the claim area, look for cultural material with methods no more intrusive than test pitting, and deliver samples of the artifacts recovered, along with a written science report and site development proposal, to the Nova Scotia Museum. We needed several artifact samples to demonstrate that this was a heritage site, and once we'd done all that, we'd receive the coveted excavation permit. Within a few weeks, we all met in Halifax, toured the site from shore at Phantom Cove, as it's called on contemporary sea charts, and selected a base of operations only five miles south of the site in the small harbor town of East Dover. We contracted Bill Bell, a local fisherman, to supply a boat, wharf, and local accommodations for the crew. We were getting closer.

Sinclair suggested we purchase a new Geometrics cesium vapor marine G-882 magnetometer to have on the job when needed. For a cool $50,000, it represented leading-edge sensing technology, software included. "The Deeptrek crew has a lot of mag-survey experience," he said. "We won't need to hire local operators." Although I was by no means an expert, I had gained enough electronic-survey experience on *Le Chameau* and *Auguste* to understand the principles and their application. And I knew that a magnetometer in the right hands could save us months of fruitless exploratory diving, and more important, it could see metal objects buried beneath sand, gravel, and in concretions. They would begin the mag surveys right away, while I'd go north to tend to *Le Chameau*. I planned to return to East Dover in a week's time.

When Matt Nigro, one of my lead divers, and I arrived back in Halifax, we were met by Sinclair, Captain Bell, Jay Usher, and some members of his crew. It was definitely a glum-faced delegation. "What's wrong?"

Sinclair did the talking. "Bob, we haven't found any wreckage. We've looked all over the place. There are no concretions, no targets whatsoever."

"If there were anything around," Bell added, "we'd have found it." Everyone nodded assent.

Did they not understand the directions I'd left? Of course there was wreckage. Did these guys know what they were doing? We'd already spent tens of thousands of dollars in addition to the cost of the mag that found nothing. Instead of the sarcastic comments I felt they had coming, I said, "Okay, guys, everybody relax. We'll have a nice dinner and go out there first thing tomorrow."

The War of 1812 really didn't need to be fought. There were no clear objectives, and neither side was prepared for the fight. It's true that the British were impressing American seamen quite illegally, but that legitimate grievance could probably have been settled by some means short of war had the times been different. But the British and French were battling it out on land and sea with the rest of Europe's nation states taking one side or the other, depending on the perception of their own best interests. And the new United States was more or less yanked by centrifugal force into the Napoleonic Wars. However, there was a strong political faction in the United States itching for a fight, never mind that they had almost no army and only a makeshift navy. Some bellicose figures in the press and Congress actually saw the war as the opportunity to drive the English out of Canada once and for all. So they had their war.

The troops that were sent north to attack the British were soundly defeated at the Battle of Detroit, ending American ambition, which had taken on a brutal form in the north. There was a lot of privateer action going on, and there were naval skirmishes up and down the Eastern Seaboard, but the American navy couldn't afford a beam-to-beam fight with the Royal Navy, so nothing conclusive happened. The war itself was inconclusive—until the Battle of Trafalgar. A lot of British ships sailed west, taking up bases in Nova Scotia from which to attack south. In late 1813, the British invaded the United States. The Royal Navy sailed into most any harbor they wanted and took over. In late 1813, a combined army and navy invaded New England. Another fleet invaded Chesapeake Bay. Now really for the first time, the war came home to the United

States, and it was ugly and lethal and to some extent waged against civilians.

But to follow the *Fantome* fleet story, we'll need to take a detour into Chesapeake Bay to get to the ships' end on the rocks of Nova Scotia. In 1814, the British ran raids up rivers and inlets to attack little towns, basically looting and pillaging, and there was no viable force to stop them. By mid-1814, the small British squadron was being heavily reinforced by a fleet of 21 vessels under Admiral Sir Alexander Cochrane, senior commander of the North American Station. That battle fleet was joined by another under the charge of Commodore Charles Malcolm. The combined fleets landed several thousand soldiers under General Ross. They easily chased American Commodore Barney, with assorted small vessels and about 500 men, out of the bay and into the narrow confines of the Pawtuxet River. Then Ross's army marched up the banks of the Potomac River, while warships sailed up the middle of the river, aiming at Washington, D.C.

The capital's citizens and members of Congress seemed to remain in deep denial that the British would and could actually attack Washington, despite early warnings. American intelligence had reported 4,000 troops landing at Bermuda, followed by the arrival of Admiral Cockburn, the marauder, in Lynnhaven Bay at the mouth of the Chesapeake on the first of March. After the defeat of Napoleon, intelligence had direct word that the British army was heading for America. President Madison's advisers had repeatedly pointed out the exposed position of the capital, the absence of defensive plans, and the obvious fact that capturing Washington would make sound military sense to the British. Furthermore, if this Admiral Cockburn was on the scene, there would be looting.

Finally, when the dust of the advancing British army was nearly visible from Washington, the Americans turned to General Winder to throw together a plan. He managed to collect a force of about 2,500 soldiers under General Smith and only five pieces of heavy artillery to face off against the battle-hardened Brits, who outnumbered the defenders five to one in men and guns. They would meet on a field near the little town of Bladensburg.

The Battle of Bladensburg took three hours, but the result was never in doubt. President Madison along with other civilian officers watched the battle from horseback. When inevitably the Brits flanked the Americans, General Winder ordered a general retreat, and the president and his men fled. They sent messengers to tell the cabinet, the citizens, and First Lady Dolley Madison that Washington was now wide open and helpless.

To add a bit of context to (but no excuse for) the following story of plundering, arson, and robbery, we need to remember, as Ross and Cockburn did, that the Americans had performed similar travesties on the Niagara frontier before the Battle of Detroit in 1813. Sir George Provost, the governor-general of Canada, had been demanding revenge ever since.

Dolley Madison, who was preparing for a state dinner, received word of the enemy's close approach to the President's Palace (it was not yet named the White House) in midafternoon. With help from the messengers, a couple of visitors from New York, and the household servants, Mrs. Madison loaded a wagon with whatever valuables could be moved, and fled. On her way out the door, she saved the iconic portrait of George Washington by Gilbert Stuart. Because it was taking too long to remove the heavy frame from the wall, she ordered the frame broken, and she personally carried the portrait, still in its stretcher, out to the wagon. As she fled, she could hear the rumble and clatter of the advancing enemy.

Henry Adams, grandson of the second president and son of the sixth, tells the story a bit differently in his massive three-volume history of the War of 1812. He claims that a servant saved the portrait after Dolley Madison had left the house.

General Ross and Admiral Cockburn rode into the city at eight o'clock that night with about 200 men. Only a single shot was fired, killing the general's horse. Maybe that was a sort of spark that set the mayhem in motion. The soldiers set upon the town, burning government buildings and the archives and artifacts they contained, wantonly stealing from civilians anything of value they could carry. Apparently Cockburn wanted to burn the whole damn town. Ross, we're told, was reluctant. But that's a moot point. Once the burning and looting started, neither officer could have stopped it.

Before it got under way in earnest, Ross and Cockburn and a group of officers entered the President's Palace to find the dining table set for a fine feast intended for Mrs. Madison's privileged guests. The British officers sat at the president's table, poured out generous goblets of wine to toast the king's health, ate the dinners, removed valuables (perhaps even the silver service they had just eaten from), and left—leaving behind orders to burn the place to the ground.

That night the British army, worrying about a counterattack, slipped out of Washington, during a violent rainstorm, with their wagons of loot. They retraced their march down the peninsula, past Bladensburg, where their dead lay unburied. About the time Ross and Cockburn were heading back to Chesapeake Bay and the protection of the Royal Navy, Commodore Gordon was overwhelming Alexandria just downriver, but before he could burn down the town, a citizens' committee approached under a white flag to ask for terms of surrender that might save Alexandria.

Commodore Gordon declared, "All naval stores, all ordnance, all of the shipping and its furniture, merchandise, platte of every description in the city or that which had been carried out of the place for safety, must be surrendered immediately." All vessels that had been scuttled had to be raised and delivered up to him. In other words, if the citizens obeyed, only the public and military buildings would be burned, leaving the inhabitants and their homes standing. They had one hour to think it over. They didn't need to think it over; they had no choice.

The commodore was as good as his word, or mostly. He looted and burned all public and military buildings, after he finished stripping the buildings of everything valuable. He loaded the loot aboard the captured vessels and sailed back down the Potomac to the bay. Elements of the American army harassed and aggravated them en route, but they lacked anything near the strength to stop the flow of plunder or to prevent the vessels from joining the main fleet lurking in the Chesapeake. The warships then were sent to besiege Baltimore.

Meanwhile, two of those captured American vessels—*Perseverance*, a three-masted square-rigger, and *Industry*, a schooner—along with a heavily laden British transport vessel, were dispatched to the British naval stronghold of Halifax via Castine, Maine, and St. John, New Brunswick. We know that from naval records. And of course we know that they didn't make it into Halifax Harbor.

Capture of Alexandria

On the 5th and 13th of August, 1814 to strengthen defenses along the Potomac south of Alexandria, the corporation loaned to the United States thirty five thousand dollars, upon condition it should be expended south of Alexandria. After the defeat of General Winder at Bladensburg, the corporation, by committee, waited upon the British Commander, at this city, to know what treatment was to be expected, provided Alexandria should fall into his hands. Admiral Cockburn assured the deputation that private property would be respected; that probably some fresh provisions and flour might be wanted, but they would be paid for. Without firing a gun, on the 27th, Fort Washington was blown up and abandoned by the commanding officer, Captain Dyson, who has been dismissed from the service of the United States, by the sentence of a court-martial, in the consequence of it.

On the 28th, after the enemy's squadron passed the fort, the corporation, by deputation, proceeded to the ship commanded by Captain Gordon, who commanded, and requested to know his intentions in regard to Alexandria; which he proposed to communicate when he should come opposite the town, but promised that the persons, houses and furniture, of the citizens, should be unmolested, if he meet no opposition. Next day, the 29th, the British Squadron was drawn up in line of battle so as to command the whole town. There were two frigates, the Seahorse, thirty-eight guns, and Euryalus, thirty-six guns, two rocket ships of eighteen guns each, two bomb ships of eight guns each, and a schooner of two guns, arranged along the town. The committee will not attempt to condense the correspondence and terms of surrender, but refer to it as a part of the report. One hour was allowed the corporation to decide. It was stated to the British officer that the common council had no power to compel the return of merchandise carried to the country, nor to compel the citizens to aid in raising the sunken vessels: these two points were yielded by the enemy. The enemy was requested to explain what was included in the term merchandise, which was to be taken; and, in answer, it was stated it would embrace such as was intended for exportation, such as tobacco, cotton, flour, bale goods etc. The plunder of the enemy was indiscriminate, and not confined to any particular class of individuals, and included alike, non-residents and inhabitants.

Partial estimate of loss, ships captured and destroyed: Three ships, three brigs, several bay and river craft, some vessels burned etc.

—U.S. Congress. American State Papers: House of Representatives, 13th Congress, 3rd Session, 29 November 1814, Vol. 21. *Military Affairs.* "Inquiry into the Capture of the City of Washington," pp. 1:524–599.

We do not know, however, exactly what was aboard those vessels when their broken hulls coughed their cargoes into the sea. What has fascinated me all these years is what I have sound reason to suspect is aboard the lost *Fantome* fleet. This is further supported by the recoveries sport divers made in the 1960s, including American silver dollars, and my own underwater reconnaissance of the site during the mid-1970s. There is sound circumstantial evidence that they carried loot from Alexandria and Washington and perhaps even Dolley Madison's silver service. We know that there was plenty of loot; we know that the Brits didn't leave it behind. So what did they do with it? They didn't transport it to Canada by road because there were no such roads in the modern sense of the word, and even if there were, the American army would have sniped at them all the way. No, the treasure had to go north by ship.

I've always believed the treasure was carried aboard *Perseverance* and *Industry*, the American captures. We do not know what took place during the stops at Castine and St. John. If the loot was recorded in either place and a manifest drawn up, it has never been recovered. Perhaps it was lost with the *Fantome*. Nor do we know whether the *Fantome* herself carried treasure, although it's not unreasonable to suppose some quantity of the loot was transferred to her during the stops. In any case, it really didn't matter because her cultural artifacts would likely prove priceless.

I needed the *Fantome* brig for the sake of identification. There were several ways to identify a Royal Navy warship by some piece of wreckage, such as the ship's bell or something else with her name on it. If we could identify *Fantome*, then we could be certain we'd found the American ships we believed carried the treasure.

I used to imagine my team and me standing before a big glass display case at, say, the Smithsonian that contained Dolley Madison's place settings from the dinner party that never was. And near the base of the case there would be a brass plaque that said, "Contributed by Captain Robert MacKinnon and associates." But of course there was no way to learn what those ships carried to their deaths except by recovering it.

Yet according to my new high-tech magnetometer and its operators, there were no shipwrecks in Phantom Cove. We know the sea does savage violence to things like 19th-century shipwrecks, but it doesn't expunge all evidence of metal. Frankly, I was a bit miffed at Jim Sinclair, Jay Usher, and the crew, but I did my best to hide it because they seemed upset enough. Also, I was aware of my own electronic prejudice. It's wonderful stuff that can save much expensive time and I couldn't be without it at this level. But it can also distract the diver from nautical common sense, rendering him dependent on a computer screen. I tried not to be old-fashioned.

When I arrived at Bell's boat and wharf, Jay and Jim were conferring over the MagLog software. "It's been giving us trouble," said Jay. Steve Drover, the team's mag tech, was on the phone consulting with the manufacturer in California. Meanwhile, the dive crew was impatiently waiting around hoping for a break in the electronic problems.

As gently as I could manage, I asked to see their dive logs. *Where*

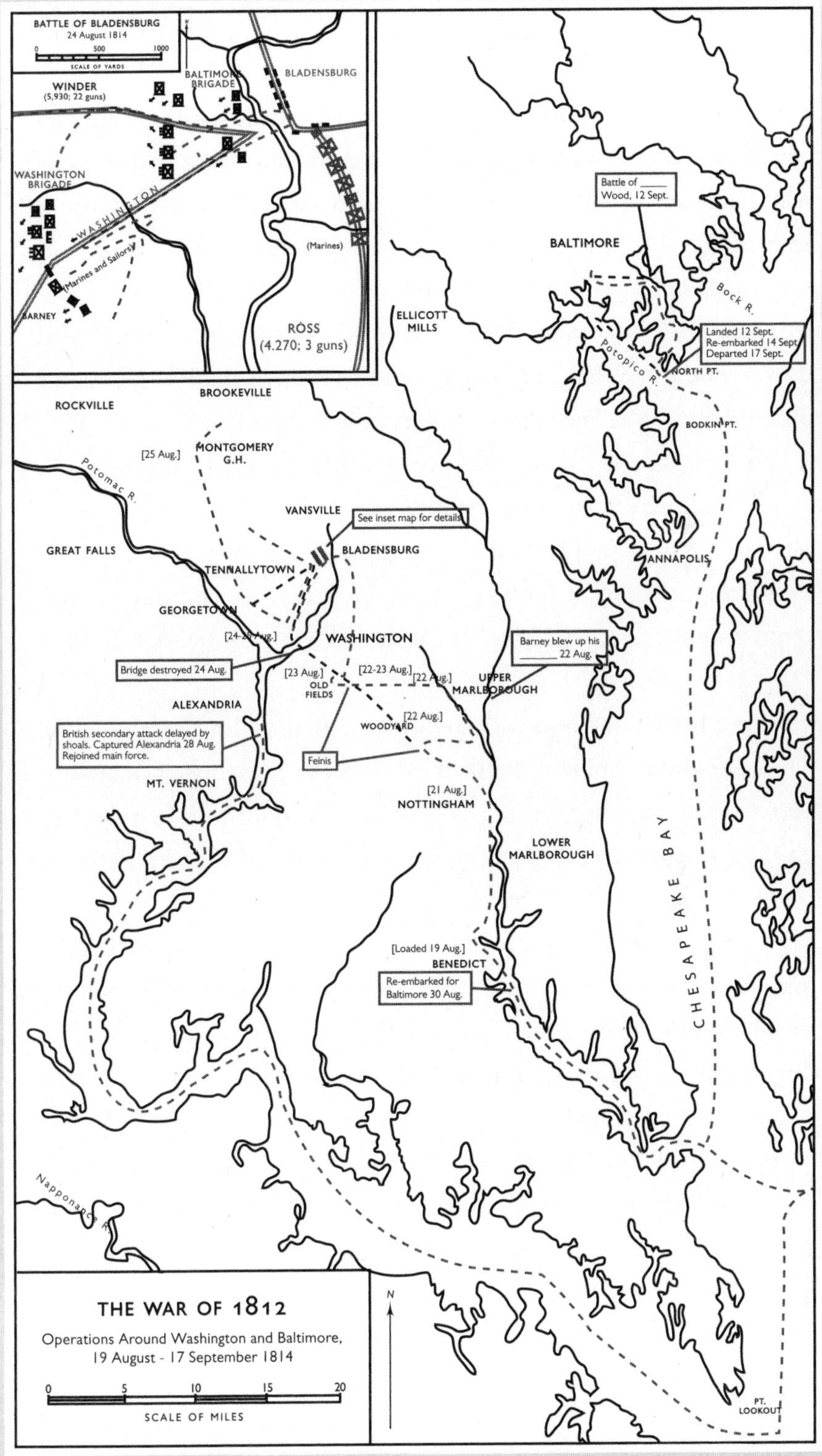

Map courtesy of the United States Military Academy,
redesigned by Vibe Creative Group *for* Capt. Robert MacKinnon

had they been searching? It took about 10 minutes to see that they had been in the *wrong* place. By a good half mile. Hadn't I told them exactly where? Okay, calm, calm. I decided to leave the mag ashore until we knew it was working properly. Then I took Bell aside.

"Cap, are you familiar with the area northeast of Shag Bay Head they call Phantom Cove? Are you familiar with the little stream that runs from the back land out over the beach in the center of the cove, the place where all the lobster traps pile up after storms?"

He looked at me, and I could see he understood immediately.

"So that's where you'll go, right? Today?" He nodded, a bit abashed. He was only trying to help. He was a good man.

I then told Sinclair to forget about the survey for now and to concentrate on diving, finding the site, and proving its cultural significance. "That is our first job," I said.

What to do now? Should I go out with them and steer them to the wreck site? I was tempted, but decided to smile, wish them luck, and let everyone calm down together. I drove back to Main-a-Dieu to look in on the *Le Chameau* site. Sinclair promised to call me with a report.

On the drive to *Le Chameau,* I was not settled, so Matt Nigro, one of my lead divers, suggested stopping outside of East Dover on the northeast side of Phantom Cove in the village of Prospect. We walked the almost two miles back along the rocky bank toward the *Fantome* fleet wreck sites. From the time we stepped out of the truck, I was engaged by the rugged terrain and shoreline, boulders and granite outcrops everywhere. As we walked toward the cove, I could plainly see that the coast offered no protection to a ship cast upon the land; it would be quickly ground to pieces dashed against the granite cliffs and boulders that in most places ran down to the waterline. As we walked toward the wreck sites, we discussed the issues with the magnetometer, continually distracted by one geologic feature or another, in agreement that not only was any ship lost on this coast doomed but most likely the debris field would be widespread, maybe for miles.

And then we saw Bill Bell's boat anchored almost directly over the wreckage I'd seen three decades ago. Divers were entering the water. We stopped walking any farther, not wanting the crew to notice us and be distracted, and retraced our steps back to the truck. As we were walking along the rock-strewn path, I stubbed my foot on a jagged rock and bent down to move it off the path and out of the way of fellow hikers. Upon picking it up I noticed the surface was rough, just like very course sandpaper. Matt and I examined it and then others that lay close by; they were all the same, some sort of coarse granite, totally unlike any we had witnessed along the shores of Cape Breton. We both came to the same conclusion almost immediately. If this type of granite rock was predominant over the wreck site, then any artifact that came in contact with it would be quickly damaged. In a high surf zone, wreckage could be abraded into nonexistence. This was indeed a troubling discovery. The *Fantome* fleet may have had the misfortune to wreck in a place where geology would play a major part in its demise.

I began the 270-mile drive back to Cape Breton with an overall sense of good fortune. There were bound to be mistakes—I'd made my share to date—and false starts, but that was only part of the process. I couldn't have been happier with the direction of my life and career. Just across the Canso Causeway that connects Cape Breton Island to the mainland, I got a call from Jim Sinclair. "Bob, we found the wreck on the first dive just where you said it was. I apologize for wasting a week but we are on it now. We found coins, lots of coins, mostly eight reales. They all predate the year of loss."

"Excellent, Jim. And don't worry about it. Please congratulate everybody for me. Great work. Did you find any cannon?" Finding cannon would prove we were on a warship, and their markings might afford further circumstantial evidence, if not positive identification.

"No cannon. But we found huge piles of cast-iron ballast ingots in a big concretion with hundreds of coins sticking out. There's probably thousands within the concretion. It's big, a hundred feet by about forty running perpendicular to shore, and it's covered by boulders. But there's everything imaginable in it. Bronze nails, spikes, rudder straps—and coins."

"Any cannon shot?" We knew *Fantome* carried 18 or 20 thirty-two-pound carronades. Shot of that caliber would offer another layer of evidence that there was a warship.

"Not yet," he said. He was clearly aware of the evidence we needed. "Do you want to come back?"

I did. But I had the delightful problem of two treasure wrecks to oversee. "It sounds like you guys have things in hand. Remember to keep the sample recovery small. Don't do any test pits bigger than a square meter. Remember, we're still in the assessment stage."

He knew that, but it didn't hurt to confirm.

I called my brother, John, who was captain of the workboat on *Le Chameau*. "Everyone's excited," he said. "We've found more of those silver plates with the cross and four globes on them." The plates and symbols were yet to be identified, but we thought they had religious purpose. "And a lot more silver coins."

"Great work." I told him the *Fantome* news.

So much material was coming up from *Le Chameau* our conservator, John Ian Cross, worried that there would soon be more work than he could handle. "If that even begins to happen, we'll hire an assistant or two," I assured him. But I didn't have to because our brilliant crew, some with real conservation experience, enthusiastically volunteered for lab work. We were like happy boys at summer camp.

But dive seasons are short in Nova Scotia. As the first successful season at Phantom Cove approached its midpoint, I began thinking ahead about the next year on both sites. Should we work these wrecks simultaneously? Should we focus on the *Fantome* fleet at least until we had all our heritage permits in place? We could put, say, 16 divers on her supported by several surface craft with advanced electronics, including side-scan sonar.

In the meantime, I asked Sinclair, when conditions allowed, to run magnetometer surveys using the main concretion area as a center point, running a line parallel to the shore from 10 feet of water or the safest operational depth for Bill Bell's boat. Then I suggested he survey out to sea for a quarter mile, making the lines no more than 50 feet apart where possible. I also asked that in shallow-water conditions, he tow the mag, flying it 3 feet under the surface, and once they achieved depths of 15 feet under the keel, to lower the fish to 5 feet with at least a 100-foot layback to avoid prop noise. "Watch out for sunkers!" I warned.

We were learning that the *Fantome* fleet site was enormous, so much so that we began to suspect the presence of additional wrecks, Nova Scotia layering. That's why I wanted a really tight magnetometer survey.

Then one fine day when I was in East Dover examining the recovered items for delivery to the lab, Jim Sinclair and Jay met me at the dock, all smiles.

"Bob, we've identified her as a British warship. The test pits are turning up bronze fittings, copper nails, and pieces of copper bottom sheathing, all stamped very clearly with the broad arrow ownership mark of the British navy. One small section of sheathing has a refit stamp on it from the naval dockyards at Deptford on the Thames dated 1811, a year after *Fantome* was captured from the French. I did a quick search, and what do you know? *Fantome* underwent a Deptford refit in 1811. That's not absolutely conclusive, I know. It's not the ship's bell, but it's pretty damn solid evidence."

"Yeah, it is. It's great. But I'm still concerned about no cannon. I'm also concerned about officialdom. I don't want to make the slightest mistake." But I was a lot less worried when, after Jim submitted his report along with sample artifacts, we were granted a Class B excavation permit, without the usual Special Places Protection Act hassles. Finally we were being treated like the professionals we had proven to be, time and time again. Alas, I later found out the manager of Special Places was on a long vacation and our permit requests were being vetted by a duly qualified and conscientious employee of the Nova Scotia Museum. Our euphoria, however, over this fair and equitable treatment would be short-lived, ending upon the manager's return.

For the moment, we had all the time we needed. We could work the site for a decade, or longer if we wanted. We could go at recovery as meticulously as possible. There's an understandable temptation for a treasure hunter to get it all, but that urge needs to be repressed. The only sensible process is to work square meter by square meter, which requires us to narrow the focus of the search. That's another reason why I wanted to find those cannon. They should be in one main pile, unlike on *Le Chameau*, and there was no record of the brig's crew trying to lighten ship, hoping to float her free of the rocks. The *Fantome* seemed to have sunk quickly; if so, we'd find cannon in one general area, and their disposition would be a clue to the location of the main wreckage. Although I was still not absolutely positive we had found the warship, the discovery of the 1811 Deptford tag made me 99.9 percent sure.

On the other hand, the days of all Cape Breton's wrecks are numbered. It's likely that a casual sport diver could have swum over one and not noticed that he or she was on a wreck site. Any artifact left exposed on the sea bottom right after the wreck would have quickly been swept away, gone forever. That's why concretions have relative importance, although even they are prone to serious degradation. They're a pain in the neck for treasure hunters, but they add a layer of protection for both precious and nonprecious artifacts. However, all it takes is one 50-knot blow to lift a 50-ton boulder and drop it on the concretion. Once broken, due to the conditions that create marine concretions, they will not readily reform. So any artifacts thus exposed will be lost. Nothing on the near-shore bottom of our ocean remains in situ for long. In addition, artifacts left in the water are continually undergoing chemical reduction through electrolysis and physical damage from wave action. It's staggering to imagine just how much has already been lost. So the time to recover what's left is not endless. In fact, for most shipwreck artifacts, the remaining time can be calculated in years not decades.

But recovery is a slow process. We learned by the close of the first season that our suspicions were true. There were more shipwrecks here than the three we were looking for, and not necessarily from the same period. This meant that we'd need to recover everything and sort it out in the lab, but that was fine with everyone.

Then with hints in the air of the autumn onshore winds to come, Jay Usher and his crew, while mechanically reducing one of the larger concretions, found a field of round shot weighing 32 pounds. The evidence mounted. Further, the mag crew found strong hits leading east-northeast from the main concretion field. These, we believed, were the long-lost cannon. Sadly, we had to leave all of that until next season.

Not long before the easterlies blew us out, Jim called. "Bob, we have some American copper coins and a lot of silver eight-reale coins [big nose Charlies] all dated well prior to 1814, the latest 1811, the earliest 1796. There are a lot of *fancy* furniture handles sticking out of the concretion, both silver and bronze, definitely not ship's furniture. These came from somebody's parlor. Like, say, from Washington, D.C."

We laughed with delight. We might be able to prove where those things came from, maybe even from Mrs. Madison's table, as we recovered them. Next season, we said, next season.

Gold single and double louis d'or recovered from the *Auguste* site in 1977

Courtesy of Robert MacKinnon

New England and Spanish coins recovered from the HMS *Feversham* site during the mid-1980s *Courtesy of Robert MacKinnon*

A pine tree shilling *Courtesy of Robert MacKinnon*

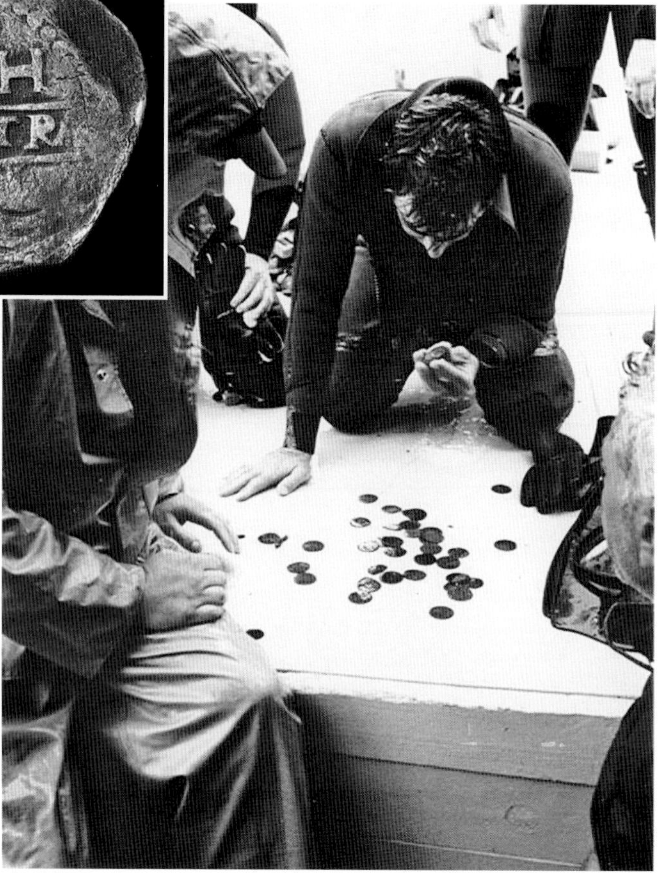

ABOVE: A silver eight reale coin

Courtesy of Robert MacKinnon

RIGHT: Divers examining coins, 1985

Courtesy of Joe Fiorentino

Cannons located on *Feversham* site *Courtesy of Joe Fiorentino*

Rare ships' fittings containing approximately 22 percent gold; recovered in 2005 from the *Joseph* transport, part of the *Feversham* fleet lost in 1711

Courtesy of Robert MacKinnon & Company

The cover of a *Stack's* auction catalogue, 1999

Courtesy of Stack's Bowers Galleries

Single and double louis d'or—gold French coins

Courtesy of Robert MacKinnon & Company

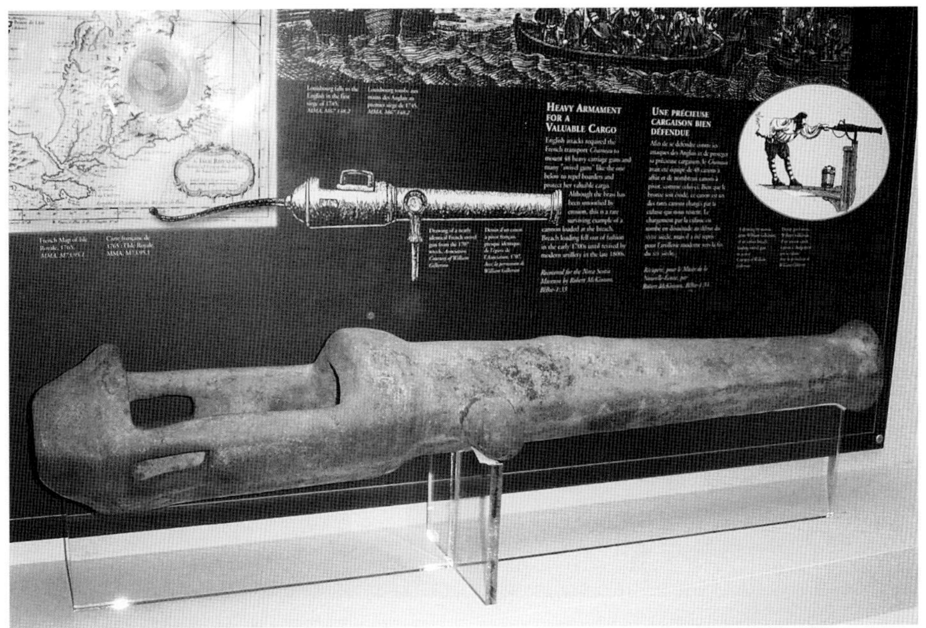

A bronze rail gun recovered from the *Le Chameau* site; on display in the Nova Scotia Maritime Museum of the Atlantic, courtesy of Robert MacKinnon

Courtesy of Mary Margaret MacKinnon

A 1724 double louis d'or—a rare French gold coin

Courtesy of Robert MacKinnon & Company

A silver religious seal depicting John the Baptist on the Sea of Galilee
Courtesy of Robert MacKinnon & Company

A collage of drafting instruments, a silver buckle, a sword hilt part, and a silver 8 L ecu *Courtesy of Robert MacKinnon & Company*

LEFT: An underwater picture of a rare bronze rail gun on the *Le Chameau* site
Courtesy of Joe Fiorentino

BELOW: *Le Chameau*–site archaeologist Rob Reedy working near the main baseline, 1995
Courtesy of Joe Fiorentino

Gold coins, single and double louis d'or, surrounding a gold and inlaid enamel cross of the Order of St. Louis, dated 1693
Courtesy of Robert MacKinnon & Company

An underwater photo of a badly worn cannon from another wreck inside the *Le Chameau* claim at Woody Point *Courtesy of Joe Fiorentino*

Divers returning to the main workboat on the HMS *Fantome* site, 2006
Courtesy of Joe Fiorentino

Kelpy Cove complete with Port Nova Island and Chameau Rock in the background *Courtesy of Joe Fiorentino*

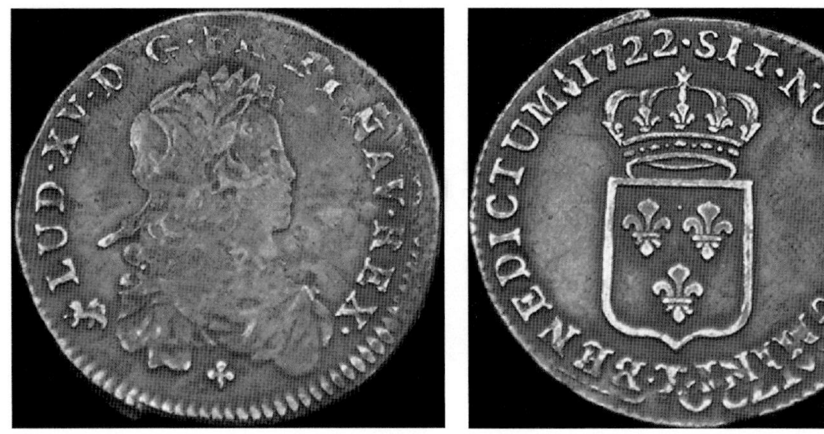

Silver French ½ ecus *Courtesy of Robert MacKinnon & Company*

A large mortise or font recovered from the *Le Chameau* site
Courtesy of Robert MacKinnon & Company

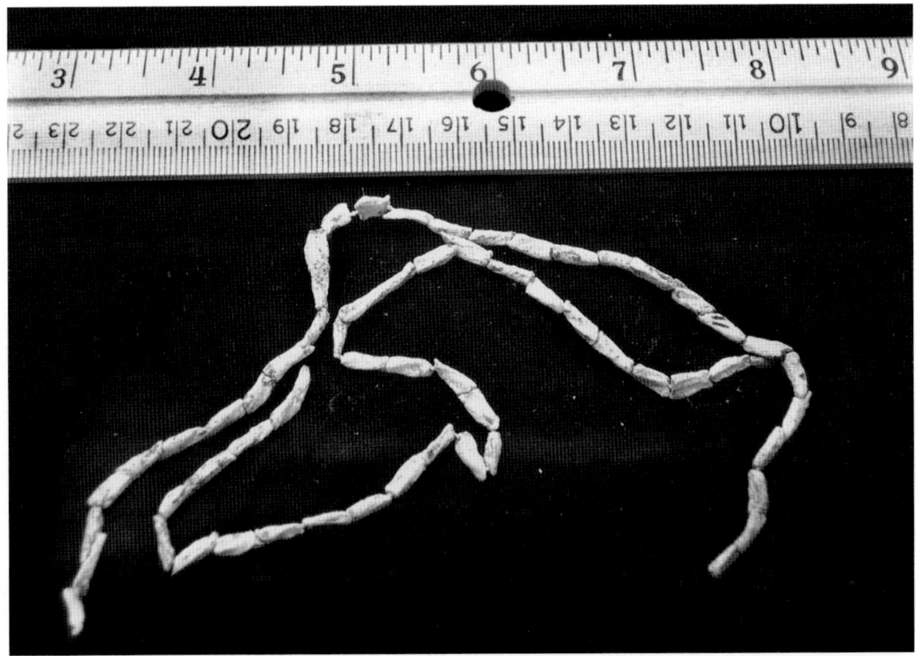

A lead mortar fuse *Courtesy of Robert MacKinnon & Company*

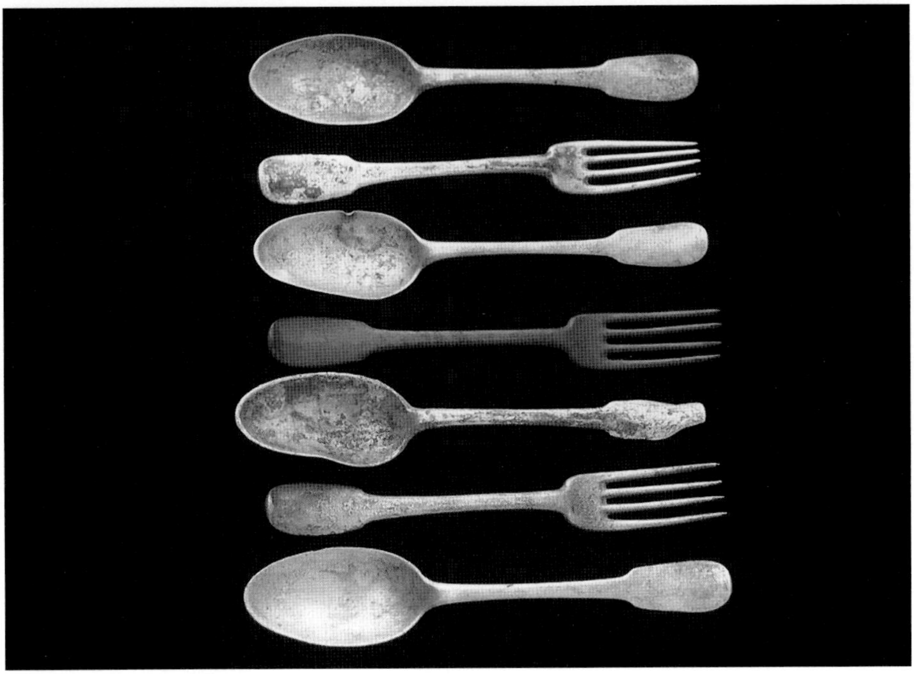

Silverware, a sample assortment of hundreds of pieces recovered from the *Le Chameau* site *Courtesy of Robert MacKinnon & Company*

Robert MacKinnon standing by the unofficial memorial to the *Fantome,* near Phantom Cove *Courtesy of Joe Fiorentino*

A Spanish silver eight reale recovered from the HMS *Fantome* site in 2005
Courtesy of Robert MacKinnon & Company

Reverse side of a Spanish silver eight reale recovered from the HMS *Fantome* site in 2005
Courtesy of Robert MacKinnon & Company

A silver Spanish coin and naval buttons recovered from the HMS *Fantome* site in 2005 *Courtesy of Robert MacKinnon & Company*

A silver American coin on the HMS *Fantome* site, 2006
Courtesy of Joe Fiorentino & Company

Fantome site concretion complete with coins and silverware, 2006
Courtesy of Joe Fiorentino & Company

Divers returning to the *Fantome* site tender, 2006 *Courtesy of Joe Fiorentino & Company*

Spanish (Latin American) and American copper and silver coins dating back to 1793, on the HMS *Fantome* site, 2006 *Courtesy of Joe Fiorentino & Company*

Bronze pins, nails, lead shot, and coins, 2006 *Courtesy of Joe Fiorentino & Company*

ABOVE: The crew setting site anchors on the *Fantome* site, 2006

Courtesy of Joe Fiorentino & Company

RIGHT: Silver coins in concretion, recovered from within the general *Fantome* site (Prospect claim)

Courtesy of Robert MacKinnon & Company

BOTTOM RIGHT: Silver coins recovered from the same concretion within the general *Fantome* site (Prospect claim)

Courtesy of Robert MacKinnon & Company

CHAPTER FOURTEEN

New Discoveries

The dive season in Nova Scotia is always abbreviated and tightly bookended by bad weather. Spring doesn't settle in completely until late May, sometimes not until mid-June if the year is particularly stormy. It was mid-July before we could return to East Dover, but by then we had the practical matters firmly in place. Captain Bill Bell would supply the same services—boat, wharf, and accommodations—as in 2005. We had an excellent team, rich with experienced divers, conservation staff, and support crew, all itching to go. Jim Sinclair would act as chief archaeologist, and John Cross would be our conservator. The Nova Scotia government had enthusiastically approved both of these scientists to represent the *Fantome* fleet wreck site. The logistics had been complex, and it would be a relief to get in the water. To focus our work on the *Fantome* fleet required us to move our base of operations, including our boat, equipment, spares, and people, from Cape Breton to East Dover, south of Halifax. With all that accomplished, we became a self-contained and self-sufficient operation. Everything we'd need was either stored on board Bill Bell's boat, our main dive boat (the *Ocean Viper*), or in designated buildings near the wharf.

The first task was to do a bottom analysis, using the boat's enhanced depth sounders and the MaxSea mapping system to record the topography and an onboard differential GPS to fix precise geographical positions. I wanted to know, among other things, the makeup of the bottom—was it sand or rock or both?—but what I most wanted to know was the exact location of shoals, reefs, and sunkers that might have played a part in the loss of the *Fantome* fleet. It's always useful in analyzing the distribution of wreckage nearly 200 years after the event to understand as clearly as possible how the vessel wrecked in the first place. Research can sometimes help, but the *Fantome* records, including court-martial proceedings, are not especially clear about the details. That's why a seaman's eye is useful to observe the area from the surface; I considered the sailing conditions and imagined myself aboard the brig as she approached the shore on that night in 1814. After I'd seen the survey results, I decided to place our starting point just outside the large concretion area about a quarter mile off the beach and marked it with a 350-pound day mooring.

During the first few days on-site, I took the dive tender (rubber chase boat) right along the shore looking for natural areas where wreckage could have been deposited, but I soon realized there were too many nooks and crevices and boulders ideal for capturing artifacts from the wave action. I then tried some drift experiments.

Investigating the causes of the wrecks I'd explored thus far, I noticed one purely nautical aspect that appeared time and again. Tidal current. In the days of sail, as I mentioned earlier, acts of seamanship that seem awesome to us today were routine. Those guys were excellent. The local profusion of shipwrecks didn't accrue from incompetence. Rocks ultimately killed the ships, but often, I speculate, it was the tidal current that set them down on the rocks. To understand the tidal dynamics, I used a low-tech, age-old method: I set lightly weighted buoys to float over the site area from both directions, at various states of the tide and in different wind conditions. I wanted the floats to ride "between wind and water," as we say, mostly submerged and therefore less exposed to the wind's influence than that of the tides. Most of our floats drifted onto the shore near Shad Bay Head to the west-southwest of Norris Rock, affirming that old lesson that wreckage in shallow water subject to tide and waves most always moves shoreward. Local fishermen who'd found lost gear on this shore further affirmed the lesson.

At the east-northeast end of Prospect Bay, beginning at Norris Rock, which separates Phantom Cove from Prospect Bay, there is a channel about a quarter mile wide or less running inside Betty Island and the mainland, appropriately called Privateer Passage, though some call it Ryan's Passage. The northeast end of the passage leads into Pennant Bay, which provides access to the entrance of Halifax Harbor around the Sambro Ledges. For a northbound ship such as *Fantome*, heading for Halifax, Privateer Passage would be a tempting shortcut or tactical diversion.

Since my first dive in 1975, I'd believed (and so did the old captain who had reprimanded me) that *Fantome* was heading for the passage when she led her charges onto the rocks. In an attempt to understand what part the passage may have played in the loss of the fleet, if any, we took the main dive tender, *Ocean Viper*, on a research mission. After a careful reconnaissance, we located what seemed the most likely route to gain Halifax Harbor. Ryan's Passage (as it is called on contemporary sea charts) was bloody dangerous and, at first glance, undoable without local knowledge. Was this really Privateer Passage? But then we began to see that there was a navigable channel between Betty's Island and the mainland.

Fantome's role as a dispatch vessel meant that Captain Sykes had been in and out of Halifax, and maybe he'd used the passage before when approaching from the south. The position of the wreckage indicated to me that he had been setting up to enter the passage. Maybe he felt perfectly safe threading that needle, and maybe he would have been, except he never made it to the passage. The tide or leeway (the tendency of a sailing vessel to slide downwind) or both in concert set him too far to port on his shoreward side and led his charges to their deaths.

According to what we know about the required compass course through the passage (east-northeast) and the direction of the breeze (southeast), Sykes had a decent sailing angle, but it was nighttime. The three ships behind were following the stern lamp of the ship ahead. Nifty shortcuts in close quarters at night are impressive bits of seamanship—as long as you make it. If you don't, someone will be bound to wonder why you didn't stand offshore until daylight. Anyway, the *Fantome* fleet, I've always thought, was set down by the tide inside Norris Rock at the end of Dollar Shoals.

Then over time and storm, the wreckage spread out along the shore toward Shad Bay Head to the west-southwest. Most of the debris field was captured by the unique geology in the middle of Phantom Cove, which encompasses the major concretion fields worked on in 2005. However, we still had to find the area I discovered in 1975, but time was on our side. Our treasure trove license was valid for several more years before we needed to renew it.

A small crowd gathered on the shore most every day in fine weather. This is a very scenic stretch of coast, and though the going is pretty rough, it's a popular walk recommended in the Nova Scotia tourism guidebooks. Many hikers were stopping for a while to sit on the rocks, watching us working barely a quarter mile offshore.

One day several guys in high-end hiking duds tried to attract our dive tender operator's attention. There was something about their body language I didn't like, so I sounded three blasts on the boat horn, the prearranged signal for the tender to return to the dive boat. When John pulled alongside, I asked what it was all about.

"I don't know. They say they're from some media company—they got cameras and stuff. They want to come out here and talk to you and the archaeologist, they said they deserve to know what you are doing."

"What did you tell them?"

"Nothing."

"Fine, go back and tell them this is a heritage shipwreck reconnaissance project. We are authorized and working under provincial permits and licenses. If they have any further questions, they should speak to the Nova Scotia Museum's Special Places manager, Robert Ogilvie. After that, don't answer any questions, just leave."

After a brief conversation that didn't seem friendly, John returned to the dive boat.

"It was weird. You know what they said? They said they had contact with the media, and that they weren't going to stand by while Americans raped a Canadian heritage site."

"Americans?"

"That's what they said."

"What did you say?"

"That we're Canadians."

I didn't know then what to make of this, but this incident gave me cold chills. And there was more when I got ashore.

Bill Bell took me aside. A reporter from a national TV news agency had showed up on his wharf like he owned the place. "What was going on at Phantom Cove?" he demanded. The reporter stated he had asked the Royal Canadian Mounted Police, but they didn't know, so he'd come for answers, and he wanted to talk to whoever was in charge. He was really pushy.

"What did you say?"

"Well, Bob, I surely hope I didn't make a mistake. But I told him along with his snooty attitude to get the hell off my wharf before I'd throw him off."

"I can see that." You didn't address Bill Bell or any other lobsterman like that on his own dock without getting wet. "No problem, Bill." I told him about the shoreline incident and the "American" business.

"But we're a Canadian team with a few American support divers!"

"What's going on, Bill? Have you heard anything?" Locals in these small fishing towns know things before they happen.

"No, but I'll ask around, ask people to keep an eye on outsiders. Sounds like someone's trying to stir up trouble but *why*?"

In many respects, HMS *Fantome* was typical of the Napoleonic period in both her design and her career. Launched in October 1808 at the French Naval Shipyard at Le Havre, she was one of 57 vessels in the *Le Cygne* (swan) class. She was rigged as a brig—that is, she had two masts both carrying square sails. Called a *corvette* by the French, *Le Cygne* class vessels were 90 to 103 feet long on deck (between perpendiculars), not counting the bowsprit, which on brigs was extremely long. Her beam was 30.6 feet, her draft 13.6. For a fast ship of this size, she was fairly heavily armed (ported for 20 guns), with those big carronades we'd been searching for. (Talking about the HMS *Beagle*, the vessel Charles Darwin made famous and that began life as a brig, one reputable marine historian mentions that this was a skittish, hard-to-handle rig.)

Though *Fantome* was built by and for the French navy, she was turned over to "private persons." This meant that she was a privateer, which is to say that France gave her permission and a degree of material support to go attack the enemies of France on the high seas. It was a good deal for the home navy—privateers were essentially surrogate warships—and for the privateer; there was enough potential profit to enrich a lowborn sailor. But it was dangerous work. There was always the chance of encountering a superior force, as *Fantome* did on May 28, 1810.

According to British admiralty records, she was intercepted and captured in the mid-Atlantic by the British frigates HMS *Melampus* and HMS *Driver* after a long chase and short engagement. In a letter to the admiral in command of Halifax Station, Captain Hawker of the HMS *Melampus* described *L'Fantome*, to Admiral Sir John Warren, at that time the commander in chief of the Halifax Station, as follows: "a fine French corvette brig, letter-of-marque, burthen 300 tons, with ports for twenty heavy carronades, and a complement of 74 men. She had made three captures."

The Brits incorporated her into the Royal Navy, and in this her story is typical of the time, when every side—English, French, and American—drafted captured ships into their home navies, making them one of their own. This muddies the ownership questions. Was *Fantome* a French ship or English? The *Industry* and *Perseverance* were American ships before the British seized them. Anyway, after a stop in Halifax where she was surveyed and found adequate for the Royal Navy, we next hear of her in 1811 in the Deptford Dockyard. From those records, we learn that her original armaments were replaced with 18 or 20 thirty-two-pound carronades.

In 1812 the brig was sent back across the Atlantic to blockade Eastern Seaboard ports and interdict commerce. During that winter, transferred to the British North America Station at Halifax, she conducted interdiction and blockade operations along the American northeast coast.

She nabbed four American ships (*Gustavus*, *Hannah*, *Christiana*, and *Racer*) during that winter. Captains and crews in all navies had serious motivation to capture, not sink, enemy vessels. Prize ships were eventually either enlisted in service or sold along with the cargoes, and the capture crews were paid prize money. Of course, the officers got the biggest cut, but many a common sailor made enough prize money to move ashore, open a tavern or store, and live a reasonably civilized life compared to that in the navy. Possible prize money was used as a recruiting tool. *Fantome*'s prize money came to some $70,000, a fortune, but by the time her crew got paid their shares in 1818, she was on the bottom near Dollar Shoals.

On April 1, 1813, the *Fantome* was deployed with the British warships *Statira*, *Mohawk*, and *Maidstone* and the tender *Highflyer* in the Chesapeake Bay off the Rappahannock River interdicting merchant shipping. Under Rear-Admiral Cockburn's command, she was ordered to pick her way up into the small rivers that feed the bay, such as the Elk and the Bohemia, to attack shipping and seize anything of use or value from towns and settlements. On the evening of April 28, the *Fantome* and a few other vessels raided Havre de Grace, driving out the defenders and seizing 51 field guns, a lot of small arms, and a quantity of payroll money for the American troops. Most of the local houses were put to the torch. *Fantome* proceeded four miles farther up the river and seized the local Principio cannon foundry, which had all of its machinery, buildings, and partially completed guns destroyed. Five schooners and a large store of flour were also burned.

On April 29, 1813, at the mouth of Chesapeake Bay *Fantome* intercepted the British brig *Endeavour*, which had previously been captured by an American privateer while bound from Guernsey to Gibraltar with a cargo of wine. The American prize crew was placed in chains and five men of the *Fantome* sailed the recaptured brig back to Halifax. This sort of thing happened a lot. Under other circumstances, it wouldn't have been surprising if the French had recaptured *Fantome* or if they had then run her up on the rocks, instead of the English. On October 5, 1813, she captured the American privateer schooner *Portsmouth Packet* off Matinicas Island, Maine. The *Portsmouth Packet* had originally been the famous Nova Scotia (British) privateer *Liverpool Packet*.

During August and September of 1814, the *Fantome* was designated as the dispatch vessel between the flagship of the British Chesapeake flotilla, HMS *Tonnant* (Rear-Admiral Cockburn), and Halifax Station. She took a few more prizes during her shuttles, with Lieutenant Thomas Sykes in command. On November 20, 1814, *Fantome* departed St. John, New Brunswick, for Halifax, Nova Scotia, with the American ships *Perseverance* and *Industry* and a heavy naval transport vessel under escort. Only the transport survived to enter Halifax Harbor.

Somewhere around the middle of the season, Jim Sinclair called me on the boat. "Bob, have you ever heard of the American periodical *Archaeology*?"

I had not.

"Well, I have a recent article here and the thrust of it is that all of us working on the *Fantome* Fleet Project, including the approved scientists, are a bunch of plunderers raping Canadian cultural material for profit. Frankly, I think it's libelous."

"What's going on here, Jim?"

There sure seemed to be a very select group in the federal and provincial government and maybe in the museum who may have wanted commercial treasure hunters out of the picture entirely, no matter how scientifically diligent they were.

Of course I knew their position, the "in-situ types" who'd rather leave the artifacts in the ocean to be destroyed. But I never really understood their complaint. Here we were paying the high cost of the scientific recovery of stuff, much of which we would be giving to the province. And if we didn't make the recovery, no government body would because they couldn't afford the time and money. But a media slur—that I'd never imagined. Remain calm, I told myself, think.

"There's more," said Jim. "Duncan Mathewson sent me an e-mail containing a similar but no-less-disturbing story in the Canadian print media, this one in the *Toronto Star,* dated November of 2005—quoting a guy named John Wesley Chisholm. He's a filmmaker; I think I met him once. Really, he certainly failed to do his homework here. The article is full of inconsistencies, including his vague assertion the HMS *Fantome* was directly involved in the raid on Washington.

"Bob, Chisholm is off base by a country mile. Although his real intentions remain unknown, he totally misrepresents the work being carried out on the *Fantome* fleet site. The article casts a negative light on the project but, more so, on the scientists and salvers involved.

"Based on this story, he is launching a crusade to stop American treasure hunters from working on the site and selling artifacts on eBay. He goes on, calling for the repeal of the Nova Scotia Treasure Trove Act, but hopes to film the site for a future documentary. Obviously he did not bother to consult with the Nova Scotia Museum in an attempt to get his facts straight. If he did, he would have discovered the recovery project is science based and permitted by the jurisdictional authority, with over fifty percent of all artifacts recovered retained by the people of Nova Scotia.

"Bob, speaking as just one of the professional scientists involved in the project, what certainly appears to be an agenda-driven attack really infuriates me. By using words like *scavenging* and citing the possibility artifacts recovered from the site could be sold on eBay, he seems to intend to place our project in a bad light. It seriously concerns me that no one representing the Nova Scotia permitting authority has come forward in the local news media to set the record straight.

"He claims he has a government permit to dive on the site. It is amazing for a filmmaker with all the research capability he must have at hand to state in the public media that the project is run by ugly Americans intent on stealing Nova Scotia's heritage. All he had to do was call the Nova Scotia Museum to find out the project is run and mostly owned by Nova Scotians. He states in the *Toronto Star* article that the Treasure Trove Act should be abolished. I fear he may have an agenda to do so using our project as a weapon. Too bad he would not cite the truth or at least get his facts straight.

"Bob, who gave him this permit, the Nova Scotia Museum?"

"Jim, the museum can't issue a permit to anyone other than the license holder."

"Of course not. But let's find out if they did. We only have this guy's word for that. However, I have unearthed some very relevant information during one of the days we were blown off-site. Another valuable piece of the shipwreck puzzle.

"From what I can ascertain, only two artifacts from the raid on Washington and the subsequent plunder of the President's Palace, the first White House, are known to have been recovered—a painting of George Washington, rescued by then–First Lady Dolley Madison, and a jewelry box returned to President Franklin Delano Roosevelt in 1939 by a local Canadian who said his grandfather had taken it from Washington in 1814."

"That is interesting. My original maritime attorney, Donald Kerr from Halifax, told me that artifacts taken from the Washington raid in 1814 cropped up every now and then in Nova Scotia estate sales."

Anyway, I couldn't concentrate on that. We had enemies. Enemies who were quite willing to go to any lengths and misrepresent our work, including the science involved. I was stunned, not so much by that fact—I'd seen the federal government's behavior before on *Auguste*—but by the realization that I hadn't known any of this was going on. I'd been surprised by the daily spectators on the beach. We had been really isolated in Cape Breton. We hardly ever saw another boat near Scatarie Island, let alone spectators. Besides, being literally underwater most of every day tends to put one out of touch. I felt angry, yes, but also sad. Now I'd have to pay attention to this—whatever it was going around—in order to protect our work and my name. I didn't want to do that. I wanted to keep my head underwater, where it was always most comfortable and engaged. So that's where I went, back in the water.

We had two broad problems to address that 2006 season. We were all but positive that one or more ships had wrecked in this cove, perhaps on Dollar Shoals, *before* the *Fantome* fleet. We found in the water and on the beach a range of round shot, from 8 to 32 pounds, too vast to have come from our three ships alone. That and other incongruities, including the very size of the site—which as we saw it sprawled over two kilometers from Shag Bay Head back toward Halifax Harbor and Norris Rock, convinced us that this was another case of layering. I have something near 100,000 pages of shipwreck research in my files. Not only about the *Fantome* fleet but about many other wooden shipwrecks in the vicinity of Halifax, some very close to Shag Bay Head. We've found reference to earlier wrecks, but that's not so surprising. Numerous ships could have died here with all hands in, say, the 1740s, when no one was around to give witness. They just vanished; it happened all the time.

After receiving strong metallic targets on the Green Shoals and one major target off Norris Rock, we dove to investigate and found wreckage from a wooden ship of some considerable size. Another set of magnetometer runs at the other end of the site along the high granite cliffs that make up Shag Bay Head turned up serious metallic targets. Divers found fittings, bolts, and other pieces of sailing-ship hardware—and a field of cannonballs of smaller caliber than *Fantome*'s 32-pounders. It would take years to solve the identity of those other ships.

Joe Fiorentino and Matt Nigro, my two lead divers, suggested that we dive at set intervals all along the shore for almost two miles. After only a morning's dive, they found bronze pins, cannonballs, and copper sheathing close to Norris Rock. "Bob, the hits are so strong they are vibrating the 'bone phones.' This whole place is one big wreck graveyard. What do you want us to do? Dig down to the hits for visual identification or keep surveying with the handheld detectors?" Joe said.

Because there was so much wreckage and the season was flying along, I decided it was time to pick one part of the site and survey it for the upcoming excavations. We settled on that large concretion field near our original reference point. We set up dive teams to go as far shoreward as the evidence of ship wreckage existed and another team to work seaward until the wreckage disappeared.

Joe Fiorentino and I dove on a concretion bed over five feet thick, and almost immediately, we saw a hole in the bed about five feet in diameter and over three feet deep. At the bottom of it we observed a stack of uniform ingot-shaped ballast blocks, each weighing about 200 pounds. I noticed the exposed tops of the ballast blocks were worn to a shiny surface that almost resembled polished brass. Rolling around loose in the hole, affected by the moderate wave action, were several softball-size granite rocks. I picked one up to examine it. Even wearing neoprene gloves I could feel the rough texture. These resembled the same type of abrasive rocks Matt and I discovered on our walk back along the shore to the wreck site in 2005. At the time, we surmised this geologic abnormality might extend to the wreck site; here was proof positive it did.

Swimming away from the concretion for a short distance, I noticed the uneven bottom was littered with thousands of these same granite rocks, from small stones up to great boulders the size of compact cars and beyond. I quickly realized what had polished the ballast blocks. I also knew this type of stressor on fragile artifacts would quickly reduce them to dust. I returned to where Joe was hand fanning around in the hole looking for markings on the ballast. Since he gave me no sign of success, I left him to it and swam around the concretion, trying to determine its extent.

After some diving experience, one grows keenly sensitive to any incongruity among the rocks, sand, and kelp; incongruity leaps out at the eye. It was a large round copper alloy plaque about 1 inch thick and 18 inches in diameter mostly obscured under a layer of concretion and corrosion that caught my eye. I fanned most of the lighter debris away. The plaque was encrusted with marine growth, but I could clearly make out the words "Of the United States." And that familiar, always pleasing bolt of excitement shot through me with a shiver. Then I saw a date—1789. With even more aggressive hand fanning, not wanting to disturb the artifact, I made out what appeared to be maybe an eagle perched on a round object, perhaps a globe. Then a few engraved stars, three above the figure and several more on one side of it came into focus. There were four holes spaced equally around the rim, which I took to be bolt holes for mounting the thing on a wall. What was it? Only recovery and restoration would answer that question, but it seemed clear to me that it was something official, the sort of plaque mounted at the entrance of an important government building. Obviously, the British thought it important enough to remove it from its mounting and carry it off. It had no intrinsic value, so it must have symbolically represented victory to the Brits.

I was so sorely tempted to recover it. I rationalized doing so on the grounds that any curious sport diver, attracted here by all the attention, wouldn't hesitate to take a prybar to the thing and mount it on his recreation room wall. But in the end, I didn't touch it. We could only do so under the terms of the recovery permit that we did not have as yet. (They had told our archaeologist more than once when he inquired that it would be coming in a day or two.) Now I wish I had recovered it.

The chilly easterlies that signal the arrival of autumn kicked up a nasty surf that made diving a challenge. However, the excitement among the crew sustained everyone, although a sense of urgency settled over us. We were in the water every possible hour. I closed out the last days on-site looking for the area of treasure, cannon, and ballast bars I first saw in 1975. Meanwhile, divers searched close inshore on both sides of the concretion in only a few feet of water. I joined them inshore, and we found brass pins, coins, lead shot, brass rings, and other pieces of wreckage carrying right into the surf line. I kept thinking about that plaque, and more than once decided to recover it, only to change my mind. We'd have time next season and the next, and we still didn't have our Class B Heritage Permit to begin recovery.

Then, at the very end of the season, Matt made a thrilling discovery near Norris Rock at the end of the Dollar Shoals while searching for the illusive carronades. It was a silver spoon with an eagle engraved on the handle. Matt hurried to the surface to ask what I wanted to do with it. He said it was just barely stuck to a small chunk of concretion a few feet under the sand and gravel—the first storm might well sweep it away.

The crew looked at me for direction. It was clear what they wanted to do; my decision was just as clear.

"Don't touch it but mark the spot and we will take a DGPS fix, Matt."

He complied and went down like a cormorant. Had we found the First Lady's table settings? We couldn't know until Jim Sinclair had a long, close look, but we sure wanted to believe it.

Jim was excited to hear about the spoon, and as we made plans for him to come see it in situ, I asked what he'd heard about the permit. "Nothing," he said.

"I'm about to close down for the season."

"I'll give them another call right now."

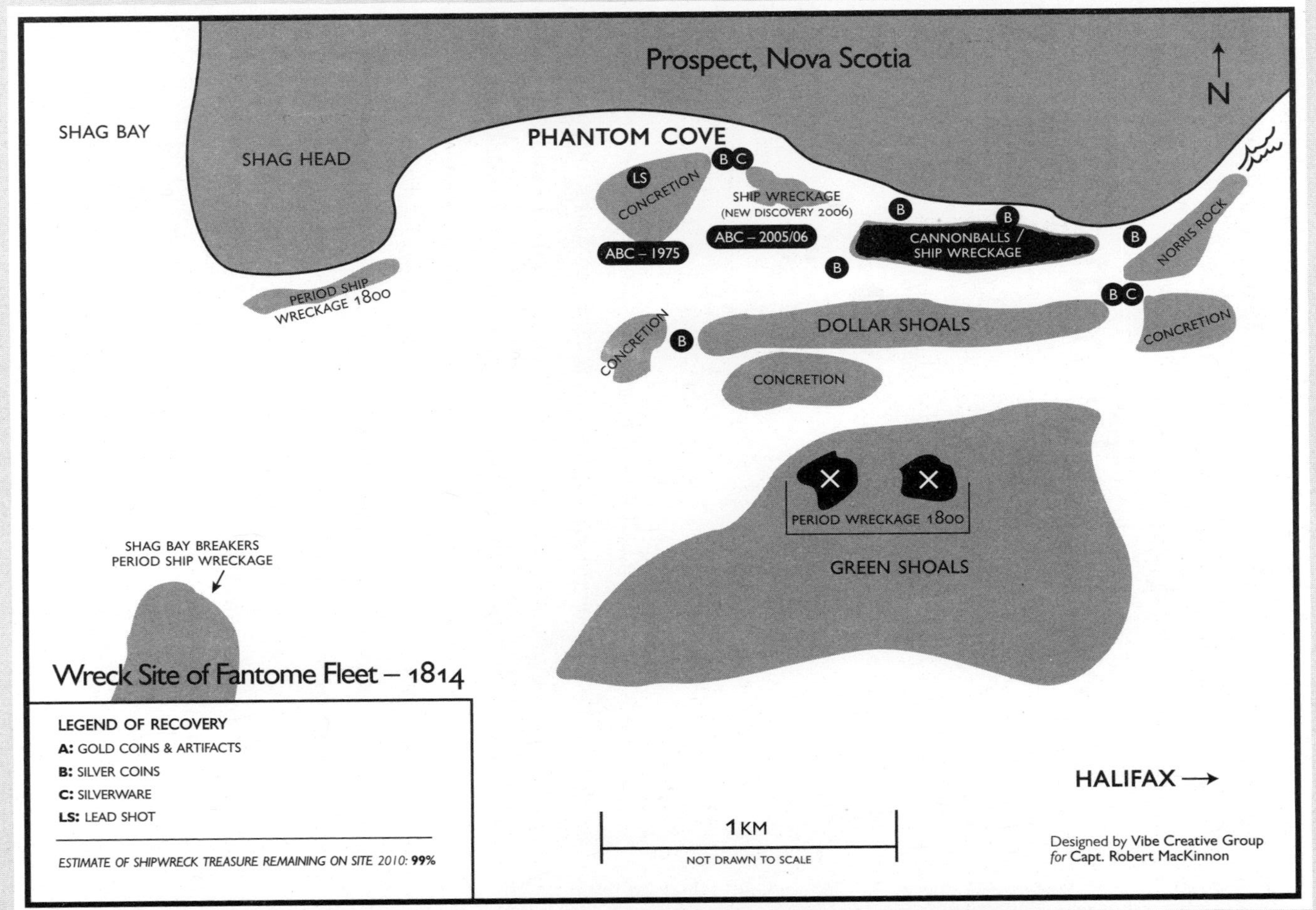

Wreck Site of Fantome Fleet – 1814
Prospect, Nova Scotia
N
SHAG BAY
SHAG HEAD
PHANTOM COVE
PERIOD SHIP WRECKAGE 1800
LS
CONCRETION
ABC – 1975
B C
SHIP WRECKAGE (NEW DISCOVERY 2006)
ABC – 2005/06
B
CANNONBALLS / SHIP WRECKAGE
NORRIS ROCK
CONCRETION
DOLLAR SHOALS
CONCRETION
CONCRETION
PERIOD WRECKAGE 1800
GREEN SHOALS
SHAG BAY BREAKERS PERIOD SHIP WRECKAGE
LEGEND OF RECOVERY
A: GOLD COINS & ARTIFACTS
B: SILVER COINS
C: SILVERWARE
LS: LEAD SHOT
ESTIMATE OF SHIPWRECK TREASURE REMAINING ON SITE 2010: 99%
1 KM
NOT DRAWN TO SCALE
HALIFAX →
Designed by Vibe Creative Group for Capt. Robert MacKinnon

CHAPTER FIFTEEN

Sovereign Immunity

By September 1, we had disassembled and stowed our gear and removed our moorings and marks, leaving no footprint on the land or in the water. I'd paid all outstanding bills around town, and by late morning, the delivery crew left East Dover in my boat bound for Cape Breton. Now there was nothing to do but say our good-byes and go our separate ways. It was a sad parting after a season of such close quarters and camaraderie. It's always a sad parting, but this time that pure feeling was leavened by anxiety.

Everyone recognized that trouble was brewing. We hadn't gotten our permit, despite repeated phone calls in which they told us "any day now." After that our trust in our own government, federal and provincial, was much diminished. We didn't expect the best of our own government after our *Auguste* experience. Our worst fears were that *Fantome* was not an isolated instance of duplicity but part of a pattern and that this delay was not bureaucratically induced but that it was intentional.

There were people, we had no doubt, lurking somewhere behind those libelous magazine articles and perhaps that "American" nonsense. The fact the provincial authority never publicly corrected these slights in the media against a longtime client of the province seemed to support this contention. "Don't worry," we told each other. "After all, we had the treasure trove permit, and it was good for five years. They couldn't just take it away from us, not without breaking their own laws."

So we shook hands, embraced, and turned away from East Dover until next season. That's the other thing about these end-of-season partings. We abruptly cease being treasure hunters for about eight dark, frozen months. Most of my guys work other jobs in the winter, some go diving in the subtropics; I go lobstering.

Anyway, I didn't make it 20 miles up the road before my cell phone rang. It was my lawyer, Jim Gogan, on the other end.

"Maybe you ought to pull over, Bob."

I did pull over.

"There's a new development. Well, new to us. England has claimed sovereign immunity over the *Fantome*."

I'm glad I pulled over. England was claiming the *Fantome* as a British-flagged vessel lost in foreign waters during wartime.

"I hear that the matter was discussed in Parliament, at *Whitehall*. Your name was mentioned along with Rick Ratcliffe's. The British High Commission made the sovereign immunity claim through our Department of Foreign Affairs. All salvage activity is to be stopped immediately. I'm sorry, Bob."

Worst fears realized, I stared at the road while the news settled in. The following conversation is cleaned up considerably for polite readers.

"I think England and Ottawa have been talking since last spring," Jim said. "That's why they've been stalling us, waiting for the actual claim to come. We know how this happened, don't we? Members of

Parliament didn't just perk up one day and decide they'd better claim the *Fantome*. There was a lot more international media than we knew. Apparently, the British press ran lurid stories about how Nova Scotia was allowing anyone with a dive tank to pillage British war graves. It upsets me personally to think that no person or department head representing Nova Scotia and a client in good standing failed to correct this injustice as soon as they were made aware it existed."

"Okay, wait a minute. They're claiming sovereign immunity over *Fantome*, right? The ships that wrecked with her were American captures. So they take *Fantome*, and we keep *Perseverance* and *Industry*."

"Won't work. They're claiming the whole site. This is partly because you've been giving them such honest reports about how the wreckage from several ships is all mixed together."

"Look, I'll call you back, okay? I need to absorb this for a while."

"Sure, anytime. Talk with you later—Wait, Bob, hang on. Are you there?"

Now what?

"Bob, my secretary just handed me a faxed copy of a letter from Bill Greenlaw [director of the Special Places arm of the Nova Scotia Museum]. It says your permit applications for the *Fantome* fleet claim have not been approved. Now that it's official, I'll start making some discreet inquiries."

"What recourse do we have, Jim? Any?"

"It says here you can contact some guy in England named Tate if you disagree with the finding. That's ludicrous. But here's a possibility. If England and Nova Scotia have in fact been talking about closing you down for several months now without informing you, then they've acted in a prejudicial manner. That's illegal. You have close to a million dollars invested in this project. I think we can make that case, but it won't get you back on *Fantome*."

I couldn't take any more. "I'm going to call Rick Ratcliffe at Natural Resources."

"Good idea. Call me back. I'm sorry, Bob."

Still parked along the side of the highway, traffic whizzing by, I called Natural Resources, where Rick served as the person to go to concerning any issues that might arise with the rights vested in current treasure trove licenses. I started to tell him about the letter that the Special Places director, Bill Greenlaw, sent to my lawyer from the museum, but he stopped me, saying a copy of the letter I referred to had just arrived on his desk.

"It's outrageous. But I'm not terribly surprised in retrospect. I've been hearing rumors for like six months now that certain Nova Scotia government officials, representatives of Parks Canada and Justice, both federal and provincial, were talking to a *third party*."

"For six months?" So Jim was right about that.

"Yeah, and now England is suddenly claiming sovereign immunity over a wreck none of them ever heard of six months ago."

"Who got to them?"

"I'm not sure. There was that negative publicity. It put some pressure on them, but how did false, negative publicity get started? Did you hear that they talked about you in the halls of Parliament, Whitehall no less? You see, you and your partners were caught in the middle of an interdepartmental war within Canada and are now dragged into international diplomatic relations between Canada and Britain. Then there's the museum. Here we have the Museum Group, the provincial authority you guys must deal with to get heritage permits. They're supposed to be acting in an unbiased manner. Meanwhile, they've been attacking the Treasure Trove Act itself. Remember their website back when, several years ago, they were attacking the act directly? Remember all that in-situ preservation nonsense?"

"Yes, but back then, I thought my legal rights would protect me."

"Yeah, I did, too. I should tell you I've been hearing other rumors about the Treasure Trove Act. It may well be that refusing you the *Fantome* permit is really part of this broader movement to get commercial treasure hunters out of the water entirely."

"Let the sport divers do it, huh?"

"Yeah, right, Parks Canada or the province sure aren't going to do it. When I first heard the third-party rumors, I asked my boss if we couldn't sit down face-to-face with all the parties, and hash something out."

"So what happened?"

"Nothing. The powers that be quashed the idea. I shouldn't be talking like this, Bob, except that we're friends, and the obvious injustice stinks. And one other thing. The Museum Group's own head archaeologist warned them that they'd better keep the clients' rights in mind or risk losing a lawsuit. Obviously, they ignored him."

"What do you think about the Treasure Trove Act?"

"About its future?"

"Yeah."

"I don't know anything for sure, but I've been hearing the word *repeal* a lot lately."

What a melancholy drive it was back to Main-a-Dieu. It felt like I'd come full circle to something like an ending. Except for lobstering, nothing else gave me the pleasure I derived from treasure hunting. I didn't want to stop. It was so simple when I was young, or it seemed so, since scuba gear and the techniques of its use in rough, shallow water were in their infancy. So were marine archaeology and shipwreck artifact conservation.

Discovery back then seemed like a kind of abstraction; it was the search, the diving that thrilled my friends and me. We wanted treasure, of course, as the object of the search, but we also wanted the activity itself, the doing—the career. That's why I never felt that employing a real scientist or following careful protocols was a burden imposed on me by meddlesome bureaucrats. Like research, it was part of the fun. But then we found treasure, and things got complicated. I attracted determined enemies among the very people who stood to benefit from my recovery and who would trample on my rights to get their way. And never mind that their way was no way at all; under it nothing would be recovered, ever. And then I remembered something; it's ironic, I guess. I fell under the romantic spell as a boy listening to the reporting about a court fight over who owned the treasure. Maybe I should have known it would come to this.

Instead of going straight home, I pulled up and parked near the dock at Main-a-Dieu, but I didn't get out of the truck. There was Scatarie Island lying low in the haze, where we'd spent so many seasons, that exquisite nautical death trap where so many ships, sailors, and passengers were killed. We'd seen, let alone recovered, only the tiniest sliver of what's still out there now, still at the mercy of the sea. My boat was in her place. The delivery crew hadn't been home long. They were still adjusting lines, and as I watched, sadness turned to anger. Dammit, I had a letter duly signed by the minister for Natural Resources that said as clearly as words could state a thing that my rights would not be interfered with as long as I was in compliance, and I was always in compliance. That had to count for something. My partners and I had already spent millions on the assumption that it did. I called Jim Gogan.

"I want to take them to court," I said.

"Good. I suggest we petition the court for what they call a judicial review where the judge will decide whether or not your rights have been infringed. If they find in your favor, which I think they will, then in a separate action we'll sue for lost opportunity and damages."

"Do it."

"First thing tomorrow morning."

Meantime, I was still an active treasure hunter. It wasn't over yet. In 2007, with last year's excellent team in place, we carried out reconnaissance and archaeological assessments on Scatarie Island. We found what we believe are the remains of the Walker fleet's pay ship, *Joseph*, wrecked along with the *Feversham* and the two other transports in 1711. And in the spring of 2008, I asked our science team to apply for heritage research permits to go back on the old *Le Chameau* site. Dr. Mathewson and Sinclair returned to oversee the scientific aspects of both the 2007 and 2008 field seasons. My dive crew stayed intact. It was like the old days.

At the end of the 2008 field season we located a new treasure wreck site at the west-southwest corner of the original Kelpy Cove claim at Woody Point. The new site began to give up American copper cents, silver dimes, and half dollars, all dated pre 1836 and all the way back to 1794, the first year half dollars were minted in the United States. We found these unique coins along with a few silver Latin American cobs dated 1776 and British crowns dated between 1800 and 1820. The discovery was topped off when Joe Fiorentino found a short-barreled cannon and a major debris field very close to shore, in 10 feet of water.

The following season, I had the great pleasure to work with Greg Stemm and Mark Gordon, leaders of the famous Odyssey Marine Exploration (OME), to explore wrecks off Sable Island. Part of Canada, Sable Island is a glorified sandbar lying out on the edge of the continental shelf, 150 nautical miles east-southeast of Halifax (44 degrees north, 59.5 degrees west). Because it's low lying, often invisible in the fog-prone waters, and sited right on the Great Circle route between Europe and North America, it's called the "Graveyard of the Atlantic," though I think Scatarie could give it a run for its money. The Odyssey guys are noted for doing brilliant work on very deep wrecks with a proper research ship and the latest in advanced electronics, including remotely operated vehicles. Though our styles are completely different, we recognized our interest and sensibility—and our long-standing shared desire to work around Sable Island.

In June 2009, I received permission to survey the area, the first-ever sanctioned by the Nova Scotia government. OME chartered a boat out of Halifax, moved a crew and equipment aboard, and—when weather permitted, a big proviso—ran an outstanding electronic survey. Though inconclusive without eyeball investigation using divers, the survey turned up one tantalizing hit after another.

In the off season of 2007, we went to court, the Supreme Court, in fact. And we won. They found that our rights had in fact been infringed upon, and the judge in open court reprimanded the province for their unsavory behavior in doing so. This was a nice moral victory, but under Canadian law, judicial reviews decide only whether an injustice was done. They do not award lost-opportunity or other damages. For that, we'd need to bring a separate suit against the province.

I put it to my investors, but instead of asking when do we start, they asked how much it would cost. Jim Gogan estimated considering the volume of work, the need for professional witnesses and legal opinions from various sources, and a host of other considerations, the cost could exceed several hundred thousand dollars. That was a fraction of the money they had invested in the *Fantome* fleet site, and with something close to $1 million of my own money and that of other small investors already spent, I begged my investors to proceed. But the world of treasure-recovery investment had changed along with treasure hunting itself, and as part of a diversified corporation instead of a group of like-minded people in it for the excitement, not only the return, they didn't want their money tied up in protracted court proceedings. Because I had nowhere near the resources to bring the suit myself, I was out the money.

And then in mid-2010, I heard the bad news announced by the provincial government. The long-standing Treasure Trove Act was set to be repealed at the end of that year. Somehow its opponents had convinced a body of like opinion that it made sense to preserve Nova Scotia's cultural artifacts by leaving them in the surf. This indifference to fact, leading to total neglect, is a travesty. We waited anxiously for the final decision.

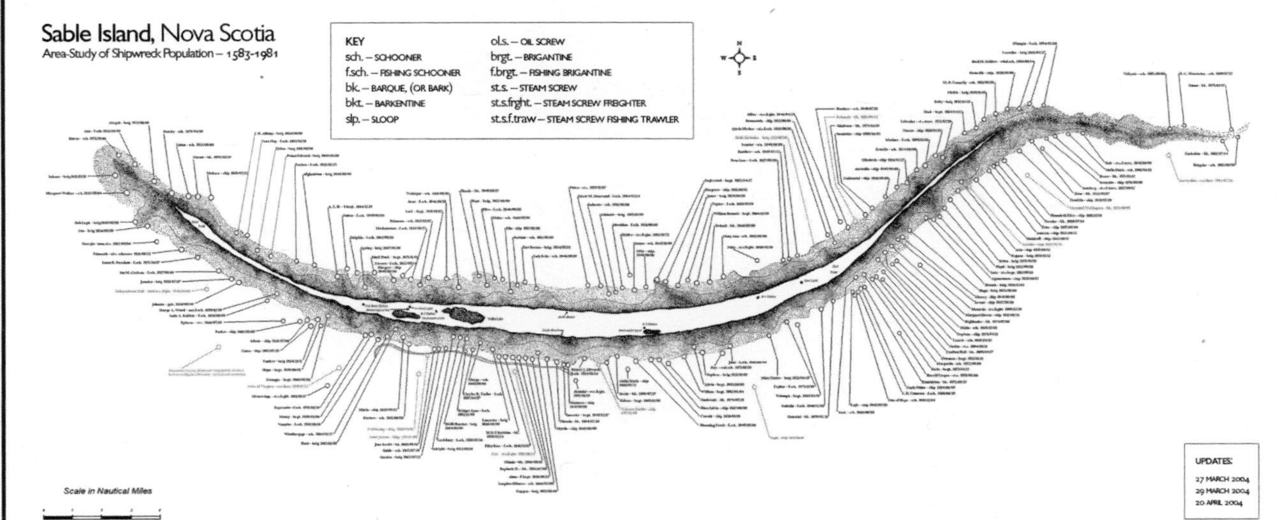

LIST OF VESSELS STRANDED AND/OR LOST AT SABLE ISLAND THAT ARE NOT PLOTTED, SHOWING NAME, RIG, AND DATE OF INCIDENTS:

ALBATROSS – sch. 1855/04/18
ALECTO – brgt. 1870/05/02
ARGO – brgt. 1860/09/10
ARGUS – sch. 1851/12/08
AURORA – ship 1777/08/28
BALGOLEY – bk. 1882/08/13
BRIDE – sch. 1880/11/28
BROTHERS – sch. 1826/01/22
BUCHANAN – ship 1757/04/22
CATHERINE – snow 1737/07/17
COMMERCE – ketch 1856/07/02
CONQUEST – bk. 1891/00/00
DELIGHT, HMS – galliot 1583/08/29
DELPHIA – brig 1826/00/00
EAGLE – sch. 1855/04/18
EURO-PRINCESS – ol.s. 1583/08/29
FAME MURPHY – ship 1779/00/00
FRANCIS, HMS – slp. 1799/00/00
FROLIC, HMB – brig 1823/00/00
GUSTAVE I – brig 1851/04/09
JANE – ship 1780/00/00
JOHN & MARY – ship 1725/00/00
LALEHAM – st.s. 1894/05/27
LEGERE, HFM – corvette 1746/09/14
LONA – sch. 1862/00/00
MANHASSET – st.s.frght. 1947/07/04
MARIE ANNE – f.sch. 1852/12/16
MARSHAL FOCH – f.sch. 1922/11/11
MARY & JANE – galliot 1633/00/00
MICHAEL WALLACE – brig 1836/00/00
MIDDLESEX, HMCS – corvette 1946/05/00
MINEHEAD – ship 1766/00/00
ORB – brig 1795/01/06
PLYMOUTH – sch. 1853/10/07
POTOWMACK – ship 1781/00/00
RAMBLER – ship 1792/00/00
RANGER – f.sch. 1852/12/18
REINDEER – sch. 1828/01/14
SAINT NICOLAS – ship 1861/04/15
SOPHIA – ship 1773/00/00
SWANSEY – ship 1771/00/00
TELEMACHUS – ship 1786/00/00
THOMAS & MARY – brgt. 1857/00/00
TROTT – ship 1801/00/00
UNIDENTIFIED – f.sch. 1760/12/00
VIVID – f.sch. 1891/08/18
WYOMING – st.s.frght. 1873/09/15
UNKNOWN BRITISH WARSHIP – 1760/11/17
5 FRENCH SHIPS OF THE FLEET OF DUC D'ANVILLE (3 WARSHIPS, 1 TRANSPORT & 1 SUPPLY SHIP OF WHICH HFM LEGERE IS ONE) – 1746/09/14

THE FRENCH FLEET WAS RETURNING FROM ITS UNSUCCESSFUL ATTEMPT AT REACHING LOUISBOURG TO RELIEVE THE LOCAL GARRISON FROM THE BRITISH SIEGE.

Redesigned by **Vibe Creative Group** *for* Capt. Robert MacKinnon

Original Map Courtesy of Nova Scotia Department of Tourism

AFTERWORD

Of course, they did in fact repeal the Treasure Trove Act. In-situ preservation, which is no preservation at all, has won the day. I suppose they would say that the repeal protects shipwrecks and their cultural artifacts from the raping of commercial treasure hunters like me until the province or the federal government gets around to respectful recovery. Let's assume that that is their reasoning (never mind that I worked under their own rules and with their approved scientists, never mind the absurdity of in-situ preservation itself) and take it at face value. All expenses considered, excavation and recovery have cost the investors about $10,000 a day. Do the now-victorious opponents of commercial treasure hunting really believe that they can raise that kind of money from taxpayers? Well, then, maybe they plan to defray costs by *selling* the coins, the gold, and the artifacts at, say, Stack's Auction House. If so, what makes them different from us? No, it doesn't make sense on any level; it's blind ideology.

The repeal of the Treasure Trove Act puts me out of business, but it has a broader impact. It means that nothing will be recovered. Under the terms of the act before repeal, the Nova Scotia Museum received 10 percent of the precious items recovered and all nonprecious artifacts. Now they'll get nothing because nothing will be recovered. That spoon we found on the *Fantome*—did it come from Dolley Madison's table on the day the British burned down the President's Palace, the first White House? And what about that round plaque with the bolt holes? Was it taken from the facade of a government building in Washington, D.C.? Will we ever know? (I still don't understand why no one in the U.S. government evinced any interest in such priceless historical artifacts.) We'll probably never know about the contents of this wreck, one of thousands, unless the Canadian government recognizes the folly and repeals the repeal.

My boat is ready to go lobstering. I've tuned the engine, changed the oil, loaded 275 traps aboard; the season opens the day after tomorrow. I'll be setting some of my traps in the very same waters that claimed wrecks I discovered, since lobsters like to hide among the very reefs, ledges, and sunkers that killed so many ships. But I'm still thinking of myself as a treasure hunter, and there are glimmers of hope that I'll be able to act like one before long.

Via its claim of sovereign immunity, England now owns the *Fantome* site. Perhaps even now, they're readying a team of qualified archaeologists and divers with intimate knowledge of these waters. Perhaps they've hired a boat and a shoreside support crew and arranged lodging for about 50 people in East Dover. But if not, perhaps they would be interested in engaging one who has already done those things to work the *Fantome* fleet wreck site. There is talk along these lines, but my friends and colleagues would not like me to discuss details. We shall see.

The engine sounds excellent at all rpms. The traps are rigged and ready with buoys attached. It's tough work, lobstering; you have to tend every trap every day beginning about three in the morning. The projected price of lobster is down, the cost of bait is up, but there's nothing new in that over the last two centuries. Still, I love life on the water. That was one reason why I wanted to go treasure hunting in the first place.

APPENDIX 1

Treasure Hunting: The Techniques of Discovery and Recovery from Shallow-Water Shipwrecks

Shipwrecks that took place during the days of sail occurred throughout the world's oceans and beyond, in any place a ship could travel, including rivers, lakes, and inland waterways. Most were wrecked close to the shores of a recognized landmass, in shoal water. For sailing ships wrecked in the shallow waters along Nova Scotia's over 7,000 kilometers of coastline, the result was usually tragic for the vessel, cargo, crew, and passengers. The foreshore of Nova Scotia is polluted with dangerous reefs, sunkers, and thousands of offshore islands and low-rising sandbars—a prime example is Sable Island, the famous "Graveyard of the Atlantic." That's a name it richly deserves, reflecting not only the enormous loss of ships this small offshore sandbar has claimed over the centuries but also the thousands of lives lost by those unfortunates who sailed on them. The inshore waters of Nova Scotia provide a no-less-daunting record, with over 10,000 shipwrecks known to have occurred. Maybe even as many are unknown and unrecorded. As a result, tens of thousands of passengers and crew members lost their lives and millions of tons of cargo never reached their intended ports of destination.

Around the world, marine, geologic, weather, and tidal conditions differ greatly. Some areas have deep sand covering the seafloor, running from the high-water mark out to sea, many miles from shore. Others offer a shoreline predominantly made up of exposed bedrock, reefs, hidden sunkers, and cliffs, some rising hundreds of feet out of the sea. The latter is what Nova Scotia offers any unfortunate ship that finds itself tangled in her maritime web, totally dominated by such destructive forces. The territorial seas of Nova Scotia are susceptible to hurricane-force winds and vicious, unrelenting storms that can last for days, tossing great walls of water on her shores. Strong tides run constantly, converging at times to create some of the most dangerous rips and side currents this planet has to offer. It is in these very waters I honed my craft as a treasure hunter, hard-fought experience gained over decades of diving in miserable weather conditions, strong tides, unpredictable winds, and unrelenting swells born in the deep ocean that constantly pound the exposed shoreline.

A treasure hunter is not born as such; he or she evolves and grows within a marine environment, gaining skills and experience that are not easily attained as much as hard earned. That is the lot of a serious treasure hunter; nothing comes easy. Instinct plays a major role in success; luck plays another. My experience—and it may differ from that of other successful salvers—is to try to live in the moment, transcend to the time the wreck occurred, long before I consider any in-depth research.

So the first step is to try to visualize the ship, the area where it wrecked, and the conditions in which it wrecked. Form a mental image of the event, letting it come alive in your mind and going over all possible aspects of the tragedy, again and again. In the end, the treasure hunter will feel an affinity with the shipwreck and the area where the event took place. When you finally arrive on the wreck site, after its discovery by physical or electronic means, you will recognize the area immediately and quickly sense what has to be done to effect a successful recovery. This premature and private psychoanalysis of such a historic event is always key to understanding it in a modern context. It is also the key needed to unlock the secrets of a shipwreck, firmly secured, dispersed, and hidden by the sea, for perhaps centuries.

Research

Research can be a double-edged sword; in most cases it is invaluable. However, when researching certain shipwreck events using contemporary sources, you can find inaccurate if not downright misleading information. You have to consider when using research as an aid to finding a shipwreck that current information may be incomplete and challenged by contemporary information only available at the time the wrecking event occurred. Research after discovery however becomes an invaluable tool not just for sorting out the story behind the shipwreck but for helping with artifact identification.

A vast majority of the shipwrecks lost within the jurisdictional waters of Nova Scotia carried contraband in one form or another, precious metals, specie, and gems not officially listed as cargo. The reasons for this are as obvious as they are misleading when considering the true value of a shipwreck from the colonial period. For example, the actual cargoes that may have been carried by the *Fantome* fleet and the pay ship *Le Chameau* at the time of loss still remain far from understood. Ships during the colonial period also carried private consignments of bullion and specie. They even carried riches taken as prizes of war, acts of piracy, and the actions of sanctioned privateers, much of which went unrecorded.

In the case of the *Fantome* fleet, there is real mystery as to the treasure source and the part the captured American vessels may have played in this maritime event, including where they were captured. We only know they were registered from the port of Alexandria prior to 1814, so we strongly suspect they were taken during the raid on Washington at Alexandria. We also know that on their final voyage to Halifax, the ships were leaving Castine, Maine, escorted by the brig HMS *Fantome*. The brig was lost, with all records of the voyage going to the bottom with her. What does that mean? It means there was a court-martial, but no treasure was verified in the testimony of the brig's captain for probably very sound reasons. These reasons might have included admiralty security concerns or possibly the fact contraband was involved.

In my professional opinion, only a naïve individual would think or state there was no treasure involved, no value to the site. Especially not after all the fuss made over the fleet and strong irrefutable evidence supplied by the first to final salvers who investigated this site, from the 1960s to 2006. This includes the vast amount of treasure I witnessed firsthand during those three dives in 1975 and later in 2005 and 2006.

In fact, a large hoard of silver coins was reported as recovered from this site directly to the Nova Scotia government by a previous treasure trove license holder. This happened during the mid- to late 1990s, a recovery that, as declared, exceeded 10,000 mixed coins.

This disclosure was never followed up on by the Nova Scotia authority responsible, although it had periodic communications with the individuals involved. This failure on the part of the provincial licensing authority to validate the salvers' claim and demand delivery of the treasure trove involved is a direct departure from terms and conditions of the Nova Scotia Treasure Trove Act.

So the story takes on yet another mysterious twist: Where did these coins come from and where are they now? Were they part of the fleet's treasure, the very same treasure we witnessed spread all over the claim site in 2005 and 2006? All of this information was included in our many official site reports and map logs, submitted to the permitting authority.

Finally, during a lecture concerning my relationship with the *Fantome* fleet that I gave in Halifax several years ago at the Nova Scotia Maritime Museum of the Atlantic, I became aware of other substantial treasure recoveries from this claim. In front of approximately 200 in attendance, local divers admitted to recovering everything from coins to silver ingots from this site. They even had pictures of the recovered treasure to support their contentions. To simply say all of this *Fantome* fuss is over a barrel of coins, as has been reported in the province's print media, surely comes from the minds of the *great unwashed.*

In the case of the pay ship *Le Chameau*, the whole issue surrounding what precious cargo she actually carried is overshadowed by the fact it came from both public and private sources. Most of it is traceable as to ownership and amount, but a good portion might have been placed on board in France by private interests without the benefit of written record.

Research before and after discovery becomes an invaluable tool to help sort out the story behind the shipwreck, and post-recovery research is an important aid in artifact identification. To say proper historical records and reports were not kept would be a wildly inaccurate statement. To say such shipping records are always 100 percent complete would also be a wildly inaccurate and careless statement. In the end, such a mind-set defeats the reality our recovery operations have proven to be true beyond any and all reasonable doubt.

Personally I do not profess to be a research expert. In fact, I come from the old school of salvers basing my shipwreck knowledge on what I see underwater and in the end recover from these precious maritime sites. This is not to say I do not place a very strong emphasis on background research, I do. Research is a tool, one of the many a salver has to have aboard should success be the motivation. However, nothing is more important than transcending back to the time a particular ship was wrecked, creating the scene over and over in your mind until you can clearly visualize it, giving it life.

Research and the **Fantome** *Fleet*

There is another aspect to pre-recovery research that many salvers overlook. That is, why would the cargo of any shipwreck be worth considering, beyond the obvious assumption that it carried some form of treasure? The answer is simple. If a salver knows there may be very rare artifacts, including specie, involved, versus the normal array of silver and copper coins, research is truly invaluable.

In the case of the *Fantome* fleet, my research turned up some very interesting numismatic facts. The *Fantome* fleet carried plunder in many forms, taken from the young United States during the War of 1812. There is one group of precious artifacts we have proven to be involved: coins minted in the United States prior to 1814. That alone would not be earth-shattering compared against coins minted in other countries prior to 1814, except for one reason: The United States did not begin minting coins until 1793. This goes to rarity.

Using the *Guide Book of United States Coins* as the reference per se, a savvy treasure hunter dealing with a loss of rare coins such as the *Fantome* fleet represents, involved in commerce raids against the United States, would key in on what is valuable and what is not. Once this is accomplished, proving that even one rare coin would be worth the effort, an experienced salver would lay out a search and recovery plan.

In the overall recovery of early American coins a salver would expect to find on this wreck site, he or she may come across extremely rare samples of those first coins minted after 1793 or just prior. In fact, the salver may find a Brasher doubloon minted in New York and dated 1787. The Brasher doubloon is a very rare American gold coin that is worth in today's market over $750,000. Even in G to VG condition—the numismatic symbols for *good* and *very good*—such high values could be expected at auction.

Piquing my professional interest even further are the many unsubstantiated reports that the 1804 silver dollar, the rarest silver coin in the world, was found on this site. In fact, two 1804 silver dollars were reported as recovered in the late 1960s. There is a lot of controversy over whether or not 1804 silver dollars were minted and found their way into circulation in 1804. United States mint records prove over 19,000 were minted in the first quarter of 1804. This seems proof positive that even a few of these rare coins could have been stored in the treasury at Washington or the customs house in Castine, Maine. It is not really *impossible* to believe that some of these rare coins actually found their way onto one or more of the vessels involved in the loss of the *Fantome* fleet at Prospect, Nova Scotia, in November of 1814.

The mysteries surrounding the origin of not just these 1804 silver dollars but also the 15 or so that are known to exist in collections and museums have transcended time, with a few specimens sold at auction. According to Krause Publications' *Standard Catalog of World Coins* (the bible of coin collectors), there are 15 known specimens of this 1804 Draped Bust dollar. In fact, at least one sold at Child's auction for $4,100,000 in August 1999. Even American coins of lesser rarity from this period, such as quarter eagles ($2.50 gold pieces) and half eagles ($5.00 gold pieces) minted between 1796 and 1810, could fetch over $100,000 at auction. Rarer pieces may even fetch several thousand more.

Based on these numismatic facts, it is not hard to understand the attraction. The right mix of early American copper, silver, and gold coins recovered from the Phantom Cove claim could easily top well over $200,000,000 in value, well worth the investor's risk!

Late News

Just recently, on January 4, 2012, a copper cent struck at the Philadelphia mint in 1793, called a Chain cent, was offered for sale in Florida by Heritage Auctions and sold for an astounding $1,380,000. Now, the treasure hunter in me knows full well that coins of this lesser value in 1793 would be common on period shipwreck sites such as the *Fantome* fleet represents, carrying plunder back to Halifax during the latter part of the War of 1812. In fact, in 2006 our divers witnessed, supported by photographs, copper coins that resembled in every possible way the 1793 Chain cent.

It concerns me, as it should all Nova Scotians, that here on this particular site, very rare colonial coins, many of which are American, all predating 1814, are destined to be lost forever. In fact, most are laid out in the open unprotected, strewn all over the Phantom Cove claim site. These rare coins, really rare and valuable maritime artifacts, will be lost due to a general and unchallenged indifference. How can this not be scientifically immoral, especially where our maritime culture is concerned?

Research in Reverse

It had been rumored for years that the pay ship *Le Chameau* carried, as part of her precious cargo, valuable religious artifacts. It was believed that lost along with her cargo of coins, a salver might expect to find gold and silver chalices, crucifixes, and other rare ornaments. It was not until the 2004 recovery season that we came across what we positively identified as precious artifacts belonging to the Catholic Church.

In an area between the main impact site near Chameau Rock and the shore to the north-northwest, we began to recover a very different type of silverware, ornate with strange symbols on the handles, unlike any we had recovered previously. In the same area we located and recovered scores of silver plates bearing the same crests and symbols and then a silver crucifix.

Once these items were cleaned in our conservation lab, the archaeologist had a better chance to examine the markings. This led to the discovery that they were in fact religious utensils placed on board *Le Chameau* for delivery to the churches of Quebec and Fortress Louisbourg. Again, research played an integral part in artifact identification.

Investment

After discovery and qualifying the intentions of making a claim and developing the recovery plan, a salver is faced with a big decision: how to financially support such an undertaking. This business is not for the foolhardy daydreamer *or* the magazine-inspired treasure hunter. It is a business filled with more disappointments than rewards, based on one very simple principal: The recovery has to be of a type and quantity to justify both the time and the investment involved. This happens in only the rarest of cases. That is why treasure hunting, in whatever form it takes, is considered one of the highest-risk investment scenarios one could ever become involved in.

To lessen the risk considerably, the investor needs to know the person or group in which the investment is to be directed. Two considerations are never invest until you speak with the person in charge, and check for proof of prior experience and related discoveries and recoveries. Failure to adhere to these very basic investment principals places any loss of investment squarely in the hands of the investor, *not the salver.* As an investor, you want to make a profit using your money. The treasure hunter, intending to hunt for treasure, seeks investment capital to help make this happen. If the investor does not understand the risks and rewards 100 percent, the responsibility for any subsequent loss lies totally with the investor. The investor *must* build in checks and balances concerning the investment that need to be clearly understood by both parties. Investors would be advised to stay away from any party that cannot prove at least one major recovery.

One final issue for the investor to consider is the long-term need for and the expectations of continued financial support that the project will most likely require to achieve completion. Project completion is the key to success. Short-term projects are subject to many uncontrollable factors that limit recovery, and limited recovery has a direct effect on the reward side of the equation.

As a rule of thumb, short-term projects should be financed as exploratory recovery opportunities only. Unless there are other extenuating circumstances, success alone should warrant further major investment. Once there is a bond of understanding and trust established between the salver and the investor, both parties may want to consider the benefits of taking their operation public. If the opportunity looks solid and the need for capital will span a period of perhaps many years, this is a better way to raise funding, but it comes with its own set of reporting requirements and government restrictions. Simply put, do not invest if you are not fully aware of the ongoing planning and operational strategies. Second, don't invest in the treasure-recovery business if you can't afford to take the associated risks involved, risks every investor needs to clearly understand and evaluate.

Technique

The word *technique* surely covers a wide range of complicated and technical subject matter when it comes to describing the actual everyday business of treasure hunting. The scope of just how complicated is governed by one important factor: Has the shipwreck been found or is the main object to find it? This deciding factor is closely followed by two other very important considerations: If the wreck has been found, what are the water depth and the wreck's location? If not located, what is the planned intensity of the search program?

When you know the value of a shipwreck site, especially when it's in shallow water, the dynamics are a little less complicated. If the shipwreck is known to you but it exists in deep water, over 150 feet, the project takes on a completely different set of development considerations. When the exact location for the shipwreck of interest is not known, a very different thought process on the part of both the salver and investor is required. The cost to find the wreck can easily mirror the cost of recovery.

Recovery projects in the early 1970s to late 1980s consisted of some very simple operational principals and techniques. On most hard-bottom sites you will almost certainly be required to deal with huge boulders, some weighing over one ton, sitting on areas you wish to explore. This condition is all too common and difficult to deal with. Our method of choice has been either to work around the obstruction or, when that is not possible, to move the object slightly to one side or the other of the area planned for excavation. Another method is to excavate up to the object in question and then move it back into the area already excavated; this is the more scientifically approved and sought-after solution.

Once clearing a general work area has been achieved, then baselines and sometimes grid sectional squares made of iron rebar are set in place to give greater control over the excavation and tie in the location of artifacts throughout the recovery process. It is at this point that a prudent salver will set out certain initiatives, employing drift tests of free-floating objects to see where they end up in a variety of surface conditions. Here it is important to understand the effect of tide and wind on wreckage debris. The first drift test uses objects that are floating high on the surface of the water, which are affected mostly by wind. The second drift test involves a wooden object of some considerable size—for example, a large wooden crate weighed down so it floats low in the water with no more than 10 percent of the structure exposed above the surface. This test is intended to let you observe where wreckage affected almost entirely by tidal flow would normally track. The drift experiment needs to be repeated during the normal tidal conditions prevalent to the area of interest. It is also important to know, if possible, the phase of the moon at the time the ship wrecked. This information will confirm a period of flood or slack tides. One or the other will have a major effect on the overall distribution of wreckage, both sections of wreck under the surface and those that may have been floating free, high in the water.

Site Development

Site development is a very spacious term. Here is where most salvers and even more investors see money and opportunity lost, investing in a myth or some story that was contrived to gain investment where the opportunity could not be properly proven as worth the risk. It's common to think of the process as first you find it, then you finance it, and then you develop it—not so! You need a development plan *before* you seek investment. This path will direct the amount of investment required and the time line over which it is needed. Site development consists of four major components: research, sensing, establishment of site boundaries, and sample recoveries resulting from sensing or initial discoveries, all combined with a solid and ongoing operations plan. Finally, knowledge of what you may find is paramount, including the value and venue for final distribution at a private sale or auction. Knowing and understanding these very simple rules protects the investor and salver alike. These are the initial factors that help guarantee success.

Developing a proper research, sensing, and recovery plan long before the major operations investment capital kicks in is prudent, if not the only sensible way to proceed. Initial limited investment to help set up the operations (lab equipment, sensing operations, and initial research) is an acceptable expense. This investment should be considered part of the cost of doing business.

A precolonial or postcolonial wooden ship that was lost in shallow water, constantly attacked by the turbulent forces of the open ocean, requires a totally different development and recovery plan from a ship lost in very deep water. The issue here surrounds the size of the debris field. In shallow water, it could be immense, covering up to or over one square mile. In deep water (over 250 feet), the shipwreck or wreckage will most likely remain fairly confined within the area where the initial event occurred, maybe even confined to an area no larger than 500 square feet. Once an experienced salver locates the shipwreck's main impact site or related debris field, the development and implementation of a well-thought-out operations plan is the first order of business. Initial concerns should cover jurisdictional and employee issues, local labor laws, closest hyperbaric chamber, hospitals, transportation links, accommodations, and so on. Really, the list can be endless.

Excavation

The main method of excavation involves the employment of a tried and long-proven method known as *hand fanning*. On some sites it is necessary to employ a rather time-consuming plan that involves removing by hand almost all of the existing boulders, rocks of a medium size, and larger cobble from the area intended for excavation. The reality and practicality of cleaning the work area before excavation begins serves two purposes. The first benefit is not having to continually move material around inside the excavation area. The second is all about having a better control in place, especially if a valuable and significant recovery is involved. Oddly enough, when you discuss this methodology with an investor, nine times out of ten he or she will ask you to skip the initial site setup process and get right down to recovery. It is impossible to work with that type of investor, one who will try to push a project to places that will only put the money and the overall project at risk. Faced with such outside pressure, a savvy salver must walk away until his or her advice is adhered to.

Finally, when it comes to the technology of starting the search and recovery process, you must have a proper datum point securely located in the bottom, which is *never* moved for any reason until the project is over. We usually use, when possible, a major geologic feature, such as a reef or ravine. It does not matter as long as it will remain as a constant to the excavation. This same concept holds true for surface electronic surveys; a constant datum point, usually a large buoy or major feature on shore, is beyond essential.

Underwater Handheld Metal Detectors

The subject of underwater metal detectors is the material for a book of its own. I will, however, make a few observations based on my experience. Underwater metal detectors have their place in the survey and recovery plan, but, and that's a big *but*, the operator needs to know how to properly use one. There are many brands available, capable of different results, from poor to excellent. Without going into which brand we prefer and why, there are some facts to consider when looking for coins, especially single coins: the size of the coin, the metal involved—gold, silver, or copper—and how it may be situated within the subsurface matrix. You also need to consider how deep in the overburden of rock, sand, gravel, and shell hash you expect to find artifacts. Here success is determined by what depth the detector has to penetrate to find a single coin. This dynamic changes greatly if the target is made up of a large clump of coins, a large iron object, or lead. The larger the metal object—the deeper in the subbottom for the discovery. A basic rule of thumb would be that a metal detector fully charged and tuned should be capable of finding a silver dollar–size coin in one to two feet of sand and gravel and a group of dollar-size silver coins in two to three feet of sand and gravel overburden.

However, there is another sensing dynamic at play here. A trained operator must take into consideration: How will the object, especially a coin, present itself to the search coil? Will it lie flat in two feet of subbottom material, presenting a fairly large target, or will it be on edge only, presenting only a very small target? The recovery results can differ greatly, and many valuable coins can be missed. This loss of such interpretive wreck data may mislead the recovery operations away from hot spots to locations of little value within the search area.

When coins, for example, present themselves on edge versus lying flat, the type of metal and the signature it reflects become extremely important. Even though they are still an alloy with a slight copper content for hardness, gold coins, as a rule, give off a very weak electronic signature. Silver, on the other hand, presents a very strong electronic signature. Turn a small gold coin on edge and the detector will have trouble registering the hit in more than one foot of subbottom cover. Often, a salvage master will direct the top layer of overburden (rocks and gravel) be removed to lessen the depth the metal detector has to penetrate. If the precious artifacts and coins have worked themselves down to bedrock in a location where the overburden is deeper than three feet, this practice is definitely warranted.

On-Site Conservation Protocol

On-site conservation protocol is a complicated subject. However, for our purposes, one rule needs to be strictly adhered to: Do not, *in fact never*, let an artifact recovered from a saltwater shipwreck remain on deck. It must be stored in a suitable saline solution or it will begin to dry out. There are two major concerns at play here. First, the artifact begins to deteriorate immediately after being introduced to fresh air. The second concern is really based on common sense: All artifacts recovered from a saltwater environment—even gold—require a certain level of conservation. This should be accomplished within the confines of a suitable conservation lab set up for this express purpose and placed in the hands of an experienced maritime conservator. If an artifact is delivered to the workboat and left to dry out in the fresh air, the conservator's work is needlessly multiplied. The final result may be reduced from what it could have been if the artifact was handled and stored properly *from the very second* it was discovered. The process to protect and conserve cultural shipwreck material really begins underwater.

Shipwrecks or Grave Sites

Many professionals and sovereign owners of naval ships laden with treasure at the time of loss profess the ludicrous idea that a shipwreck site is indeed a grave site and as such it should be left alone, the cargo protected from treasure hunters. In some cases, the presentation of this theory has been useful to stop treasure and nontreasure artifacts from being legally and scientifically recovered by the private sector. It has universally muddied the waters of controlled scientific excavations funded and carried out by the private sector, the only really viable source of venture capital currently available.

It is a fact that a shipwreck site is the grave site of the ship; however, the wrecking process distributes almost every part of the wreck—including the unfortunate people who perished—far from the original impact site. In shoal water, most of the passengers and crew who died on a shipwreck would have been tossed up on the beach to be either buried or consumed by the sea and sand. In the case of the *Auguste* and *Le Chameau* shipwrecks, most of the victims were washed up on the beaches immediately opposite both wreck sites. Many more were washed ashore miles from the shipwreck. Some were washed back out to sea by tide and wind, there to be consumed at depth. The only exception may be sailors trapped in pressure vessels, like submarines, but of course in time their tomb will fully deteriorate and their remains will be claimed by the sea.

Accidents on our highways claim thousands of lives every year, yet the thoroughfare is not abandoned; the accident scene is cleared away and traffic resumes. When terrorists destroy our buildings, claiming innocent lives in the process, we do not cease the resumption of normal activity; we raise a fitting memorial and honor the dead. This is the sensible way to remember the passengers and crew of a single ship or the entire maritime losses of a certain geographic area. Interfering with a process that acts to preserve our cultural maritime history under the guise or myth that somehow a shipwreck site represents a graveyard is a deceptive and extremely misleading theory or policy.

APPENDIX 2

A Brief History of the Provincial Silver: The First Coins of Colonial North America

The story of money in the Americas covers a period of over three centuries. It begins with the settlers of New England. They carried on a fur trade with the friendly Indians, using a form of exchange referred to as wampum—mussel shells fashioned into beads, usually threaded on a belt or leather thong. During those early days, the colonists had no to very little use for money in the form of coin; they developed a strong barter system for dealing with the procurement of their everyday needs. When they began to trade in earnest with foreigners from Europe, traders preferred coin (bullion) over wampum, the local medium of exchange. As a result, the colonists petitioned England to provide them with gold, silver coins, even their own form of small-change currency.

England ignored the plight of the North American colonists, continually denying their request for hard currency. Their agitation to gain a standard coinage reached its peak in 1651. England was on the brink of civil war between the Puritans and the Royalists, and thus ignored the colonists, who eventually took matters into their own hands. Although coins from the Sommer Islands (now Bermuda), called hogge money, were provided from around 1616 onward, they could not meet the colonies' demand for a standard hard currency. Finally, in 1652, the General Court of the Colony granted the minting of a series of silver coins—shillings and half and quarter shillings, known as Massachusetts shillings—and sixpence and threepence coins. Silver bullion was first procured from the West Indies, then from local sources, including melted-down silver items such as silverware, clipped foreign coins, and certain foreign currencies of a lesser face value.

The authority was granted to John Hull in the Massachusetts Bay Colony to begin minting silver coins only in 1652. Joseph Jenks, owner of the Saugus Iron Works, north of Boston, was given the job of making the dies (punches) for the first coins. Hull was appointed mint master, and Robert Sanderson, his assistant. Although Spain established a mint in 1535 at Mexico City, the shillings minted near Boston in 1652 were the first coins minted in the English Americas. At that time other colonies, such as Maryland and New Jersey, had coins minted in both England and Ireland for specific use within that jurisdiction. The New England coins of 1652 became the official currency of the colonies, minted from 1652 to 1682. The minting of New England coinage was abandoned in 1682, and a petition to renew the coinage in 1686 was denied by the General Court of the Colony. All coins minted had the same date, 1652, to give the impression they were minted during the English Civil War, when Cromwell was in power.

The first coins minted were called NE pieces or NE shillings; they were stamped with a single impression on each side. On one side the coins showed the initials *NE* in the upper quadrant; on the reverse, the stamp contained the roman numeral *XII*. The six- and threepence coins had Roman numerals *VI* and *III*, respectively, on one side, and the *NE* on the opposite side remained standard.

The Tree Series of New England Coins—1652

The next year, to avoid clipping of the NE shilling, an act the simplicity of its design invited counterfeiters to commit, a new series of coins were introduced from 1653 to 1682. They are commonly referred to as the New England tree coins. The willow tree was the first insignia of a tree to be used. It was followed by the oak tree and finally the pine tree. The mint maintained the same spread of denominations, except in the oak tree series, which included a twopence piece dated 1662. The coins were crude by design, minted on a very thin silver flan, easily corrupted by excessive usage, physical damage, clipping, or immersion in salt water.

Many of the shillings were purposely bent into a shape that resembled a wave in the silver. Such coins were called witch pieces and were rumored to ward off evil. The deformed coins were reported as popular in the Salem and Gloucester areas. However, they still maintained their legal value and were traded for goods throughout all of the colonies. As time passed, the New England coins mixed in with the other common silver coins of the era and were used throughout the colonies. This grouping became known as the *provincial silver.*

The Spanish milled dollar, valued at eight reales—commonly referred to as the pillar dollar or piece of eight—is linked with romantic fiction in a way that no other coin has ever been. The time-honored coin and its fractional parts (half, one, two, and four reales) were the principal coins of the American colonies. They were the precursor of the American silver dollar. Even after the first coins were minted in the young

United States, beginning in 1793, the pillar dollar remained legal currency in the States and continued to officially circulate until 1857.

The Historic Significance and Numismatic Value of New England Coins in Modern Times

Although examples exist of almost every coin in the New England series, they are considered to be the rarest silver coins minted in North America. Only one coin stands out as a rarer specimen, having the greatest value of any silver coin known to collectors today: the 1804 American silver dollar. From a history standpoint, the story behind the New England coins minted from 1652 to 1682 signifies the colonists' continuous struggle to be recognized by the English Crown as a viable entity within the existing British Empire. Those coins, once they were introduced into circulation in 1652, allowed the colonists to gain much needed control over trade and development within New England. Their introduction opened up worldwide markets that demanded payment in bullion currency. Their very existence and use throughout the world added strength to the colonists' bargaining position, enabling them to do business on a global scale. The old barter system, although it still existed in New England, soon became reserved for the benefit of the local economy, much as it exists today.

Massachusetts shillings (New England coins) and their fractional counterparts are some of the most sought-after early coins minted in North America. They are rare and always in demand. Some of the more common are coins from the pine tree series, which, depending on condition, usually sell for several thousand dollars each; rarer varieties sell for much more. The oak tree coins are also desirable, although there are fewer available for sale. Thus the price they fetch at auction is usually higher than that of a similar pine tree coin. Because far fewer willow tree coins were minted between 1653 and 1660, they are the rarest of the tree coins, some selling at auction for over $100,000 each, again depending on rarity and condition. Finally, the NE shillings, the first series of silver coins minted by John Hull at Saugus, Massachusetts, from 1652 to 1653, are generally considered to be the rarest and most sought-after silver coins minted in colonial America. Collectors consider it a privilege even to have the opportunity to bid on such rare coins. This sentiment is much stronger in the United States due to the coin's connection to the nation's colonial past.

APPENDIX 3

Nova Scotia's Cultural Shipwreck Resources

It is generally believed that between 10,000 and 20,000 shipwrecks occurred within Nova Scotia's Territorial Sea over the past 400 years. I believe the number is closer to 20,000, considering the unknown, unrecorded shipwreck events that took place at remote places, such as Sable Island, St. Paul Island, and Scatarie Island. Even with the current technology available to the salver and scientist, only a small percentage of these wrecks have been discovered or will be discovered. I believe this figure represents less than half of 1 percent, and that is being generous.

The end result of my professional assessment is obvious. Over 99 percent of the shipwrecks lost within the territorial sea of Nova Scotia will go undiscovered; thus they will be lost to the knowledge of humankind forever. Nova Scotia, in fact Canada in general, working with outdated, archaic maritime management programs, has struggled to both protect this resource and attempt to address private-sector involvement. The provincial legislative initiatives in the form of the Nova Scotia Treasure Trove Act and the Nova Scotia Special Places Protection Act, although in need of reform, represent very progressive and positive attempts to protect this cultural resource in favor of the people of Nova Scotia. Within Nova Scotia's territorial sea, jurisdiction is not an issue, nor should it be. The confusion comes into play when outside conventions such as sovereign immunity are introduced. This only enhances the gray areas surrounding the rights of the original owner versus the claim holder and the jurisdictional authority of the province to manage such cultural resources.

Around 2005, serious cracks appeared in the long-standing use of the Nova Scotia Treasure Trove Act allowing a salver to legally lay a time-controlled claim over a predetermined geographical portion of seabed within the territorial waters of Nova Scotia. This system is based on the same principals used to allow claim staking in the land-based mineral industry but also extends to offshore petroleum claims and more. The Treasure Trove Act was not designed to protect shipwrecks. It was designed to control access and protect the interests of the people of Nova Scotia. It was also designed to collect appropriate royalties and related fees from an approved ministerial license holder.

The Special Places Protection Act does not represent the jurisdictional authority. Its main purpose is to protect Nova Scotia's cultural resources. Shipwrecks over 50 years old fall under the designation of a *historical cultural resource*, which this legislation effectively controls.

The act includes a strict science protocol through which a series of research permits allow for varying levels of resource disturbance and recovery; permits can be applied for by the approved and licensed claim holder. The only situation that does not require the involvement of an archaeologist is the opportunity for a proven individual or group to receive a Class A Reconnaissance Research Permit. However, this heritage permit comes with its own unique set of guidelines and reporting requirements.

Over the past 25 to 35 years, this combination of checks and balances provided by both forms of provincial legislation allowed scientifically controlled, legal access to the shipwrecks of Nova Scotia. This system worked rather well, and those who chose to work within the system found it relatively easy to respond to both the provincial requirement and the ongoing industry concerns. Recently, many outside forces, mostly made up of agenda-driven individuals who do not or, through indifference, choose not to understand the benefits of the existing legislation, have been calling for the repeal of the Nova Scotia Treasure Trove Act.

The province has responded on more than one occasion by adopting interdepartmental studies, public meetings, and periodic legislation revisions, but to no avail. Within the past few years the province decided to place the whole Treasure Trove Act issue and how it interfaces with the Special Places Protection Act into the hands of an unbiased third party (under contract) to study the issue and provide solutions. This study has been completed, and the report, referenced as the Blackstone Report, was recently presented to the province with its recommendations. Although the general public is not privy to internal recommendations, industry intelligence understands that the Blackstone Report respects the existing legislative status quo. The main focal point of the report makes observations and offers constructive suggestions that would see both acts reformed to better serve the provincial clients involved.

I realized many years ago that the current Special Places legislation was never designed, at least in its present form, to manage the maritime cultural shipwreck resource with which it had been tasked. On the other hand, I believe that both pieces of provincial legislation, with some modifications, are adequate and proactive tools that allow for private-sector involvement. Repealing the Treasure Trove Act and leaving the

Special Places Protection Act to deal with this issue is a recipe for disaster, leading to an even greater loss of what is left to be recovered from a finite cultural resource.

The private sector needs a clear and concise opportunity, one that is easy to understand, one that is not fraught with controversy or susceptible to instability and constant change. If you take private industry and the financing it brings to the table, even though it is a for-profit group, out of the equation, everyone loses. The remaining maritime cultural resources left for collection are condemned to total degradation, lost forever.

A small province like Nova Scotia, with a limited tax base, will never have the funding available to scratch the surface to even look for—not to mention scientifically excavate—these shipwrecks. More to the point, it cannot commit the multimillions of dollars that the discovery and recovery operations of only one ancient shipwreck could eventually cost. Thus taking the private sector off the table and allowing the current opportunity to make a profit (a foul word to the purist being paid from the public purse) represents draconian thinking, resulting in the loss of a significant aspect of Nova Scotia's maritime history.

The position now of the hands of the maritime clock represents the final opportunity to save what can be saved. They are surely and scientifically proven to be close to the eleven o'clock hour. The clock continues to tick away to the inevitable—midnight and the close of day for this resource and the overall loss it represents to Nova Scotia and the world. This is a needless and most unfortunate condition that denies the opportunity (worldwide) to salvage what remains of valuable resources for scientific collection. In this case, *if* the provincial legislative regimes enacted for the main purpose of protection were allowed to work within the intended duality of their purpose, what is left of this Nova Scotia cultural resource and who would reap the benefit? The current legislative model has industry and government working together toward a common and no-less-lofty goal. The status quo truly represents the interests of all Nova Scotians, and thus, in the end, maritime heritage *lost* that could have been saved is no less than unforgivable.

Other Major Discoveries

Over the last thirty-five-plus years, I have either discovered or investigated at least 100 treasure-laden ships wrecked along the shores of Nova Scotia, Newfoundland, New Brunswick, Maine, and Massachusetts. Most were lost during North America's colonial period. For this book, I picked five treasure sites that seemed appropriate as to time spent on each in research, recovery, conservation, and final dispensation of the artifacts involved.

In the early years diving with Ronnie Blundon, we were finding a shipwreck of value every other month. This location process carried on when Jim Mullins began to dive with me in the mid-1970s, leading to the discovery of *Auguste*, lost in Aspy Bay in 1761. One of the most valuable shipwrecks I discovered with Jim Mullins back in 1976 lies halfway between Woody Point at the southwestern end of the *Le Chameau* claim and the entrance to Baleine five miles north of Louisbourg Harbor. Research and identification of the artifacts found indicate the following high-value discovery, one we never really had the opportunity to excavate:

> Marie sans Pareille, *of Marseille; left Que. for L.R. on 3-11-1745 under Capt. Henry Vincent with a valuable cargo of furs & specie profits [registered at over one million livre] for La Compagnie Rouennaise De Niganiche, (agent for the Compagnie des Indes), after wintering at Que., and was lost at Baleine, several leagues north of Fortress*

Louisbourg; owned by Joachim Suriam; J.N. BEAUJON had her heavily insured.

—Parran (Bx.) 22-11-1747 (printed); Archives nationales, Paris, Fonds des Colonies, C11A 38 fol. 262, 83 fol. 363.

L.R.—La Rochelle.

A few years earlier, Ronnie and I found a major French treasure ship in a small cove, just south of where Grand River meets the sea, twelve miles south of Point Michaud. We only had the opportunity to make a few dives on this site. We observed thousands of silver and gold coins in concretion, silverware, cannon, ships fittings, anchors, round and lead shot. We made a claim on the site but time never allowed us to actually begin a meaningful excavation. I was still involved with other treasure wrecks closer to home that were much less costly to work on. This site has never been excavated. I estimate from what I observed and know now, almost thirty-five years later, that the recovery value of this site mirrors that of the *Auguste* and *Le Chameau.*

Finally, during the early 1970s I came across a shipwreck research document connected to the Orbit Group's initial discovery of *Le Chameau*, provided by the local shopkeeper who sold me my first diving gear. It was included in a bound file he suggested might be of some value although the wreck involved was lost off the coast of the United States—Cape Ann, Massachusetts, to be precise. In brief, the ship was French, belonging to the Compagnie des Indes, and bound from Martinique to France via Louisbourg. The ship, which I will not name for security reasons, ran afoul of three British warships in the 1740s off the coast of Nova Scotia. A chase ensued, but severe weather hampered the attack, with all vessels on a southerly course, heading toward Maine. Two days later, the French ship, after suffering some damage, fell in with a French privateer, and they both continued their journey along the coast of Maine and into the waters off Cape Ann. The bad weather lay in the south and east, eventually forcing the larger vessel ashore, where she was abandoned. The privateer, the document indicated, stood by until it rescued the crew, with the ship breaking up on a reef just offshore. The loss in treasure carried on board this ship, loaded in Martinique, amounted to 2,000,000 pesos in Mexican silver dollars.

On an extended long weekend pass, I left Toronto with my diving gear and took the long drive to Gloucester. From there I followed Route 127A north looking for a landmark that related: the Twin Light Motor Inn, just south of Rockport. Without much trouble, I found the inn and checked in for the night. The next morning I took out the map included in the research package and tried to match the shoreline with where the ship was lost. After a few hours of driving up and down the coastal road, the only offshore reef I could find that matched lay less than a quarter mile back south from the motor inn. I could see it clearly while standing on the road that hugged the shoreline.

That was it. I parked my car in an area adjacent to the reef and small cove that set off toward Gloucester to the south. Here I put my wet suit on and carried my tank and weight belt to the rocky shore. After entering the water, the first thing I saw was an old ship's anchor in about twenty feet of water. How lucky was this? I swam in a search pattern but found nothing else. My air gave out and I returned to shore.

I went back to the car and retrieved another tank, the last one I had with me. This time I took a closer look at the reef, how it ran and the distance from shore. It became evident that the ship this anchor belonged to lay wrecked on either the north or south side of it. I was working on the southern side. Entering the water again, I decided to stay on the south side of the reef but swam into the small cove. There it was, spread out in front of me: a trail of huge iron cannon.

With time under the water now of the essence, I took in as much of the wreck site as I could. It led right up to the high rock shoreline in about fifteen feet of water. I turned back to the open ocean; the wreckage extended for some distance, fading out in near fifty feet of water.

In what I considered the middle of the wreck site, I saw several large brass cylinders, about three feet long and approximately one foot in diameter. I recognized the cylinders to be part of the ship's pumps and bilge evacuation system. Moving the two that were the closest, I saw that underneath lay a handful of silver eight-reale cobs, although at the time I did not recognize them as such. I hand fanned around and found more, but I had already gone on reserve. Returning to shore, I came across several bronze cannon and another huge anchor. Once on the beach, or I should say the top of a small cliff, I laid in a landmark. I intended to come back.

It would take almost thirty years before the opportunity would arise again. By then, in Nova Scotia at least, such work was becoming a bureaucratic nightmare by design. On a trip to New York, returning via Boston with Joe Fiorentino and my new partner Steve Farrell in tow, I made an appointment with the state archaeologist. All the way to his office I felt the trip would be less than productive. His name was Vic Mastone.

As soon as we were introduced and led into his cluttered office, I could feel a sense of well-being. Here before me was a man who knew his business. He began by saying, "Welcome to Boston, Bob, I am glad to meet you; I am familiar with your work and the fact you are a friend of Bob Cembrola. He is a very highly respected marine archaeologist within our circle of influence. In fact, I have consulted with him over the years on various shipwreck projects. Great stuff! Now, what can I do for you?"

To say I was taken aback would be an understatement. This guy was friendly, he was professional, and he was courteous, but foremost, it was obvious he wished to talk and deal with us on equal and level ground.

Not knowing if a foreign salver would be welcome in state waters, I told him the story of the shipwreck and my dives there many years earlier. Without missing a beat, he stated, "Bob, that is great, we can go about this two ways. You can go to the site and retrieve enough evidentiary data in the form of a few artifacts we can examine for historical significance. The other route is, make your claim to me, lay out a simple map of the area, and I will take it to the state board for approval." This he said would be a simple and painless process that should see me on the claim within a month.

I was not used to this level of cooperation back in Canada, with one glaring exception: dealing with Rick Ratcliffe, the provincial registrar of treasure trove claims at Nova Scotia's Department of Natural Resources, and his immediate staff. Vic also added this one codicil: "Bob, once we have your claim secured, I will post it with the state police who travel Route 127 all the time. They will look after your claim until your return and when you are working the site. Do you think you could be up and running this season?"

I told Vic that I was working two historic shipwreck sites in Canada, but once I was finished, I had a very strong desire to return to Cape Ann and begin recovery operations. We left it at that, but not before I asked if he would mind if I introduced him to Rick Ratcliffe in Nova Scotia. He said, "No problem, anything I can do."

When I returned to Nova Scotia, I contacted Rick and told him about Vic Mastone and the way they did business in Massachusetts: the right way. In time Rick contacted Vic, which led to a face-to-face meeting. Rick hoped to gather enough positive information, really a new master plan of how another jurisdiction was dealing with shipwrecks, a positive example he could bring to his superiors. He did just that; apparently it fell on deaf ears.

At the end of the day, *Fantome* happened. I never returned to the wreck site off Cape Ann. Now that Nova Scotia has repealed the only act that truly protected our maritime heritage in a progressive way involving the private sector, the future is bleak from both an operational and a cultural perspective. For me, I am seriously looking forward to re-acquainting myself with a land where courteous professionals like Vic Mastone are the norm, not the exception.

The True State of Nova Scotia's Shipwrecks

You may wonder how some of the artifacts described in this book could survive in such incredible condition. This includes coins that look like new and other artifacts that do not seem to have suffered the ravages our harsh maritime environment should have imposed on them. This issue is also what drives the in-situ preservation argument, realizing that no matter the stresses suffered, some gold artifacts will always be available for collection in near-perfect condition. I say *near-perfect* because once anything man-made is absorbed by the ocean, for whatever reason, it begins to deteriorate. The rate is conducive to myriad dynamics, all controlled by nature and the activities of people.

My experience and that of others involved in the recovery of cultural shipwreck material, scientist and diver alike, realize one alarming fact: Only a mere percentage of what was originally a time capsule of its day is left to study and recover. This condition of continual degradation is ongoing and unstoppable. Shipwrecks lost in the shallow waters of Nova Scotia, especially wooden vessels over 100 years old, are now nothing more than a discontinuous assemblage of artifacts, either mixed in with other maritime events or, if left in the open, subject to a total and complete destruction.

In reality no organic items can or do stand up to the forces inflicted on them by the ocean. Only large metal objects have a chance to survive for a few hundred years or more. Such items include cannon, anchors, and artifacts made of gold or some other noble metal. Nova Scotia's rich maritime history is being lost every day, every hour, every minute it remains undiscovered, unrecovered, and unconserved. There is no logical, scientific, moral, or agenda-driven argument that can support otherwise. Nova Scotia was light-years ahead of other similar maritime jurisdictions, with solid, innovative, and protectionist legislation in the form of the province's Treasure Trove Act and Special Places Protection Act.

The real problem, sad to say, is the failure of those administrating and enforcing those acts to render them effective. This is an issue that lies firmly at the directors' level, the failure to appreciate the benefits private-sector initiatives provide and enhance. This attitude serves only to placate the minority at the expense of the majority, and has a negative and final effect on the resource.

After the Repeal

Almost a year has passed since the Nova Scotia Treasure Trove Act was repealed by the current New Democratic Party government of the province. Another year of degradation and unforgivable loss has also passed for Nova Scotia's ancient shipwrecks, lost during the days of sail. In that short but precious period of time, no proactive plan has been implemented to save even *one single* shipwreck artifact or to conserve one shipwreck site. In fact, the long-term plan seems to be to abandon this precious cultural resource. Why? Why, indeed. Money! With the private sector removed from the equation, the very authority responsible to the people of Nova Scotia—that is, to make wise and time-sensitive decisions—have turned their collective back on the province's finite maritime history for one sound reason: They cannot afford to deal with it.

Other maritime-related events, both positive and negative, enriched the global news media in 2011. In Ontario, it was reported that the province, finding itself in a deepening financial crisis, laid off its only full-time marine archaeologist responsible for all things shipwreck related in the Great Lakes. On the positive side, it was reported that the government of the Bahamas has now taken a more enlightened approach to its cultural maritime heritage. Sad to say, Nova Scotia, prior to the repeal of its Treasure Trove Act, was light-years ahead of what has to be declared a very enlightened approach by the Bahamian government to involve the private sector. Kudos to the visionaries involved.

Titanic Woes

Recent news reports in Halifax's print media and on national television center around a controversy involving Nova Scotia's Maritime Museum of the Atlantic's refusal to display recently recovered artifacts from this famous shipwreck. Artifacts recovered from the *Titanic* will be auctioned off in April 2012, but the registrar for the museum, Lynn-Marie Richard, is quoted as saying, "The museum will never consider displaying any of these artifacts—even as a temporary exhibit." To do so, she explained, would fly in the face of conventions the Maritime Museum of the Atlantic entered into with the International Congress of Maritime Museums. Over 5,000 extremely rare artifacts are involved.

The Nova Scotia Maritime Museum of the Atlantic's registrar is right. The staff of the province's museums who signed into the ICMM convention see artifact collection as something almost spiritual. This attitude reaches an agenda-imposed frenzy if cultural artifacts are not scientifically collected. However, there is only a slight distinction between ethics and common sense, really a slippery slope if the people of the province of Nova Scotia come out on the losing end. In the case of shipwreck artifacts, due to the fact that the Nova Scotia Treasure Trove Act was repealed in 2010, they most certainly did and will from this time forward. To make a blanket statement using the word *never* is very shortsighted. The public museums in this case belong to the people of Nova Scotia, not the museum staff. In any event, public museums should not be tied to unrealistic, unreasonable conventions.

Let's look into the future to see where this sort of isolationist policy could lead. At some point in the future, a tourist in Nova Scotia walking along a beach in Cape Breton sees the sun glint off a metallic object. Upon further examination, the tourist finds a cache of ancient artifacts. That person gathers them up and places them in his backpack. The tourist forgets about the find and eventually he returns to his home outside Canada. A few years pass and by some coincidence the tourist becomes aware his find that day in Cape Breton may have some real historic significance and thus real monetary value.

The tourist takes the artifacts he found in Nova Scotia to an auction house for appraisal. He finds out the artifacts are unique; they are Viking in origin. His rare find may prove Vikings settled in Cape Breton as they did at L'Anse aux Meadows, in northern Newfoundland. The tourist's discovery, once confirmed as to Viking in origin, would have worldwide historic implications. The artifacts, of course, would be priceless both in historic and monetary value, but more so to the people of Nova Scotia. No matter the circumstances surrounding their *by chance* discovery and the fact they were now being considered for sale in another jurisdiction, what position would the Nova Scotia Maritime Museum of the Atlantic take? Really that is the question, one the people of Nova Scotia deserve to have answered before ethics in the *Titanic* artifact case continue to overshadow the common good.

Is there an answer, some common ground on this issue? As a person who's been involved with the maritime cultural resources of Nova Scotia for almost half a century, I truly believe there is. Putting all the banter, fearmongering, and agenda-driven hypotheses aside, the solution as I see it surrounds the need for a new vision on the part of everyone involved. To disregard cultural artifacts recovered *intentionally* or *by chance* outside the arena of science is unethical.

At the same time, the public good is better served if science is involved. However, in the case of recovering shipwreck artifacts, the job is expensive beyond any public servant's imagination. It is surely beyond the ability of the taxpayer to support and, in some cases, exceeds the private sector's purse. In fact, the precious few cultural maritime resources that remain for sanctioned collection now require the resources and goodwill of both groups.

Shipwreck Artifacts, Royalty, and Final Disposition

Nova Scotia has retained thousands of conserved shipwreck artifacts taken in royalty selections from as far back as the early 1960s. It is only very recently that a few such items found their way to display cases at the Maritime Museum of the Atlantic, Halifax. After following a deeply entrenched policy of don't display for the fear of *inciting uncontrollable treasure hunting activity*, one visionary changed the rules. It all came down to a past director of the Maritime Museum of the Atlantic who was willing to buck the system: Michael Murray.

APPENDIX 4

Legal Opinions and Related Court Decisions

Over the rather short history involving the recovery of treasure trove from ancient shipwrecks lost within the territorial waters of Nova Scotia, three of the more prominent—*Le Chameau*, the *Auguste*, and the brig HMS *Fantome*—have triggered the requirement of formal judicial reviews. In the case of the *Auguste*, legal opinions were submitted to Parks Canada on behalf of the salvers, once Parks questioned ownership. It was dealt with outside the courts. To fully understand the history of treasure trove recovery and related activities, where Nova Scotia claims it holds sovereign jurisdiction, you need to be taken on a brief tour through the complicated world of salvers' rights. What actually happens when such rights are unjustly interfered with? The pay ship *Le Chameau* appeal court decision was a judicial review to sort out the application of partnership law to settle a dispute among the original partners before and after recovery.

The 1971 decision handed down by the Appeal Division of the Nova Scotia Supreme Court regarding *Blundon et al. v. Storm* is not directly related to anything more than the attempt by those involved to seek a final judicial settlement. Certain issues had developed in regard to the rights of the original partners, known as the Orbit Group, versus the rights of those who finally recovered a hoard of treasure from the shipwreck of *Le Chameau*. The process to see this accomplished was long and in some cases drawn out in the province's courts for almost six years. The final decision of the appeal court judges delivered a verdict that recognized the rights of both parties involved and rendered their judgment accordingly.

By reading the Supreme Court decision handed down in 1971, one can easily review the history of events leading up to the need to seek third-party intervention. That is, who discovered the wreck and who made the recovery of treasure trove? One can also get a sense that the salvers involved followed the due process in place to claim a shipwreck and any cargo that might be eventually salvaged. That is, they registered their initial claims to the local receiver of wreck invoking Part X of the Canada Shipping Act. They also applied for and were granted a license under the Nova Scotia Treasure Trove Act. This legal government instrument recognized their ownership of the claim and all it contained but only while the license was in force. By applying for this license the salvers recognized the province's interest and jurisdictional authority.

The *Le Chameau* court case was the first highly visible public event that brought the recovery of treasure trove out of the shadows and to the forefront of issues that would shape the future of treasure trove recovery in Nova Scotia. It did not set any new precedent under Part X, but it qualified a process we would follow on countless occasions, claiming the rights to recovered treasure trove until 1995. After 1995, the authority of Part X came into question over that of the true jurisdictional authority,

Nova Scotia. This abrupt change in jurisdictional protocol set the scene for even more industry confusion.

The Justice A. David MacAdam Decision

An official letter from the director of the Nova Scotia Museum was delivered to our lawyers on September 1, 2006. After being issued ministerial licenses and disturbance permits by the province of Nova Scotia in 2005 to carry out scientific excavation operations inside the Phantom Cove treasure trove claim, our rights, as a direct result of this one letter, were unjustly denied.

On March 1, 2006, England approached Canada's Foreign Affairs Department in Ottawa, requesting that all licensed activities inside the Phantom Cove claim cease. We were not officially made aware of this request or the intergovernmental discussions it created. Ottawa was intent on forcing the province of Nova Scotia to refuse the issuance of the heritage research permits we needed to exercise our rights under the current treasure trove license we held for the Phantom Cove claim. The main intent, to stop us from carrying on with excavation activities approved in 2005, was put forth in a letter signed August 31, 2006.

The formal notice came more than halfway through the time left available in the 2006 recovery season. We had applied for both Class A and B Heritage Research Permits in March and early May of 2006. The March application for a Class A Reconnaissance Permit was approved. The May Class B Heritage Research Permit was not approved, with no formal notice received by the claim holder until September 1, 2006.

In early April, almost a month after England's first notice, a note was sent to Daryl Eisan, representing Nova Scotia's Intergovernmental Affairs Department, advising Nova Scotia of England's diplomatic request. On May 17, 2006, Louis Simard, representing Federal Foreign Affairs, wrote to Daryl Eisan wanting to know Nova Scotia's position referencing the fact that England claimed sovereign immunity not only over the brig HMS *Fantome* but over another naval vessel lost at Cape Breton I held a claim right over, the HMS *Tilbury*. On May 29, 2006, the manager of Special Places made his recommendation to his director that no excavation license be issued for 2006 until ownership was established. The client did not receive official notice until September 1, 2006. Over three months had elapsed since the manager's recommendations and almost six months had passed since England first made Canada aware of its contentions. England asserted it had a sovereign right in the claims being worked on or slated to be worked on by Le Chameau Explorations Limited.

On more than one occasion I made the Nova Scotia government fully aware both in writing and in various telephone conversations to the Nova Scotia Department of Natural Resources that Le Chameau Explorations Limited, the client, had no interest in the ship HMS *Fantome* whatsoever. As a consequence, the company would not expect to be barred from any other benefit inside the Phantom Cove claim because that ship might be wrecked there. We asked for, and then later demanded, the issuance of the appropriate permits to continue with the recovery operations initiated in 2005. These requests were refused, as were requests to meet with everyone concerned, once we were made aware of the province's refusal to issue further disturbance permits at the end of August 2006. This last issue may be the main grievance we had in dealing with England's claim, in that we were denied a place at the table while our fate was being decided by both federal and provincial governments.

I spoke to the registrar of claims (at the NSDNR) on several occasions regarding this affront by the Nova Scotia government. He agreed with me that there should be a meeting set up with all parties involved, noting he had made several high-level requests for exactly the same thing. The main purpose would be to try to sort out any issues that might let the client continue with work in its claim. The registrar realized, as did one other government official who was part of the permit-approval process, that this particular client had a long history of total compliance. To blatantly deny a ministerial-approved, provincially licensed opportunity, without any consideration for the client's long professional relationship with Nova Scotia, was at the very least a denial of procedural fairness.

The person I refer to was at the time the head archaeologist for the province of Nova Scotia and offered a very viable solution. He proposed that a conditional permit be issued referencing England's request to stay away from the HMS *Fantome* while working on this site. Included in the permit conditions would be the instruction to record any artifacts relating to the HMS *Fantome* but to leave them in situ. This indeed was a very solid approach. The client would be afforded the opportunity to continue working the claim, but in recognition of the British interest, until it was proven one way or the other, this new condition would apply. The client would be instructed to avoid, where possible, wreckage from the brig. In fact, this would be a win-win proposal for everyone.

In addition, the client, Le Chameau Explorations Limited, was advised in early 2006 that an official of the U.S. State Department met managers of our affiliate in the United States at a maritime conference held in Florida. This official advised that he intended to interfere with the *Fantome* salvage project at Prospect, Nova Scotia. He had already made contact with English officials along with others interested on both sides of the Canadian–American border. He contended he took this action to Ottawa and across the Atlantic to ensure this happened. It did.

Even before England made its position known to Ottawa, the United States, as it is reported, made its position known to England. This unwarranted and blatant interference in the inherent rights of the province of

Nova Scotia leaves room for some serious conjecture on the part of the salver involved. Just as there should have been conjecture on the part of the officials of the province of Nova Scotia after we advised them of this breach in international protocol. They obviously mishandled this case and in a big way, leading the client to seek justice in the Supreme Court of Nova Scotia. Justice initially denied was eventually handed out with the delivery of Judge MacAdam's written decision on March 28, 2008.

Judge MacAdam got right to the heart of the matter. He recognized that regardless of the issues that surround the power of a director of the Nova Scotia Museum to make decisions for or against a client of the province, a client in good standing was subject to due process. Once treasure trove licenses and heritage permits were approved by the ministers of the crown, that client, if compliant, deserved to be treated with unbridled respect and professional fairness. In this case, Le Chameau Explorations Limited and those it represented were denied "procedural fairness and natural justice," all at the recommendation of one man—the manager of Special Places, who had the discretionary power to do the right thing in this case and extend an established client the benefit of the doubt. This would have ensured the opportunity that at least meetings would have been held between all the parties involved. If England had declined, then he could have asked his superior, the director, to issue the appropriate permits immediately. England could not just make a claim without proving the site; this was yet another contentious issue. That responsibility fell to England, not the claim holder.

In 2005, Le Chameau Explorations Limited, along with its American affiliate (Sovereign Exploration Associates International), raised and invested close to $750,000 in the Phantom Cove claim. Here the decision of one man placed the legal rights of several companies and the investors involved in serious jeopardy. After the permit was denied in 2006, I urged the partners to sue the province in a lost opportunity suit.

They reviewed the suggestion. After the decisive Supreme Court decision of Judge MacAdam, clearly finding the province guilty of denying the client natural justice, I counseled my partners once again to consider a strong legal response. It was now obvious my partners should review their previous decision of not taking further legal action even after winning the 2007 court case.

We discussed the issue at length with our lawyers in 2008, to determine if we had a strong case. They agreed we did but counseled the need to consider the massive costs versus the return of such an undertaking. Taking the province of Nova Scotia, the jurisdictional authority in this matter, to court could possibly produce as many negatives as positives. The province would rely on the taxpayer to pay its legal costs; the client was left to its own devices costwise. Further, a protracted case could take years and cost in the high six figures, a fact we had to consider after the extreme cost associated with the 2007 court case just to have a legal opinion rendered.

The other factor that demoralized everyone involved came when we were informed the Nova Scotia government was seriously considering the repeal of the Nova Scotia Treasure Trove Act. If this repeal came to fruition, the result would be no less than catastrophic for the client. Eventually, in 2010, the province issued a press release that on December 31, 2010, the Treasure Trove Act would be repealed, the legislation struck down. As a result, our rights and opportunity ceased to exist after December 31, 2010. Even after 35 years of full compliance and business development based on the written promise that our recovery rights would never be unjustly interfered with, the province of Nova Scotia sacrificed them for far less than the greater good.

APPENDIX 5

Shipwreck Artifacts In Situ

The Fallacy of In-Situ Preservation by James Sinclair

In the past few years, mostly in response to an increasing inability to manage collections of archaeological material, a concept has surfaced that has, we believe, dire ramifications for shipwrecks and the collection of artifacts that may be found on such sites. This dangerous idea is *in-situ preservation*. The net effect of this concept—if accepted—will be the continued deterioration of the underwater cultural heritage. This idea is the inevitable outcome of some extremely rigid and misguided preservation policies that require every single object from an archaeological site to be cataloged and stored whether it is from the period of interest, modern detritus, or is among tens of thousands of identical specimens, thus filling repositories with objects of less-than-optimal informational value. It must also be noted that resources for this type of endeavor are finite, especially in the public sector—that is, government and/or academia.

Budgetary cuts and restrictions have in many cases eviscerated once-thriving public programs of this sort. The call for public-private partnerships is increasingly being touted as the wave of the future in a multitude of studies surrounding the ocean, including underwater cultural heritage management.

However, many of the professional societies concerned with cultural resource management and archaeology have codes of professional conduct, ethics statements, and bylaws that preclude nearly all involvement with private enterprise in its various forms. As a consequence of this, these same professional societies are promoting in-situ preservation as the method of choice in the spectrum of management options aimed at underwater cultural resources.

In-situ preservation does not work when it comes to the majority of shipwreck sites in the world. The oceans are vast planetary recycling mechanisms. Objects of nearly any makeup that are lost into it will eventually reach a state of complete dissolution. Whether hard against a cobbled shore in Nova Scotia, like the *Le Chameau*, or in the abyssal depths, such as the *Titanic*, this deterioration is an ongoing process. This can be abundantly confirmed by any materials scientist. These are facts that much of the historic preservation and archaeological community choose to ignore.

We as archaeologists are interested in the contextual information artifacts that these sites contain. However, the contexts that are so very important for the interpretation of the sites are being lost due to the ongoing deterioration of artifact collections associated with these sites. If we as scientists are concerned about historic preservation and interpretation, we must be concerned for not only the site but its constituent parts—an aspect that those who promote in-situ preservation as the management method of choice fail to take into consideration or disclose.

Let us look for a moment at the well-preserved, documented shipwrecks that have been investigated in the world. These include the *Vasa* (1628), the *Mary Rose* (1545), the *Hamilton* (1813), and the *Scourge* (1813). There are also a number of nicely intact shipwrecks in the Great Lakes and other freshwater lakes around the world; however, the estimates of numbers of wreck sites in the world are given as approximately 3 million, according to the United Nations Educational, Scientific and Cultural Organization (UNESCO). The overwhelming majority of these wrecks occur in high-energy surf zones and more often than not exhibit a highly discontinuous scatter pattern that can be perceived only through the most careful mapping and recovery of the endangered artifacts. These zones are most certainly not conducive to any sort of in-situ preservation.

Certainly *Le Chameau* (lost in 1725) falls into this latter category. The wreck is scattered widely over the section of coast where the initial disaster took place. One would be hard-pressed to imagine a more inhospitable section of the coast.

With submerged geological features (the locals call them *sunkers*), exposure to the worst weather patterns, and a depositional environment that is one of the harshest imaginable, the *Le Chameau* is truly an endangered wreck site. Enormous wave action from North Atlantic swells is almost constant. The cobble bottom and shell hash is in a continual state of motion. What survived are metallic objects that have become secreted in among the more stable cobble or somewhat protected by the very geologic structures that were the initial cause of the wreck. Mixed in with *Le Chameau* materials are artifacts from what appear to be four other period wrecks.

In some environments (Florida, and others) there is a natural process of encrusting that takes place. This is caused by the attraction of calcium ions that free float in seawater, adding to the oxidation processes of iron. A white concrete-like material is deposited over the surface of the deteriorating object, mitigating somewhat the deterioration process. There seems—for whatever reason—to be much less of this phenomenon happening in the northern waters around Nova Scotia. As a consequence the iron components of these vessels continue to deteriorate. In some instances, the iron deterioration products *are* the concretion matrix, shielding other objects from the brunt of the ocean's effects. Needless to say the chances of survival of the wooden construction components in such an environment are nearly nonexistent.

As an added stressor on artifacts in these environments, there is the compounded situation of ice. There are years that these sites are completely covered in pack ice. This stressor must be taken into account when assessing the dynamics of the ongoing deterioration of the *Le Chameau* site and others like it. In shallow areas such ice would extend from the surface to the seabed, scouring the bottom with unimaginable force. This is undoubtedly the reason that the 135-foot steel-hull vessel that was wrecked on the shore here is gone.

Perhaps one of the greatest examples, certainly the most high-profile proof that in-situ preservation is a very bad idea, is the situation surrounding the ironclad vessel *Monitor.* This very important historic vessel was located in 1973 off the coast of North Carolina. It was immediately made into the first National Marine Sanctuary in the United States. There it sat for over a generation. In the mid-1990s investigations showed that the wreck site was in an advanced state of deterioration—large sections of the ship that had been intact were missing. Response from the U.S. National Oceanic and Atmospheric Administration (NOAA) was immediate and a multimillion-dollar project was launched to recover important sections of the vessel.

Much more could have been saved if efforts had been made when the ship was discovered to recover the artifacts. This is the same situation we have on *Le Chameau* and, for all intents and purposes, all the ancient shipwrecks of Nova Scotia. Deterioration is ongoing. *Now* is the time *to save what little remains* of these vessels.

Undiscovered, unrecovered, unconserved, and unreported underwater cultural heritage—is a lost cultural heritage.

Prepared by James J. Sinclair, MA, RPA,
for Captain Robert MacKinnon

James Sinclair acted as an alternate marine archaeologist and site conservator under renowned marine archaeologist Dr. Duncan R. Mathewson III for Mel Fisher during the famous recovery of the *Atocha* treasure off south Florida. James was the first archaeologist to officially visit the deep wreck of the SS *Titanic* in the submersible *Mir II*.

James acted as my alternate to Dr. Mathewson in Nova Scotia and became principal investigator in charge of the *Fantome* fleet operations of 2005. He remained on standby in 2006, ready to continue scientific investigations at Prospect, Nova Scotia. His long involvement with historic shipwrecks worldwide is legendary.

No other maritime scientist is more qualified to render a scientific opinion on the lunacy of in-situ preservation within an ocean context, except for classical maritime conservator John E. Cross. His professional assessment and clinical laboratory analysis are included in the next section, which was part of his yearly conservation report from 2004, sent to the province of Nova Scotia on my behalf.

Conservation Report, *Le Chameau,* 2004 by John Cross

The facts of having a custom-designed conservation laboratory along with the opportunity to be part of a team who have worked successfully together for many years have made for me a most rewarding and satisfying year.

One of the most refreshing aspects of this year's work has been the cooperation of all members of the recovery team, allowing ideas and knowledge to be freely exchanged. This is of benefit to all and without doubt of benefit to the whole conservation process.

In this regard I would personally thank the salvage master—Captain Robert MacKinnon. The archaeologists—Dr. Duncan Mathewson and James Sinclair—my friend Captain John MacKinnon, and all members of the "Science" team.

Before completing this report, I would like to add some notes and observations on the condition of artifacts recovered from the wreck site of the French *flute Le Chameau*—lost in 1725 near Louisbourg, Nova Scotia.

I have had the privilege of working with material from the *Le Chameau* wreck site since the 1995 recovery season and have observed a marked deterioration in the overall condition of artifacts in this time. This in no way is a reflection on those making the recovery but a function of the environmental conditions in which artifacts are buried.

This deterioration may be accounted for in two ways:

A. Chemical Deterioration

B. Mechanical Deterioration

A. Chemical Deterioration

The electromotive series of the metals most commonly found in shipwrecks of the 18th century places them in the following order from the most noble to the base metals:

	POTENTIAL	COMMENTS
Gold	+1.51	Little deterioration
Silver	+0.80	Pitting
Copper, cuprous	+0.55	Deteriorated
Copper, cupric	+0.36	Deteriorated
Lead	-0.13	Marked deterioration
Tin	-0.14	Marked deterioration
Iron, ferrous	-0.44	Virtually missing
Iron, ferric	-0.04	Virtually missing
Zinc	-0/07	N/A

I have added comments as to the metals occurrence on the *Le Chameau* site. These measurements apply to pure metals in laboratory conditions, and it must be remembered that the metals of the 18th century are not pure; even the gold coins encountered are only 93 percent metallic gold. All metals met, being in effect alloys, are subject to electrochemical corrosion, a galvanic cell being created with the seawater acting as an electrolyte. Corrosion will continue until the baser of the two metals is completely destroyed. This may be observed in the silver plates from this past season's recovery, where the alloying copper metal has been completely destroyed, leaving the major element, silver, brittle and fragile.

We find little in numbers of iron artifacts from this site, the corrosion having been given time to be complete and many valuable artifacts lost. The copper alloy artifacts of originally tertiary alloys (three metals) are now only remaining in a binary alloy form and deeply pitted and fragile—examples of which are the so-called billon coins. All this is due to electrochemical corrosion which *will* continue until the complete destruction of the artifacts is reached.

Perhaps the most noticeable aspect of metallic corrosion in recovered material from this site is the presence of corrosion products that can only occur in the presence of free oxygen. This inevitably will lead to the complete destruction of artifacts. Free oxygen is present in the seawater on this site, as it is in any shallow-water site, due to continual agitation of the water due to currents, tide actions, and storm situations. This same situation can be readily observed also in copper and silver alloys from the site.

We even see on close examination of gold coins the effects of this galvanic cell action in the presence of oxygen—the copper metal alloyed with the gold being slowly but inevitably destroyed.

In short, all metals from marine sites of shallow depth will be eventually destroyed, and action should be planned now for the recovery of this material while there is still anything of note worth recovering.

I have personally noticed a marked increase in this type of corrosion over the past 10 years on this historic site and urge all concerned to make efforts to recover this cultural material while there is still something to recover.

B. Mechanical Deterioration

As noticeable as chemical deterioration is the deterioration that can be attributed to mechanical action. By this I mean the constant moving of artifacts and rocks on the seafloor. Metal artifacts show more signs now than in the past of recent mechanical damage; this is usually exhibited by scratches so recently formed that corrosion of the underlying metal has not as yet taken place. This damage is caused by tide, current, and storm action, and is uncontrollable and hence will continue.

Additional damage undoubtedly has been caused both by pack ice conditions and fishing activities.

Ceramic pieces when examined show much wear on fractured surfaces and to areas of glazing, and it is amazing to consider how many pieces of ceramic and glass the *flute Le Chameau* must have carried and how few pieces have been recovered.

Conclusions

There can be no doubt that all shallow-water shipwreck sites are in danger and that slowly but inevitably all traces of the vessels and their cargoes will be lost. All such sites should be closely examined and, where desirable, recovery made. Unless action is taken soon, there will be nothing left to recover, and this destruction is inevitable and unstoppable.

Prepared by John E. Cross, conservator, March 2005,
for Captain Robert MacKinnon

John E. Cross is a highly respected conservation scientist. He was educated at the University of London, among other respected academic institutions, and originally retained by the British Museum Systems as a metals conservator and restoration expert. John is a qualified radiologist, among other achievements both technical and educational—all too many to mention.

John has worked with shipwreck material for most of his long career. He supervised the metals section of Parks Canada's Conservation Labs in Ottawa, Canada; taught students of conservation; and designed and supervised the construction of both field and permanent conservation labs in North America and Europe. John has worked as a senior conservation expert for several governments and related international institutions. Over the years, he has been invited to speak on the subject at many maritime conservation symposiums worldwide.

John has supervised conservation protocols for recovery projects from the Canadian Arctic to the Mediterranean and almost everywhere in between. He does not make his observations either lightly or without years of evidentiary proof.

It is just as important for *you* to understand what both scientists, Jim Sinclair and John Cross, are trying to say as it is for the provincial and state authorities responsible for the management of our finite maritime cultural resources. Simply put, our ancient shipwreck sites and the artifacts left for collection are in the final stages of degradation. Even now, only less than 1 percent of the original ships and their cargoes remains to be discovered, recovered, and conserved.

Many maritime archaeologists are promoting the in-situ preservation theory, which holds that because some shipwreck artifacts have been somehow stabilized in the place they now find themselves—the ocean—this is protection enough. That is until some new, as-yet-unknown technology comes along to expedite their safe recovery. However, the ocean does not work on a time clock waiting for miracles; it ravages such precious artifacts every day. No enlightened professional could in good conscience support such a ludicrous theory, one that has not been scientifically proven nor in fact could be.

APPENDIX 6

Overview of Shipwreck Recovery and Site Survey Maps

For the select few fortunate enough to discover treasure on land or a rich shipwreck under the sea, life will be forever remembered in two ways: *before* and *after*. Before discovery, a treasure hunter is filled with anticipation and a blind faith that the object of the search actually exists. After discovery, the treasure hunter is filled with a sense of awe and satisfaction when the dream—the obsession—becomes reality. This memory footprint is now embedded in the awe and excitement of that first discovery, including the time it happened and who was there when it happened. It could be the first gold coin or some other precious artifact lost to the memory of humankind that will drive and nourish the truly dedicated professional, manifesting itself in the need to experience, again and again, the anticipation and thrill of new discoveries.

Introduction

The initial and ongoing distribution of historic shipwreck artifacts after an unfortunate vessel makes contact with the hard shore, reef, hidden sunker, or some other obstacle in shallow water, breaking apart and spilling its contents into an angry sea, is a very complex and diverse study. A successful treasure hunter will strive to understand the dynamics of what we commonly refer to as the wrecking process. There is a need to investigate how and why certain artifacts scatter, with some traveling far from the original point of impact.

Involved in this distribution hypothesis is one constant the treasure hunter must study and firmly understand—the maritime conditions prevalent within the main area of interest, tides and other natural factors, and in some cases even the movement of sea ice. Marine archaeologists refer to this phenomenon of artifact distribution away from the original point of impact and breakup in shallow water under several terms: the artifact scatter pattern or the discontinuous assemblage of cultural material; those in the field often use the less than scientifically accepted term *debris field.*

At a high-level meeting held in Halifax during the mid-1990s between officials of Parks Canada, the Nova Scotia government, me, and legal representatives for everyone involved, Dianne Hearst, head of Parks Canada's Underwater Division, brought government policy to the table. She stated, "When dealing with historic shipwrecks, Parks prefers to perform *triage archaeology* rather than an all-out attempt to gather every last artifact, a monumental and cost-restrictive task." She went on to use as an example Parks' four-year involvement (from 1969 to 1972) in surveying the historically significant shipwreck sites of the *Bienfaisant* and *Marquis de Malauze* and the eventual recovery of artifacts from the wreck site of the French naval transport *Machault.* All three ships were lost in the estuary of the Restigouche River inside the Bay de Chaleur in 1760.

She made note that during that time, over 5,000 search and recovery dives were recorded before the project drew to a close. However, the archaeologists involved felt that they had only scratched the surface—far less than what could be considered a full recovery of the entire collection still available on-site. They believed the recovery operations could continue with real success for many more years. The issue, as she explained it, came down to cost and return. Parks strived to save a significant and representative sample of the artifact assemblage associated with the loss of the *Machault*; however, no viable ongoing project time frame or result could be verified; thus further activity could not be financially justified.

Since that time, based on my own discovery and recovery experience, which reached its zenith long before I met Hearst in Halifax, and by making significant recoveries under provincial license from many complicated historic shipwreck sites, I began to fully appreciate the wisdom of her words and the true benefit of this policy. Parks' practical understanding of the reality on the ground, so to speak, stood to save cultural shipwreck material and related scientific information within the confines of available funding. It really came down to saving a little versus losing it all, the final result of leaving shipwreck artifacts in situ.

I have chosen to explain the recovery maps in this book based on the foregoing: what was recovered, what remains to be recovered, how the ship wrecked, the initial point of impact, and what treasure *I estimate* remains on each site for future recovery. By *treasure* I mean gold, silver, and gems in other than their natural state, as referenced in the original Nova Scotia Treasure Trove Act. Although there is another and just as relevant treasure of nonprecious cultural material and site information involved with each historic shipwreck site, I did not direct projects for these artifacts. They, of course, became a by-product of my recovery operations and were always treated with equal care and scientifically accepted conservation protocols. Thousands of these artifacts now belong to the people of Nova Scotia, with a small grouping on display at the Nova Scotia Maritime Museum of the Atlantic, on the Halifax waterfront.

A. The Recovery and Survey Map of the Armed Transport HMS *Leonidas,* Lost at Scatarie Island (on Hay Island Breaker) in 1832

General Area

The eastern end of Scatarie Island comprises the region between Southern Point to the southwest and the Eastern Rocks to the northeast, a distance of 3.2 miles. It is a natural trap for sailing ships, including iron ships of the last century. This crescent-shaped landmass, along with its many reefs and hidden sunkers, represents the most eastern portion of land jutting out from the province of Nova Scotia into the North Atlantic. Ships had to sail around Scatarie Island traveling in and out of the Gulf of St. Lawrence or north and south along the Eastern Seaboard. Unfortunately, many captains never realized the dangers even the waters some distance offshore held in store for a ship that strayed from a safe and reasonably distant course to clear the island.

With the establishment of Fortress Louisbourg by the French, beginning in earnest around 1713 and occupied until 1758, only 10 leagues to the south and west of Scatarie Island, ship traffic increased considerably. Fortress Louisbourg commanded the approaches to the Gulf of

St. Lawrence. This fortified town was also the capital of the French Colony of Isle Royale and one of the most significant fishing and commercial ports in North America. By early 1750, Louisbourg was the second largest settlement in New France after Quebec, the location of which saw a major increase in both commercial and naval shipping, skirting the shores of Scatarie Island, all year round.

Countless ships laden with treasure used the Port of Louisbourg during this period. Some were wrecked within the general vicinity of the port, others captured, by the use of less than conventional methods.

Capture of the *Notre Dame de la Delivrance* in 1745 at Louisbourg

The French flag flew from the ramparts of Louisbourg for some time after the fall of the city—The conquerors hoping that French ships would be decoyed thither, nor were they disappointed. Numbers of rich prizes fell into their hands. One of the richest was the Notre Dame de la Delivrance. *Hidden beneath its cargo of cacao was found four million dollars*—nearly two million Peruvian dollars, besides gold and silver ingots and bars.*

The Delivrance, *in company with the* Louis Erasme *and the* Marquis D'Avin, *had been attacked off the Azores by English privateers. After a sharp action of some three hours the* Erasme *and the* Marquis *were overpowered. While the privateers were engaged in securing their prizes, the* Delivrance *although damaged, contrived to crowd on sail and raced for Louisbourg. When she neared her destination—duped by the fact the French Flag still flew over the Fortress port—she was captured by two English men-of-war.*

—From *Cape Breton Over* by Clara Dennis

---

*A cargo of treasure worth $4,000,000 in 1745 could easily be worth a hundred times that amount in 2010.

Between Southern Point and the Eastern Rocks alone, it is reported that over 70 ships were lost, some as far back as the early part of the 18th century. The island itself boasts the loss of over 200 ships dashed to pieces along her hazardous coastline, with tens of thousands of sailors and passengers losing their lives. Our early diving surveys of the 1970s confirm many wooden ships were lost—some on top of each other, creating a layering effect—with no existing record of the ship, date, or reason for the loss. Scatarie Island's shipwreck losses stand only second to another Nova Scotia island, Sable Island, which may well account for over 500 recorded shipwrecks, and many more unrecorded, since the first voyages of John Cabot to this region in 1497 and 1498.

Wreck Site

The British transport HMS *Leonidas* was a staunch wooden warship of the period, armed with 18 twenty-four-pound carronades and lesser deck guns. She carried a precious cargo of specie in the form of several tons of copper coins, bullion from private sources, soldiers, passengers, and general cargo bound for Quebec from both Halifax and her original port of departure in England. The *Leonidas* sailed out of Halifax around mid-August 1832; however after only a few days at sea heading north she failed to clear the outer reefs of Scatarie Island, striking the Hay Island Breaker. The breaker consists of a body of reefs and sunkers that extend from Hay Island to the east for some considerable distance, almost a quarter mile. From the first evidence we found of the wreck in the early 1970s, we place the initial point of impact—and the start of the wrecking process—between the Colombo Breaker and the outer reefs of Hay Island. Almost immediately, we witnessed the wreckage of two ships mixed together in about 25 feet of water. Both were subsequently identified from the more modern wreckage of the SS *Colombo*, lost there in

1885, mixed with several carronades complete with cast-iron gun carriage frames from the ill-fated transport *Leonidas*.

Our underwater surveys led us along the southwest side of the breaker toward Hay Island itself, where we located another group of carronades, lead shot, cast-iron gun carriage frames, iron carriage wheels, and copper coins. We followed the trail of copper coins into depths of less than five feet of water, almost to the edge of Hay Island itself. The copper coins were everywhere we looked, in mounds and buried deep in the sand and gravel, many covered by heavy cobble and large boulders. To say there were millions would be an accurate assessment. We continued to follow the trail of ship wreckage into what the locals call Hell's Gates. Along the way, we discovered a vast cache of silverware we felt came from the wreck of the transport. Here the trail of copper coins seemed to fade out.

On the southern side of Hell's Gates there is a small rock formation that sticks out of the water at high tide called Red Rocks. This is where we discovered several different cannon not related to the wreck of the transport. We found many silver coins of both French and Spanish origin, an assortment of gold French louis d'or coins, and English guineas, all circa 1720. We also found a trail of wreckage that led into the middle of Southeast Harbor. After several more survey dives heading west into the harbor we came across an assortment of small brass barrel hoops stamped with the French fleur-de-lis along with other markings and symbols. Near the brass hoops we located silverware, silver coins, and red bricks by the hundreds but no further wreckage from the *Leonidas* transport. Our investigations took us to the outer shores of Southern Point Cove. There we located many large cast-iron cannon bored for 18- and 24-pound round shot, cast-iron ballast bars, and assorted artifacts that still remain unidentified as to origin.

We exhausted our search for wreckage of the *Leonidas*, realizing that the majority of what evidence remains lies along the southwest side of the Hay Island Breaker and within the bowl that is created by the island itself leading away into Hell's Gates. I investigated the areas behind the sunkers just offshore of the island, locating tens of thousands of copper coins, many in excellent shape, protected from harm by the very rocks that claimed the ship they were consigned to.

Estimate of treasure still left for recovery on the *Leonidas* wreck site—80 to 85 percent.

B. The Recovery and Survey Map of the Cartel Ship *Auguste,* Lost off Ladies Beach, Aspy Bay, Cape Breton Island, in 1761

General Area

Aspy Bay is located just inside the very northern tip of Cape Breton Island. It is a large bay framed by Cape North and White Point to the south, approximately 15 miles across at the mouth. The inner portions of Aspy Bay are generally sheltered from most winds, except for any from the northeast around to the southeast. The seafloor of the inner bay on both sides of Dingwall Harbor predominantly consists of deep sand and fine gravel, falling off to a mud and small rock shoal bottom offshore. Aspy Bay provided limited shelter from strong winds out of the north for sailing ships intending to round Cape North and enter the Gulf of St. Lawrence. From a historic standpoint, it was virtually without the presence of people during the 17th and 18th centuries. The bay and the area surrounding it were considered part of Cape Breton Island's wilderness, with only native summer camps known to be established close to where Dingwall Harbor is located today.

Wreck Site

The *Auguste* began her career as a French merchantman captured by the British on August 18, 1756. At that time, she was sold by the British navy as a prize and renamed *Augusta*. The ship was designed to carry passengers and cargo and listed a crew of 39 when captured. The *Auguste* was ported for up to 16 guns, and from existing accounts, the ship would have been approximately 90 feet on the waterline and registered at approximately 250 tons. In 1761 the ship was chosen along with two others to bring patriots back to France, the direct result of a major defeat suffered by the French at the hands of British forces on the Plains of Abraham outside Quebec City in 1759. The British captured Montreal in 1760; as a result, New France was firmly in the hands of England, thus influencing the later creation of Canada.

The *Auguste*, heavily laden with her passengers' personal fortunes in bullion form, finally sailed from Quebec after many delays and setbacks on October 15, 1761, so late in the season there was general concern on both sides for a safe passage. The concerns were realized on November 15, 1761, after a month of storms and misadventures. The cartel ship *Auguste* ran ashore a short distance off Middle Beach, Aspy Bay. The *Auguste* and her cargo were forgotten for the next two centuries, until I was lucky enough to make the initial discovery that led our dive team to the main wreckage in the early summer of 1977.

The remains of the *Auguste* lay approximately 500 feet off the southern end of Ladies Beach in 18 feet of water, almost adjacent to a small brook that empties out of Middle Harbor into the sea. Most of the known wreck site in 1977 and 1978 was covered with over 4 feet of sand; however, the cannon and stern sections were found in the open with no sand cover, the result of winter storms exposing sections of the wreck.

It is apparent the ship struck the shoal water of Aspy Bay in one piece, confirmed by the evidence we uncovered in 1977 and La Corne's account of the loss in 1761. This became an important issue when trying to figure out the size and direction of the debris field.

The 1977 and 1978 recoveries were controlled by main baselines and offsets. Several test pits were excavated; they all showed treasure in some form and are noted on the corresponding site map by the letters *TP.* It was obvious to us that over time much of the cargo, including the treasure spilled from the wreck as it broke up and that was stored in chests and other containers, had been easily moved from the main impact site by wind and wave. The test pit at the northern end of the 1977–1978 main baseline running parallel to the beach proved to be the richest in coin and artifact. It was never excavated after the 1978 operations came to a close.

The main debris field begins several hundred feet from the 1977–1978 main baseline back to the northeast. It flows shoreward, even into the entrance of the little brook that flows out of Middle Harbor, which was possibly a small river in 1761. During this period, we recovered several thousand silver, gold, and copper coins along with thousands of other precious artifacts, silverware, jewelry, silver seals, spoon molds, three large German silver bells, and other precious artifacts within the general vicinity of the main baseline. The test-pit coordinates were incorporated within a future recovery plan that never took place. The test-pit positions on the *Auguste* wreck site map included in this book were taken from that original plan, and daily dive logs were kept by the supervisors of the dive team.

In 2001, I led a new team to Aspy Bay looking for what remained of the *Auguste* treasure. We needed to survey in the original main baseline using coordinates from the 1977–1978 season. We found the underwater monuments almost immediately and set in new baselines. This time I turned the arm of the baseline that runs parallel with the shore a little farther to the northeast, using the old SS *Kismet* anchor as the most northerly monument. This proved beneficial, with recovery of treasure the immediate result.

The 2001 field season proved to be the last time I would work on the *Auguste* site. The new team carried on for a few more seasons with some limited success. The main problem with this site, as with most other shallow-water shipwreck events, is the size of the debris field. In this case, it is fairly large, which would count out anything close to a complete recovery without the intervention of mechanical dredging. Such disturbance activities using barge-mounted dredge equipment are not scientifically acceptable excavation practices and risks blunt-force trauma damage to delicate cultural material.

This seemingly unassuming loss in 1761 of the cartel ship *Auguste* and her cargo remains by far one of the richest shipwreck treasure sites and culturally significant sites in Canada.

Estimate of treasure still left for recovery on the *Auguste* wreck site—75 percent.

C. The Recovery and Survey Map of the Fifth-Rate British Frigate HMS *Feversham* and Her Small Fleet, Lost off Southern Point–Howe Point, Scatarie Island, in 1711

General Area

The wreck of the entire HMS *Feversham* fleet occurred on October 7, 1711, just inside Southern Point, or Howe Point as it is sometimes referred to, between two sunkers that are awash at low water, the Little Sunker and the Cape Breton Sunker. Both rock structures are not large by reef standards, but they are strategically placed to trap a ship between them with devastating results. Southern Point is the last eastern landmass on the southern side of Scatarie Island. It is a violent area known for strong tides and huge swells born far out in the open ocean.

The bottom shallows very quickly from 20 fathoms only a few hundred feet from the island to 5 fathoms very close to the cliffs that line the shore. The quick change in depth during certain storm conditions can create huge waves that reach far inland, leaving the point devoid of plant life—as far back as one quarter mile from the shore. During the early part of the 18th century, Scatarie Island and the adjacent mainland lacked any sort of settlement able to assist shipwrecked sailors unfortunate enough to be stranded there.

Wreck Site

The HMS *Feversham*, a fifth-rate frigate armed with 36 cannon, and the three transports she was escorting, *Mary*, *Joseph*, and *Neptune*, were caught in a strong southwest gale and ran ashore around midnight on October 7, 1711. The frigate tried to clear the very point or pitch of the island but was forced ashore, falling prey to the two sunkers that quickly reduced her to a complete wreck. The three transports following her stern lanterns drove ashore to the west along the southern shores of Scatarie Island. All the ships except the transport *Joseph* were dashed to pieces overnight. The *Joseph* ran hard aground and remained upright for the next several days. Over half of the frigate's crew and officers were lost; however, the transports ran ashore in less hazardous waters and only a few sailors were claimed by the sea.

The frigate and three transports sailing under orders were carrying supplies and bullion in both gold and silver coin referred to as the provincial silver to aid Admiral Hovenden Walker's raid on Quebec during a period of hostilities between France and England known as Queen Anne's War. The total loss of bullion was recorded in the November 1711 edition of the *Boston Dispatch Chronicle* as $5,000,000 in gold, including all stores and armaments.

When we first surveyed this area in the early 1970s, we located huge bronze pins, some up to 10 feet long—over one inch in thickness was the norm. We located several pairs of large bronze pintles and gudgeons, cannonballs, anchors, and lead shot between the Little Sunker and the cliffs of the island just opposite. We followed the trail of wreckage along the bottom until we came to a very large bed of concreted cannonballs, approximately 30 feet by 30 feet in diameter, almost 4 feet thick and more in places. The wreckage of the frigate seemed to pile up on the eastern side of the Cape Breton Sunker, named for the loss of the steam ship *Cape Breton* that struck there in 1920, also a complete loss. This is where we later located a majority of the frigate's cannon and cargo of silver and gold coins (including Spanish, New England, French, English, Dutch, Hungarian, and German thalers), silverware, and an assortment of rare gold cobs.

We surveyed the shallow waters on the western side of the Cape Breton Sunker and located several cannon from the *Feversham* wreck—lodged under steel hull plates from the *Cape Breton*. In fact, using metal detectors outside the line of iron wreckage from the modern ship, we gained a continuous series of electronic targets right into the sand beach at the end of the cove to the west. Most of these targets proved to be silver coins, Latin American cobs of all denominations dated before 1700. No coins were found that dated after the wrecking event of 1711.

The *Joseph* Transport

In later years we continued our visual and electronic searches even farther west to the coves and small inlets on the northwest side of the reef structure known as the Western Breaker. Eventually, we were searching the shallow waters along the shore, almost a mile from Southern Point. Here I discovered a silver bell dated 1696 with the word *Joseff* inscribed in Old English writing. Very near the bell I located several ancient silver spoons and forks in excellent condition. As the years quickly passed, I would keep going back to this area hoping to find the treasure of the pay ship *Joseph*. What we did find were ships' fittings: broken pintles and gudgeons that had a considerable gold content, some up to 22 percent. This mix of metals was common knowledge to the early Cape Breton salvage divers, but its existence concerned our conservator, who needed to satisfy his professional curiosity by traveling to England to witness similar artifacts kept under lock and key in a British naval museum. As it turned out, the practice of mixing a small percentage of gold into a copper alloy mixture was not all that uncommon; it gave the object a bit less rigidity.

In 2007, while carrying out an archaeological assessment under provincial permit, we located even more coins and artifacts mixed in with the wreckage of the *Cape Breton*. We call this *site contamination* when one shipwreck's debris field is impacted with the debris field of another shipwreck. It is not necessary that one wrecking event would occur after or before the other. In fact, certain conditions created by severe storms could easily reverse the perceived time line.

In searching for the remaining transports, *Mary* and *Neptune*, we discovered what may be the oldest known armed shipwreck in Canadian waters. At the entrance of Flukes Head Cove, some distance offshore is a very large and formidable rock formation jutting out of five fathoms of water called the Ragged Rocks. On the western side of the reef formation we located several ancient cannon, a banded rail gun, dozens of thick sheets of lead sheathing about four feet by four feet square with quarter-inch square holes all around the edge, believed to be hull sheathing. We also found remnants of three large German silver bells and two main anchors in the deeper water of the cove. During the Dive Scatarie Project—back in the 1970s—my divers found silver coins between the Ragged Rocks and the island, in the shallow channel that separates them. Even earlier in my career, I found gold and silver coins in the same area. Reconnaissance reports were provided to the Nova Scotia government, who had no interest in recovering the rail gun or other historically significant artifacts, especially the bells, even after we offered to recover and conserve at our own cost.

Estimate of treasure still left for recovery on the HMS *Feversham* wreck site and the transport *Joseph* wreck site—85 percent.

D. The Recovery and Survey Map of the French Pay Ship *Le Chameau*, Lost on the Chameau Rocks at Kelpy Cove in 1725

General Area

The wreck site of the *Le Chameau* can be found almost halfway between Scatarie Island and Louisbourg Harbor on Cape Breton Island, the ship's intended destination in 1725. The local name given to the place where the wreck occurred is Kelpy Cove, although this is misleading as the cove itself is just inside and shoreward from the ship's original point of impact. The cove itself is enclosed by two points of land that form the bowl of the cove, Cape Breton Point to the north and Woody Point to the southwest. The distance over water between these geographic features is a little less than 1.5 miles. The extreme outer rim of the cove seaward is blocked by Port Nova Island, an independent landmass that creates two very distinct passages into the cove. The area where the pay ship wrecked lies inside Southern Point, Scatarie Island, six miles distant to the southeast and slightly outside the entrance of Louisbourg Harbor, nine or so miles to the west-southwest.

Wreck Site

The 48-gun French pay ship *Le Chameau* struck and wrecked on the sunken reef structure forever since known as the Chameau Rocks, located halfway between the southeastern corner of Port Nova Island and Cape Breton Point to the north, after first striking the reef known as the Virgin Rocks, located immediately south of the Chameau Rocks. The ship was fully loaded with supplies for New France: general merchandise, bullion from both government and private sources, arms, powder, and lead and round shot for the land forces. *Le Chameau* carried a complement of over 300 passengers and crew, vital dispatches, French and ecclesiastical dignitaries (including the new intendant of New France). All perished.

The ship measured approximately 120 feet on the waterline, drew over 14 feet of water, and registered at 600 tons. The *Le Chameau* was built in France, although the builders copied a Dutch design for heavy transports of this type. The *Le Chameau* and her sister ships, *L'Elephant* and *Le Portefaix*, were intended to supply the French colony of New France and the French island of Martinique with both funds and supplies from France. The *L'Elephant*, carrying a similar cargo of supplies and bullion destined for Quebec, was lost in the St. Lawrence on September 1, 1729. Both maritime tragedies almost certainly rendered a serious blow to the future of France's colonial interests in North America. The effects may have played some small part in the final days of New France, which was eventually lost to the British in 1760.

The wreck site of *Le Chameau* was first located by a dedicated group of local salvers known as the Orbit Group; however, in the mid-1960s another team made a substantial recovery of bullion under a cloud of controversy. The shipwreck and her secrets were far from understood at the time. I began to work this site in the early 1970s, carrying out my last recovery operations inside what we refer to as the Kelpy Cove claim in 2008. During all that time of continuous search and recovery dives, the wreck kept expanding in size and treasure potential. The wreck site of the *Le Chameau* must be considered a contradiction in terms. The immediate area really involves the wreck sites of several period shipwrecks within Kelpy Cove, although the French *flute* is the only historic shipwreck positively identified. There are also two other, modern shipwrecks impacting the site. They are the SS *Ragna*, lost in 1914 at Woody Point, and the SS *Cillisto*, lost in 1928 after striking the Virgin Rocks. Wreckage from both can be found inside the debris field of the French pay ship.

Supported by my personal research files, backed by extensive diving reconnaissance and two comprehensive electronic surveys carried out by renowned geophysics firms, we have proven beyond any doubt that other ships wrecked here. The Kelpy Cove claim is the final resting place of at least five historic wooden shipwrecks, at least four of which were armed with a unique assortment of cannon. The involvement of more than one such shipwreck in this area leads to serious site contamination, by which the cultural material from one shipwreck is mixed with the cultural material of another. There is practically no way to sort out which is which, unless the artifact's origin is obvious at the time of recovery.

The wreckage of the *Le Chameau*, for example, extends from the area of the Chameau Rocks all the way across to Woody Point to the southwest, a distance of one mile or more. It also flows to the north, ending just inside Cape Breton Point to the north, a distance of over half of a mile. The stern section lies even farther to the east-northeast. In all, the wreckage of the royal *flute* covers several hectares of shallow ocean bottom inside

Kelpy Cove. At the original point of impact and breakup—the Chameau Rocks—many of the ship's cannon, smaller anchors, cannonballs, lead shot, and cargo, including an assortment of bullion, came to settle. The ship quickly broke up into at least three pieces; a section of the bow and decking was driven ashore at Woody Point. The stern section, affected more by tide than wind, slipped over the reef edge between the Chameau Rocks, closer to Cape Breton Point. One main anchor, some small cannon, and a few lesser anchors spread out across the shallow reef structure that runs for several hundred yards away from the Chameau Rocks to the southwest, directly toward Woody Point. Here the water deepens to 70 feet. All along the reef that leads to Woody Point, gold and silver artifacts were recovered, including coins, silverware, jewelry, and military medals.

From the Chameau Rocks heading toward the center of Kelpy Cove, parts of the ship and cargo scattered at the time of wrecking and long afterward. Here we found another of the ship's main anchors and two large cannon located closer to Cannon Point, at the entrance of Kelpy Cove. It was this trail of wreckage that led us to the recovery of religious materials, such as church silverware, silver plates, crucifixes, and other ecclesiastical artifacts. Near the center of Kelpy Cove, in 50 feet of water, we located a shipment of fine swords, less the iron blades, with gold-gilded handles, solid-silver handles, silver and gilded hand guards, and highly decorated gold-gilded and solid-silver pommels.

Close by, one of the divers discovered the second cross of St. Louis we found on the site. The first one I found during the mid-1970s at the southwest edge of the reef structure leading away from the Chameau Rocks. The second was found by one of our science divers, Matt Nigro, in 2005. Both were recovered in almost pristine condition, gold and enameled Maltese-style crosses about 1.5 inches square, both dated 1693. This discovery also led us to find hundreds of copper alloy ship fittings, dead eyes, and lead shot leading into the very shallow water of Kelpy

Cove, with the trail ending almost at the high-water mark. In all, over the years since 1972 until 2008, under various provincial licenses and permits, including early declarations to the local receiver of wreck in Louisbourg, I recovered alone or with my team thousands upon thousands of treasure trove artifacts from the main wreck site of the *Le Chameau*. These finds included hoards of gold and silver coins. Today, many of these precious and nonprecious artifacts are held within the Nova Scotia Museum System and belong to the citizens of Nova Scotia.

The New Site

Adding even further to the mystery and intrigue of the overall Kelpy Cove wreck site is a unique site we came to refer to as the New Site. It is located in a small cove just inside the western edge of Cape Breton Point. During September 2002, while carrying out an underwater reconnaissance of the shoreline between Cape Breton Point and Cannon Point, divers Matt Nigro and Jason Day came across an assortment of motor shot the size of basketballs, just at the entrance of the small cove that lies inside Cape Breton Point to the west. They entered the cove and were astounded to find it littered with cannon of all types. When they reported the find to me, I instructed them to return to both areas and examine the cannon to try to get an accurate count.

They did so, returning with a count of 55 cannon, but noted they did not survey the entire cove, and although small in size, it was full of deep crevices with cannon piled on top of each other. Some of the crevices were virtually full of cannon, short, long, fat, and thin. I sent them back for a second count, while I dove on wreckage near Cannon Point. When the divers returned from the New Site, they agreed they had both counted 85 cannon.

As they described, many were very short, which were later identified as carronades and smashers. I then moved the team to this area and had a closer look for myself. I was awestruck by what I observed, as were the other divers, more so because only two of the royal *flute*'s cannon were observed among the many other guns. This meant, by my quick count, there were over 125 cannon more or less inside the claim, factoring in the cannon at the Chameau Rocks and others scattered around the cove from the wrecking of the *Le Chameau*.

Although we were busy excavating the main wreck site in the center of Kelpy Cove, I selected a team of divers to return to the New Site. I instructed them to begin some limited disturbance excavations to assess the cannon's origins. The result was very unexpected. The divers working to open up the concretion that seemed to lock every piece of cast iron in its grasp notified me that there were many smaller cannon under the ones visible on the surface. Other finds included blocks of cast-iron ballast and thousands of cannonballs. I looked the site over again and noticed that the small cannon were in fact rail guns, most about 36 inches in length and a few up to a foot shorter. Nearby in one of the crevices lay an assortment of cannon that were robust in design but less than two feet long. What had we stumbled on, one wreck or two wrecks? Maybe more?

In later years we tried to carry out some type of meaningful excavation of the New Site, spending weeks breaking through the concretion trying to find a clue as to the shipwrecks involved. The divers did recover silver and copper coins, even 8 L ecu coins from the *Le Chameau*, further supported by the discovery of two cannon that matched perfectly to those from the ship's original impact site just inside the Chameau Rocks. However, after a lot of effort, no definitive information identifying the wreck or wrecks was ever found. The site still remains a mystery to this day.

The New Site has proven itself to be rich in specie. The effort to unlock the treasure from the rock-hard concretion creates its own technical and scientific problems. In the end we decided to leave the New Site and spend our time trying to find the rest of the *Le Chameau*'s treasure. In fact, a majority of that treasure to date has never been found, by the divers in the 1960s or by my efforts. It was really all about opportunity versus justifiable cost; the New Site may be worth millions, but it could take millions to unlock its secrets. We had to move on. Now that the Nova Scotia government has decreed the Nova Scotia Treasure Trove Act repealed, this is just another site that will be ground to dust by the sea and winter ice.

The American Wreck at Woody Point (circa 1836)

In 2005, my divers found cannonballs, sword parts, and a single French silver jeton dated 1721 in the shallow water not 30 feet from the very tip of Woody Point on the northern side, inside Kelpy Cove. The jeton matched others we found closer to the Chameau Rocks mixed with wreckage from the *flute*. During the last week of the 2008 operations season inside the Kelpy Cove claim, one of the science divers returned to the main workboat with coins we first identified as 8 L ecus. Upon further inspection, they turned out to be American silver half dollars, dating from the early 1800s. With time at a minimum, we directed our full attention to the new find at Woody Point, and with only a week left to investigate, we recovered scores of American silver half dollars, a few British crowns from the same time period, a few American copper coins, and a four-reale Spanish cob (Lima mint) dated 1776.

The divers also found a cast-iron rail gun yoke along with thousands of bronze spikes, other ships' fittings, and thousands of copper sheathing nails. From the evidence, we deduced that there was yet another new wreck site at Woody Point mixed in with the wreckage of the *Le*

Chameau we had first witnessed in 2005. We had surely opened a Pandora's box, with the wreckage of several period wrecks migrating back and forth when storms created the perfect conditions to redeposit artifacts at will. After witnessing huge boulders of several tons or more that had moved around this cove as if they were mere pebbles, the phrase *discontinuous assemblage of cultural material* began to make perfect sense.

Estimate of treasure still left for recovery on the *Le Chameau* wreck site, the New Site, and the American wreck site—80 percent.

E. The Recovery and Survey Map of the HMS *Fantome* Fleet, Lost on the Dollar Shoals at Prospect, Nova Scotia, in 1814

General Area

The *Fantome* plunder fleet consisting of four ships ran ashore at night on and near the Dollar Shoals, approximately 3 miles south of the village of Prospect, Nova Scotia, in November 1814. These wreck sites can be found between Norris Rock to the east-northeast and Shag Bay Head to the west-southwest, covering a distance over the water of approximately 2 miles. The closest major port lies 20 miles to the northeast, Halifax Harbor, the destination of the fleet en route from Alexandria, Virginia, and Castine, Maine, via St. John, New Brunswick. The escort brig HMS *Fantome* met the other ships at Castine for the last leg of the trip to Halifax.

There is another prominent shoal just outside the Dollar Shoals called the Green Shoals, which may have played some part in the navigation error that placed the plunder fleet so close to the lee shore. The entire area making up Phantom Cove is exposed to winds from the southwest around to the east. Severe Atlantic storms are very common in this area; however, sea ice is not known to reach this far south along Nova Scotia's Atlantic shoreline.

Wreck Site

On a November night in 1814, the four ships of the fleet ran ashore south of Prospect. However, accounts in local newspapers of the time report other ships were involved and lost with the fleet. Our research accounts for only the brig, one ship, one schooner, and a naval transport that freed itself from the shoals in the morning and made it back to Halifax without further incident. Although no lives were lost, the ships were a total loss, with no chance to salvage the precious cargo they carried. The brig and one of the other vessels quickly filled with water and sank on the outer edge of Dollar Shoals. Winter storms soon broke the ships apart, distributing sections of all three, first over the shoals and then along the shoreline some 500 feet distant. Our surveys indicate that one of the ships, most likely the larger of the captured vessels taken at Alexandria, actually struck the end of the Dollar Shoals in the place where the reef drops away, creating a very narrow channel of deeper water between the Dollar Shoals and Norris Rocks to the northeast.

The area where these ships wrecked is deceiving and difficult to read from a salver's perspective. Inside the Dollar Shoals that run almost a half mile parallel to the shoreline, there is a wide gully of deep sand and gravel that runs from the shoal up to the rock walls of the mainland that are predominant in this area. There is only a small gravel beach located in the center of Phantom Cove, the name it is given on modern marine charts. The headlands, beaches, and ocean bottom for some distance offshore are littered with huge granite boulders, covering parts of the wreckage and making it difficult to search for the rest.

In both 2005 and 2006, my divers located large areas of artifact-filled concretion and trails of associated wreckage on both sides of Phantom Cove. In 2006 we began to carry out extensive electronic surveys between Phantom Cove and the Norris Rocks. Here we located major shipwreck evidence in the sand- and gravel-filled gully between the cove and Norris Rocks. Just inside Norris Rocks on the Phantom Cove side, we found what proved to be the final resting place of one of the ships involved. The divers used handheld metal detectors to locate hundreds of targets. Upon investigation, we identified their findings as ships' fittings from the period, treasure in the form of coin and silverware, chain, and ballast blocks. A bit closer to Phantom Cove, in the deep crevices found in the rock wall face near the shore, they found bronze spikes, treasure, cannonballs, small-caliber round shot, 32-pound round shot, cannonballs, chain, and cast-iron ballast blocks. One of the divers came across deep pockets of lead shot and broken ceramics. The targets recorded in the center of the gully were not investigated due to the depth of the overburden.

The work we carried out on the site, all permitted and licensed by the province of Nova Scotia, drew a lot of unwanted attention, especially from critics. They freely stated these ships carried no treasure from the raid on Washington and in fact no treasure except possibly a few coins from the customs house at Castine. However, the real truth is to be found on the bottom of the sea, not as conjecture but from the reality of our scientific investigations, which prove beyond any doubt that the ships carried cultural material, not just from the raid and burning of Washington in 1814 but from many other sources. Cargo included plunder taken from towns and seaports along the Eastern Seaboard of the United States and from prizes captured by ships of the British navy at sea.

Near the center of Phantom Cove, in 18 feet of water, we found the largest of the many concreted shipwreck-related masses: an assortment of exposed cultural material, including silver coins and silverware embedded in the surface. We recorded dozens of others between Norris Rocks and the inner beach, from the Walker's Beach area of Shag Bay Head to the north-northwest. Within the larger concretions, some of which measure over 50 feet long by 20 feet wide, and loose in the sand and gravel matrix, we found hundreds of assorted cannonballs, the majority of which were 32-pound round shot. We also found literally tons of lead, bird, and musket shot. Coins and other delicate artifacts from many different nations lie out in the open, both on the surface or suspended with the sand and gravel that fills the many crevices and gravel pits that make up the seafloor's subbottom. Thousands of rare and unique American coins from a very important time in the history of the U.S. Mint, which officially began operations in 1793, a mere 21 years before the wreck, were lost here.

As reported from earlier finds, these most likely include the extremely rare 1804 silver dollar, which refutes the belief by numismatists that these coins were minted later, in 1836. We have also seen silverware taken during the raid on Washington embedded in the concretions, other coins, and countless precious artifacts trapped inside the matrix, most mixed with ships' fittings, lead shot, cannonballs, and cast-iron ballast. The area in the center of Phantom Cove between a depth of 20 feet and the low-water mark represents a cluster of riches beyond anyone's comprehension.

The only way this site can be proven for what it really represents—plunder from the United States and prizes taken on the high seas, including cultural material taken during the raid on Washington and the burning of the first U.S. Capitol—is in its timely recovery and conservation. However, the opportunity lessens each day this material is left in the ocean, every time a storm redistributes boulders of over a ton or more, crushing and grinding fragile artifacts to proverbial gold dust.

Every historic wooden ship, wrecked in the shallow waters of Nova Scotia's Territorial Sea suffers its own unique set of destructive dynamics. At play and seriously impacting how long a single or certain group of cultural artifacts will survive are cyclonic, hydraulic, and electrolic stressors. The overall result is that these destructive forces are bent on the total annihilation of wreckage debris.

This is surely true for the area where the HMS *Fantome* fleet was lost in Phantom Cove. One of the overwhelming geologic features south of Halifax, including the Prospect area and beyond, is the overwhelming abundance of weather-beaten gray granite rocks, from pebbles to several-ton boulders. Phantom Cove, its small beaches, and the water just offshore are filled with this type of rock, the surface of which feels like very coarse sandpaper. During even the slightest of wave action, a diver working in the water close to shore can hear the softball-size granite rocks rolling around and banging into each other, giving off a very distinctive clicking sound. These rocks move almost 24 hours a day, every day, smashing against exposed artifacts and shipwreck concretions, slowly but surely exposing their precious contents. This ongoing reality reduces the total shipwreck artifact collection in situ to less of what was available only a day ago. As this natural phenomenon continues, the wreckage of any wooden ship lost in the shallow ocean will cease to exist, sooner than one may think. The thousands of fragile, rare, and historically significant artifacts exposed in the open on this site are doomed if not recovered immediately.

Estimate of treasure still left for recovery on the HMS *Fantome* fleet wreck sites—99 percent.

Research-Supported Estimates of Treasure Remaining on Each Site as of 2011

1. HMS Leonidas

The transport *Leonidas* carried over 10 tons of copper coins, which comes to millions of coins. David Dow's research reported a private consignment of specie in gold and silver coin loaded at Halifax and possibly a large shipment of silverware, most of which is still on-site as witnessed during the Dive Scatarie Recovery Project on this site. I estimate that no more than 300,000 copper coins have been recovered to date, no silverware, and only a handful of gold and other silver coins related to the loss.

2. HMS Feversham *Fleet*

The small *Feversham* fleet carried a major portion of the funds, provincial silver, gathered in New England and elsewhere to support the 1711 invasion of Quebec. This force was led by English Admiral Hovenden Walker and his fleet. Research and notices in New England papers of the time state the *Feversham* loss at $5,000,000 in gold, indicating many millions of coins are involved. Considering what I recovered from this site over the years and the new discoveries after 2005 of the fleet pay ship, the transport *Joseph*, most of the original treasure carried by these four ships still remains on-site to be recovered.

3. Le Chameau

The royal pay ship *Le Chameau* carried a shipment of government funds in the form of gold, silver, billon (an alloy of mostly copper), and copper coins from France for delivery to Quebec. However, this ship carried other funds in the form of coin and bullion, funds for private, business, and church interests. Our research places this figure closer to 2,000,000 livre. Most of the specie carried by the *Le Chameau* belonged to private passengers or was consigned by the crown to private interests. Hundreds of thousands of coins and precious artifacts from this shipwreck still remain on-site to be recovered.

There is additional treasure to be considered within the Kelpy Cove claim, the treasure carried by the as yet to be identified ship at Woody Point and the treasure remaining to be recovered from the New Site at Cape Breton Point.

4. Auguste

The cartel ship *Auguste* carried a private cargo of gold and silver bullion, most of it in coin. It was the personal property of the elite of New France repatriating back to their homeland on board the ill-fated ship. Previous research carried out during the 1977–1978 recoveries by the original salvers and Parks Canada concludes the loss on-site, in coin alone, may top 2,000,000 individual gold, silver, and copper coins. This does not include other forms of bullion or precious artifacts, such as jewelry, ingots, finger bars, and silverware. Even though the site has seen several years of unrelated salvage efforts, the majority of the treasure carried by the *Auguste* still remains for recovery.

The case of the *Auguste* has an odd twist. During its commission to take patriots back to France, English officials would not agree to let the businessmen who sailed on board the cartel ship load cargo for profit and resale in Europe. However, they seemed to turn a blind eye in regard to the bullion being loaded on board unabated. The true explanation may never be known, but a theory put forward by the archaeologist in charge of *Auguste* excavations in 1977 and 1978 makes sense. In exchange for the privilege to remove these riches, the English bartered with the patriots for their military connections and influence within the Indian nations. For this service, the British officials at Quebec gave the patriots leave to take their entire wealth on the voyage back home to Europe. It was reported at the time that St. Luc de La Corne alone was worth tens of millions, thanks to his profits of years in the fur trade and other commercial ventures, including the plunder of war.

5. Fantome *Fleet*

The HMS *Fantome* fleet was lost with no real record of what treasure the ships, including the escort brig, may have carried. The brig was lost soon after striking the Dollar Shoals, carrying all official papers of the voyage to the bottom with her. However, we know where the ships came from and that the vessels captured at Alexandria were filled with property plundered from the people of that town, surrounding countryside, and other towns and seaports in the vicinity. Since the plunder of Washington took place at this time, it is believed some of what was taken, especially specie, may have been loaded on board one or more of these vessels. It is also reported that the ships may have taken large sums of specie from the customs house at Castine. The bullion was gathered there by the English from many sources to be transported back to the naval dockyard at Halifax and eventual shipment back to England.

To further support the conjecture that bullion was carried north on board one or more of these vessels, even possibly on the brig, our recovery and survey operations in the area prove beyond any shadow of a doubt that in fact, it was. Our efforts on-site are covered in several science and survey reports now in the hands of the province of Nova Scotia, reports that should be, by rights, part of the public domain. The information they contain, including site photos, prove without the possibility of contention by any person—scientist, researcher, or expert in early American history—that the ships carried a large cargo of American riches. We also have proof that cultural material plundered from Washington by the British before they set fire to the city's official buildings and edifices during the evening and night of August 24, 1814, remains part of this shipwreck site.

Small Change, Risk, and Instinct

My estimates in this appendix are based on the "more or less" theory. There may have been several hundred thousand coins, most likely over a million, shipped on board the *Le Chameau*, HMS *Leonidas*, and the HMS *Feversham* fleet. Small change plays a decisive role in these estimations. For example, the silver eight-reale cobs of Latin America, found on many shipwrecks lost before 1800 and after, were minted in lesser denominations (quarter, half, one, two, and four reales). In fact, depending on the denomination, it could take 32 quarter reales or 16 half reales to equal a single eight-reale cob in both weight and value. A ship carrying the value of 100,000 eight-reale cobs in silver quarter reales would in fact carry 3,200,000 silver coins. Of course this is an oversimplification of the reality; most ships carried a mixture of specie, with lesser denominations in either copper, silver, or gold necessary to carry on trade.

It was a very common practice in the 16th, 17th, and 18th centuries for dollar-size silver coins to be divided into fractions by the mint. In extreme cases, as we have proven in the recovery of New England coins from the *Feversham* site, it was common practice for the public at large to alter such coins. They were clipped or divided into lesser denominations; partial one-shilling sections were recovered from the wreck site of the *Feversham*.

When a researcher finds the manifest of a treasure ship, specifically a ship carrying specie, he or she may find the cargo listed in simple terms, such as "80,000 livre" instead of a complete breakdown of the small change. (*Livre* is the French term of account; an ecu is a silver coin comparable to the Spanish eight reale in weight and value.) The wreck of the *Leonidas* is a prime example for the need of small change to facilitate trade in British North America. History dictates the ship carried tons of copper coins already broken down by selective minting into pence, halfpence, and farthings.

Finally, my estimate of what treasure remains on each site is based solely on my actual recovery experience, knowledge, and instinctive sense. This information was gained from research, test pits, and/or by electronic means. To say I know where every gold or silver coin is hidden on a shipwreck site is incorrect. I know where to look, and I know how to read a debris field. Based on my proven ability to re-create the wrecking process from the time of initial impact, I believe my assessments are plenty accurate.

Even backed with this knowledge, recovery of treasure in shallow water is a very slow and costly process. Recall that the debris field can cover an area from a few acres of seafloor to hundreds of hectares, even miles of coastline. It could take years to recover even 50 percent of what treasure a ship may have carried at the time of wrecking. The shipwreck of the *Auguste,* lost in Aspy Bay, provides a fine example. The entire cargo is not only spread over many, many acres of sea bottom; the wreck site in most areas is covered with a thick layer of sand, a condition that requires timely mechanical intervention to facilitate recovery.

I estimate, based on my 40-plus years of continuous recovery experience, that it would take a fully equipped salvage team 10 years or more of six-month field seasons to find 50 to 75 percent of the treasure the *Auguste* carried at the time of her loss.

You may think this is unrealistic. How could anyone afford to support such a recovery? In reality this is the only kind of shallow-water recovery operation an investor should support. If the cost of yearly operations is $750,000, with a contingency budget of $250,000, the total projected cost of continuous yearly recovery operations for 10 years would be $10,000,000, plus or minus.

Compare this realistic estimate of operations cost against the value of the treasure you may be seeking, both in modern recovery terms and in modern numismatic values. Just one silver coin worth $1 in the mid-1700s may be worth $100 or more in modern times. This is the norm with treasure coins versus what the coin was worth at the time of loss. Some extremely rare coins, such as the New England willow tree shilling and its subdenominations, could easily fetch over six figures at auction. It all depends on rarity and condition, with rarity being the main value driver.

Again using the *Auguste* shipwreck site as an example, the ship at the time of loss is reported to have carried at least $10,000,000 in bullion, most of which was a mixture of gold and silver coin. It is safe to say that the conversion rate of value from 1761 to 2011 would be 10 times or more per dollar value. Even at $10,000,000 times 10, the value of the treasure in 2011 would be $100,000,000. If the salver took all the time and care it really takes and recovered only 25 percent of the treasure carried on board the *Auguste*, after expenses and interest, he or she would be splitting in the vicinity of $15,000,000 with the investment group. To take this one step further, there may be rewards to equal the value of the recovery in intellectual property rights (IPRs).

In most cases, when passengers traveled on ships both private and naval, they carried personal bullion for a number of reasons. No one can be sure of the amount or in what form. Even if an official manifest is available detailing the cargo, including the bullion, the treasure hunter needs to consider the very real possibility of contraband. Specie in the form of contraband or prize cargoes taken at sea may also be involved in the recovery. Contraband and captured funds would not be recorded in the original ship's manifest.

This is the case with the *Auguste*; no manifest exists of the riches loaded on board by the passengers. This is also the case with the *Feversham* fleet loss; other than an account of funds taken from the treasury in New York, the rest of the bullion goes unaccounted for. It may consist in part of two rich prizes, one taken off Nantucket and a French merchantman taken in Cuban waters by ships from Walker's invasion fleet. Only recovery helps sort out fact from fiction.

SELECTED BIBLIOGRAPHY

Le Chameau

National Archives of Canada: Library and Archives Canada

Microfilm Collection MG1-Serie G1. *Fonds des Colonies, Depot des papiers publics des Colonies, etat civil et recensements.*

Reel no. F-804. "List of Passengers Embarked Onboard Chameau." Aug. 11, 1720, folios 101–105.

Microfilm Collection MG1-Serie C11A. *Archives Nationale, Fonds des Colonies, correspondance generale.*

Reel no. 51. "List of Ownership of Recovered Materiel from Chameau." 1725, folios 501–503v.

Reel no. 52. "Letter—Beauharnois to Ailleboust." Oct. 15, 1730, folios 211–211v.

Reel no. F-40. "Letter—Vaudreuil to Begon." Oct. 10, 1719, folios 5–6v.

Reel no. F-40. "Letter—Vaudreuil to Begon." Nov. 14, 1719, folios 124–126.

Reel no. F-40. "Letters—Vaudreuil to Begon." Nov. 14, 1719, folios 145–148.

Reel no. F-40. "Various Charges & Duties Regarding Chameau." Nov. 14, 1719, folios 149–151v.

Reel no. F-41. "Resume & Letter from Vaudreuil to Begon." Mar. 5, 1720, folios 110–114.

Reel no. F-41. "Resumes & Letters from Vaudreuil to Begon." Apr. 19, 1720, folios 236–238v.

Reel no. F-42. "Letter from Vaudreuil to Begon." Oct. 26, 1720, folios 63–64v.

Reel no. F-42. "List of Passengers on Chameau." Oct. 25, 1720, folios 221–223.

Reel no. F-43. "Resume & Letter from Vaudreuil to Begon." Mar. 24, 1721, folios 222–222v.

Reel no. F-44. "Letter from Vaudreuil to Begon." Oct. 8, 1721, folios 31–32v.

Reel no. F-44. "List of Arrivals on Chameau." Oct. 9, 1721, folios 70–71v.

Reel no. F-44. "Letter from Vaudreuil to Begon." Nov. 4, 1721, folios 87–90v.

Reel no. F-44. "Letters from Begon to Compte. De Jean Petit." Nov. 10, 1721, folios 231–238v.

Reel no. F-44. "Letter from Ramezay to Vaudreuil." Oct. 6, 1721, folios 242–243v.

Reel no. F-44. "Letter to Compte. Bradrig from De Mezy." Oct. 22, 1725, folios 405–405v.

Reel no. F-44. "Letter Regarding Loading of Recovered Material from Chameau." Oct. 11, 1725, folio 406.

Reel no. F-44. "Letter from de Ramezay to Vaudreuil & Begon." Oct. 14, 1722, folios 412–413v.

Reel no. F-44. "Letter from L. A. de Bourbon to Begon." June 1722, folio 429.

Reel no. F-45. "Letter from Vaudreuil to Begon." Oct. 14, 1723, folios 3v–4v.

Reel no. F-45. "Letter from Vaudreuil to Begon." Oct. 14, 1723, folios 61–64v.

Reel no. F-45. "Letter from Begon to Vaudreuil." Oct. 14, 1723, folios 184–187v.

Reel no. F-45. "Letter from Begon to Vaudreuil." Oct. 14, 1723, folios 202–204.

Reel no. F-45. "Letter from Begon to Council of Marine." Oct. 14, 1723, folio 205.

Reel no. F-45. "Letter from Begon to Msr. Lotbiniere." Oct. 14, 1723, folios 229–232v.

Reel no. F-45. "Letter from Begon to Capt. of Chameau." Oct. 17, 1723, folios 251–252.

Reel no. F-45. "Letter from Begon to Vaudreuil." Oct. 20, 1723, folios 253–254.

Reel no. F-45. "Letter from Begon to Vaudreuil." Oct. 20, 1723, folios 255–256v.

Reel no.F-45. "Letter from Begon to Council of Marine." Oct. 20, 1723, folios 257–258v.

Reel no. F-45. "Letter from Begon to Vaudreuil." Oct. 17, 1723, folios 259–261v.

Reel no. F-45. "Letter Regarding Embarkation of Passenger on Chameau." Oct. 10, 1723, folios 314–315v.

Reel no. F-45. "Letter from Capt. de Beauville of Chameau to Begon." Dec. 4, 1723, folios 380–381.

Reel no. F-46. "Letter from Vaudreuil to Begon Regarding Finances." Nov. 2, 1724, folios 22–23v.

Reel no. F-46. "Letter from Vaudreuil to Capt. de Beauville of Chameau." Oct. 25, 1724, folios 79–79v.

Reel no. F-46. "Letter from Begon to de Ramezay." Nov. 2, 1724, folios 159–160v.

Reel no. F-46. "Boarding Contracts for Passengers . . ." Sept. 28, 1723, folio 285.

Reel no. F-47. "Letter from Begon to Vaudreuil Regarding Wreck . . ." Oct. 31, 1725, folios 252–253v.

Reel no. F-47. "Letter from Begon Regarding Passage to France in 1726 & Mention of Wreck . . ." 1725, folios 367–367v.

Reel no. F-48. "Letter from Beauharnois to Dupuy Regarding Financial Loss . . ." Oct. 12, 1726, folios 3–4v.

Reel no. F-48. "Memo from de Ramezay re. Family Members Lost . . ." Folios 169–170.

Reel no. F-48. "Letter from Begon to Council Requesting L'Elephante to . . ." May 20, 1726, folios 206–206v.

Reel no. F-48. "Complaint of Financial Loss." Sept. 2, 1726, folios 270–271.

Reel no. F-48. "Letter from Dupuy to de Ramezay—Loss of Persons." Oct. 21, 1726, folios 283–286v.

Reel no. F-40. "Various letters from Vaudreuil to Begon." Oct. 26, 1719, folios 30–49v.

Reel no. F-40. "Letters from Vaudreuil to Begon—finances, Importations, etc." Nov. 14, 1719, folios 96-101v.

Reel no. F-40. "Letter from Vaudreuil to Begon—Finances, etc." Nov. 14, 1719, folios 120–123v.

Reel no. F-40. "Letter from Vaudreuil to Begon—Finances for the Church . . ." Oct. 28, 1719, folios 179–193.

Reel no. F-40. "Letters between Vaudreuil & Begon—Finances, Trade with N.E., etc." May 23, 1719, folios 279–300v.

Reel no. F-41. "Letters & Resume from Begon." Jan. 7, 1720, folios 31–38.

Reel no. F-41. "A Royal Memorial Re. Relegious Financing, etc." Mar. 4, 1720, folios 94–109v.

Reel no. F-41. "Letters & Deliberations of the Council of Marine—Financing, etc." Apr. 20, 1720, folios 262–265v.

Reel no. F-42. "Letters from Vaudreuil to Begon Regarding Trade." Oct. 26, 1720, folios 35–50v.

Reel no. F-42. "Certificates of Masters & Trade for Chameau." Oct. 21, 1720, folios 224–227v.

Reel no. F-42. "Letter from Capt. Voutron of Chameau Regarding Voyage . . ." Dec. 9, 1720, folios 269–284v.

Reel no. F-43. "Letters from Vaudreuil to Begon." Jan. 13, 1721, folios 67–73v.

Reel no. F-43. "Letters from Begon Regarding Council Deliberations." Dec. 2, 1721, folios 332–335v.

Reel no. F-43. "Letter from Begon to Vaudreuil Regarding Council Orders." Dec. 17, 1721, folios 360-362.

Reel no. F-43. "Letter from de Ramezay to Begon Regarding Freight Charges." Dec. 19, 1721, folios 368–369v.

Reel no. F-44. "Letter from Vaudreuil to Begon Regarding Funds, etc." Oct. 17, 1722, folios 275–279v.

Reel no. F-45. "List of passengers on Chameau." Oct. 14, 1723, folios 312–313v.

Reel no. F-46. "Letters from Vaudreuil to Begon Regarding Colonial Management, etc." Nov. 2, 1724, folios 27–42v.

Reel no. F-46. "Extensive List of Letters from Begon regarding Needed Financing, etc." Nov. 2, 1724, folios 253–261v.

Reel no. F-46. "Orders for Material to be Shipped on Chameau." Oct. 31, 1724, folios 274–274v.

Reel no. F-47. "Letter from Longueuil to Begon with Extensive Mention of Losses . . ." Oct. 31, 1725, folios 106–120.

Reel no. F-47. "Letter from L'eveque Regarding Detailed Mentions of Losses, Persons, Finances, etc." Oct. 4, 1725, folios 462–465v.

Reel no. F-48. "Letter from Beauhamois to Dupuy Regarding Cargo Shipped on Chameau, etc." Oct. 20, 1726, folios 34–41v.

Reel no. F-48. "Letter from Begon Requesting Expedited Deployment of L'Elephante, etc." May 20, 1726, folios 207–210v.

Reel no. F-48. "Letter from Dupuy to Vaudreuil Regarding Replacement of Funds, etc." Oct. 21, 1726, folios 288–296.

Reel no. F-114. "Letter from Treasurer de Selle to Msr. Nicolas Lanoullier regarding Expenses of Colonies & Loss on Chameau, etc." Oct. 25, 1728, folios 395–398v.

Reel no. F-114. "Letter from Lanoullier Requesting Data on fate of 1725 Funds, etc." May 25, 1728, folios 403–404.

Reel no. F-121. "Letter from Vaudreuil to Begon with Suggestions for Award of Cross of St. Louis, etc." Nov. 2, 1721, folios 167–174v.

Reel no. F-125. "Deliberation of the Council & Letter to Begon." Aug. 29, 1719, folios 406–410.

Reel no. F-125. "Deliberations of the Council & Letter from Vaudreuil to Begon." Nov. 28, 1719, folios 417–418.

Reel no. F-125. "Deliberations of the Council of Marine & Letter from Begon." May 24, 1722, folios 531–532v.

Reel no. F-125. "Deliberations of Council & Letter from Jean-Louis de la Corne de Chaptes." May 24, 1722, folios 536–537.

Reel no. F-125. "Deliberations of Council & Letter from Begon." May 28, 1722, folio 541.

Microfilm Collection MG18-H54. *Archives Nationale, Fonds de la famille Ramezay, Series Diverses proprietes et moulins a scie.*

Reel no. C-15684. "Copies of Returns Regarding Chameau Wreck." 1726, pages 1585–1588.

Microfilm Collection MG1-Serie C11C. *Archives Nationale, Fonds des Colonies, Correspondance generale, Amerique du Nord.*

Reel no. F-517. "Deliberations of the Council—Mentions of Chameau and Funding, etc." Mar. 3, 1722, pages 222–223.

Reel no. F-517. "Deliberations of Council of Marine—Material for Fortifications Shipped on Chameau." Apr. 12, 1722, pages 303–304.

Microfilm Collection MG1-Serie C11B. *Archives Nationale, Fonds des Colonies, Correspondance generale, Ile Royale.*

Reel no. F-136. "Memorandums by St. Ovide Regarding Wreck of Chameau." Sept. 12, 1725, folios 181–182.

Reel no. F-136. "Letter from de Mezy & Others with Descriptions of Chameau Wreck, etc." Aug. 29, 1725, folios 213–215.

Reel no. F-136. "Letters of de Mezy & de Vaudreuil to Begon re. Loss of Chameau." Sept. 3, 1725, folios 216–219.

Reel no. F-136. "Letter from de Mezy about Loss of Chameau." Sept. 6, 1725, folios 221–222.

Reel no. F-136. "Letter from de Mezy re. Ownership of Recovered Material." Aug. 29, 1725, folios 235–235v & 237.

Reel no. F-136. "Letter from de Mezy re. Ownership Update of Material." Sept. 5, 1725, folios 241–242v.

Reel no. F-136. "Particular of Property of Msr. De Goutin, etc." 1725, folios 243–253v.

Reel no. F-136. "Letter of de Mezy Concerning Details of Chameau Wrecking." Dec. 10, 1725, folios 274–276v.

Reel no. F-136. "Letter from Begon to Morpain & de Mezy re. Munitions/Material Recovered." Sept. 28, 1725, folios 284–288v.

Reel no. F-136. "Reports of Morpain Regarding Salvage of Material from Chameau." Dec. 19, 1725, folios 375–375v.

Reel no. F-137. "Letter from de Mezy with misc. Mentions of Chameau, etc." Aug. 14, 1726, folios 87–91.

Reel no. F-137. "Letter of de Mezy Regarding Wreck Material Recovered." Dec. 4, 1726, folios 97–98v.

Reel no. F-137. "Document from Controler M. Sabatier re. Disposition of Recovered Material, etc." Dec. 4, 1726, folios 130–144.

Reel no. F-137. "Statement of Friar Michel-Ange re. Internment of Bodies from Chameau." Oct. 14, 1726, folios 177–178.

Reel no. F-137. "Letter of de Mezy Inquiring about Recovered Material from Chameau." Sept. 9, 1726, folios 179–180.

Reel no. F-137. "Update Letters from de Mezy & le Normant re. Chameau." Sept. 11, 1726, folios 181–182.

Reel no. F-137. "Extensive Listing of Recovered Material from Chameau by de Mezy." Sept. 12, 14, 20, 1726, folios 184–189.

Reel no. F-137. "Additional Descriptions of the Wreck of the Chameau." Sept. 9, 1726, folios 214–214v.

Reel no. F-138. "Letter from de Mezy with Details of Recovered Material." Dec. 10, 1727, folios 108–109.

Archives Nationale, Paris

Document Collection. *Fonds de la Marine, Correspondance generale, Lorient, LaRochelle & Paris.*

Correspondence. Records of the Marine Council. Folios 209–248v.

Archives departementales de la Charente-Maritime, La Rochelle, France

Microfilm collection MG1-Serie C11B. Fonds de la Marine, Correspondence generale, Ile Royale.

Reel no. F-136. "Situation reports from de Mezy regarding loss of Chameau." Sept. 6, 1725, folios 223–228. [Trident Research.]

Walker Fleet 1711

The Public Record Office. Manuscript Report Series 140. Vol. 1. London: Admiralty 1.

Capt. Augustine Rouse to the Secretary of the L.C.A., in the HMS *Sapphire* (40 guns) at Annapolis Royal. June 24, 1712. To go with a sloop and a brig. to Cape Breton to salvage the *Feversham* wreck: "I am then to proceed with the above mentioned Vessels to Spanish River & Load them with coals for the use of the Garrison."

Rouse to the Secretary of the L.C.A., Boston, May 6, 1712. Refers to the wreck of the *Feversham* in November 1711.

The volume contains several letters from Admiral Sir Hovendon Walker and copies of letters in his hand that relate to the 1711 expedition to Quebec under his command.

The Public Record Office. Manuscript Report Series 140. Vol. 2. London: Admiralty 3.

Minutes of the Commission for Lord High Admiral. Nov. 8, 1712. Reference to slop clothes left on the HMS *Feversham* off Cape Breton.

The Public Record Office. Manuscript Report Series 137. London: State Papers 42.

Extract of Letter from Capt. Rt. Hughes, Kent, Plymouth. Aug. 21, 1711. "Admiral Walker was in Quebec River himself and had left some ships to cruise between Cape Breton and off Placentia's."

Copy of Letter from Capt. Butler, Marsham, St. Westminster. Oct. 26, 1711. Complains of ill-treatment by Walker and the return from Spanish River after the loss of the transports.

The Public Record Office. Manuscript Report Series 141. Vol. 1. London: Colonial Office 5.

Admiral Walker's Journal. June 25, 1711. Reference to the fleet off Cape Breton.

Letter from Admiral Walker to Col. Vetch. Aug. 8, 1711. Reference to the fleet off Cape Breton.

Letter from Col. Vetch to Walker. Aug. 26, 1711. Reference to rendezvous at Cape Breton.

Col. Vetch's Journal. Oct. 20, 1711. References to the Walker expedition, which proceeded to Cape Breton on Aug. 8, 1711.

Auguste

Cameron, Silver Donald. *The Wreck of the Auguste.* Ottawa: National Historic Sites Publications, 1992.

The Journal of St-Luc de La Corne. Montreal: Chez Fleury Mesplet, Imprimeur & Libraire, 1778.

Reproduction of original in: Library of the Public Archives of Canada. Microfiche. Ottawa: Canadian Institute for Historical Microreproductions, 1982. 1 microfiche (18 fr.); 11 x 15 cm. (CIHM/ICMH Microfiche series = CIHM/ICMH collection de microfiches; no. 34367.)

MacKinnon, Robert. Diver and Operations Logs—*Auguste* Recovery. 1977–1978.

HMS *Fantome*

Cockburn, Sir George. *Cockburn, Sir George, 10th Bt., Admiral of the Fleet, 1772–1853.* London: Caird Library.

Lloyds of London (Lloyds Coffee House). *Lloyds List & Maritime Gazette.* No. 4928, Sept. 30, 1814, and no. 4935, Jan. 3, 1815. Available at Phillips Library, Salem, Massachusetts.

Lossing, Benson J. *Pictorial Field Book of the War of 1812.* New York: Harper & Brothers Publishers, 1869.

Schulman, Holly C., ed. *The Dolley Madison Digital Edition.* Charlottesville: University of Virginia Press, 2004. References to sacking of the Capitol building, 1814.

Tracy, Nicholas, ed. *The Naval Chronicle: The Contemporary Record of the Royal Navy at War: Volume V, 1811–1815*. London: Chatham Publishing, 1999.

U.S. Congress. *Financial Matters—Mint Reports for 1803–1805*. American State Papers, House of Representatives, 13th Congress, 3rd Session, I:103–119. Detailed coinage quantities of the U.S. Mint at Philadelphia in reports submitted to the U.S. Treasury for the calendar years 1803–1805.

Miscellaneous

Blundon et al. v. Storm, [1972] S.C.R. 135. 1971-06-28.

Cuhaj, George S., and Thomas Michael. *Standard Catalog of World Coins 1801–1900*. 6th ed. Iola, WI: Krause Publications, 2004.

Le Chameau Exploration Ltd. v. Nova Scotia (Attorney General), 2007 NSSC 386. S. Sn. No. 277337. Sydney, 2007-12-11.

MacKinnon, Robert. Unpublished dive logs (*Auguste* site, 1977, 1978).

MacKinnon, Robert. Unpublished dive logs (HMS *Fantome* site, 2005, 2006).

MacKinnon, Robert. Unpublished dive logs (HMS *Feversham* site, 1982, 1985, 1986, 1995, 1996).

MacKinnon, Robert. Unpublished dive logs (HMS *Leonidas* site, 1975).

MacKinnon, Robert. Unpublished dive logs (*Le Chameau* site, 1976, 1995, 1996, 2004, 2005, 2008).

MacKinnon, Robert. Unpublished operations logs—*Le Chameau* silver ecus used in regulated subbottom migration experiments (*Auguste* site, 1978).

MacKinnon, Robert. Unpublished personal operations logs (*Auguste* site, 1977, 1978).

Mathewson, Dr. Duncan. Unpublished science reports contracted by Robert MacKinnon (*Le Chameau* site, 2004, 2005, 2008).

McKenzie, Natario. "$200M Wreck Furore Spurred Salvage Ban." *Tribune* (Freeport, Bahamas). Dec. 4, 2011.

The Public Record Office. Manuscript Report Series 139. Vol. 2. London: War Office 34. Trident Research.

Amherst to Albermarle. Feb. 27, 1762, folios 51–52. Gives news of the shipwreck of the St. Luc La Corne off Cape Breton.

Reedy, Rob. Unpublished science reports contracted by Robert MacKinnon (*Le Chameau* and HMS *Feversham* sites, 1995, 1996).

Sinclair, James. Unpublished science reports contracted by Robert MacKinnon (HMS *Fantome* site, 2005).

Yeoman, R. S. *A Guide Book of United States Coins, 36th Edition, 1983.* Racine, WI: Western Publishing Company, Inc., 1983.

ACKNOWLEDGMENTS

I have had the rare opportunity to work with some of the most experienced salvage and science divers, including renowned maritime scientists, ever to be involved in this business. Since the early 1970s these people added greatly to the hoard of human treasure I was fortunate enough to become involved with, sharing such a common interest. They are as follows:

American Divers

Joe Franolich
Don Villere
Dennis Manogian
Lou Chiaster
Al Daher
George Mazzoni
Jim Leslie
Mark Nowacki
Al Schetino
Carol Schetino
Craig Boothney
Ray Brown
Ed Stinson
Eric Stinson
Chris Stinson
Frank Nelson
Mike Luke
Eugene Brunelle
Dick Smith
Patricia Hart
Barry Barbara

Tom Mahon
Ed Young
Rob Moran
Mike Haas
Nick Warden
Matt Nigro
Joe Fiorentino
Joe Sommers
Barry Gross
Julie Russo
Ed Hayes
Chuck Gill
Phil Masters
Carl Brown
Bill Ward
Tom Smith
Harry Wagner
Wesley Calebrese

Canadian Divers

Robert MacDonald
Ronnie Blundon
Bill Dalton
Ed Melnick
Duane Dauphnee
Bob Anthony
Jason Day
John Webber
John Oldham
Harvey LeRoy
Steve Williams
Tim Lightfoot
Ed Barrington
Aubrey (Ace) Lynk
Jack Shumacher
Jim Mullins
Ronnie O'Neil
Terry Jessome
Bob Dicks
Russell MacDonald

Scientists

Robert Grenier
Jim Ringer
Ron Waite
Roy Skanes
Callum Thompson
John Cross
James Sinclair
Dr. Duncan Mathewson
Robert Cembrola
Rob Reedy

Operations Crew

John White
Fred Steele
Wayne McComber
Capt. Danny Gaslard
Capt. John MacKinnon
Ricky Burke
Jeffrey MacKinnon
George Steele
George Stockley
John Fitzgerald
Capt. William Bell
James Campbell
Jack Steele
Terry Dwyer
Lorne MacPhail
Clayton Dixon

Research

David Dow	Ronnie Blundon	Archie Rose
Joe Fiorentino	Ed Melnick	Phil Masters
Ed Michaud	Rob Reedy	Robert MacDonald
Robert Cembrola	John (Ian) Cross	Donald Kerr
John Webber	Dr. Duncan Mathewson	Jack Steele
Harvey LeRoy	James Sinclair	Fred Steele
Greg Cochanoff	Charlie Burke	

In accumulating the data for a work of this class, it is inevitable that a large number of people must contribute in one way or the other. Success is bound to the proper foundation, no matter the endeavor. In my case, this foundation was reinforced by the first recognized treasure hunters in Cape Breton: Ronnie Blundon and Robert MacDonald. They were partners of the Orbit Group, founders of the pay ship *Le Chameau*. The fact I had the good fortune to work with and learn from these early salvers cannot be overstated. Ronnie Blundon, in my estimation, remains the one true shipwreck visionary mainly responsible for the successes I enjoyed since we first teamed up on the Dive Scatarie Project during the mid-1970s. James Mullins also deserves very special mention; he became one of the most competent science and recovery divers I had the privilege to train and work with, now for over 35 years.

My early relationship with marine archaeologist Robert Grenier reinforced my curiosity in the ethical way to excavate shipwrecks. He was a mentor of sorts with a keen interest in the scientific recovery of cultural material related to wooden shipwreck sites. His advice and direction during the early years of our relationship proved invaluable helping shape my strong desire to save Nova Scotia's shipwreck cultural material.

During the discovery and excavation phases of the cartel ship *Auguste*, I had the good fortune to become involved with marine archaeologist Jim

Ringer and his team sent from Parks Canada to assist the recovery project. The Parks team, without question, acted as consummate professionals guiding the diving and conservation operations. They helped the salvers achieve a controlled scientific recovery, one we were and continue to be proud of.

I would be remiss here if I did not recognize Ed Barrington and his crew. By the time I first worked with Ed in 1977, he was a very experienced commercial diver with many years of experience salvaging Nova Scotia shipwrecks. He still remains a true and influential friend, a condition that reached its zenith during the *Auguste* excavations, always sharing with me the good, the bad, and, in the end, the ugly.

In later years, I had the good fortune to work with industry-renowned marine archaeologists Dr. Duncan Mathewson III and James Sinclair—the maritime scientists involved in directing the famous *Atocha* recovery. Both scientists had a serious influence on our search and recovery methodologies, introducing us to cutting-edge advancements in electronic and diver-based excavation methods. Dr. Mathewson reinforced my ambition to finish a book I had begun to write years earlier depicting, as he noted, "a unique personal and historic account of discovery and perseverance."

I would also like to single out and recognize marine archaeologist Robert Cembrola, curator of the Naval War Museum, Newport, Rhode Island. He acted as my science adviser and provided industry updates since 1995. I would also be remiss if I did not mention one other very important person, Joe Fiorentino. Joe has been a constant in the development of this story both as my lead diver and confidant since he first came to work for me in 1985. Also included, but no less important, are my other lead divers, Robert Anthony, Matt Nigro, Ron O'Neil, Phil Masters*, and Duane

*Phil Masters's team discovered English pirate Blackbeard's famous ship *Queen Anne's Revenge*—wrecked off Beaufort Inlet, North Carolina, in 1718—on November 21, 1996.

Dauphinee. To anyone and everyone else involved in my long career whom I may have failed to acknowledge, I express my sincere thanks and gratitude.

In preparing this book, I would like to especially thank my wife, Mary Margaret; Dallas Murphy; my agent, Eileen Cope; Trident Media Group; Natalee Rosenstein; and the Berkley Publishing Group. Foremost, the unwavering support of my parents, who instilled in me the true Highland Scots values of that ilk's strong sense of adventure and daring.

MacKinnon Clan Motto: *Audentes fortuna juvat* (Fortune favors the daring).